POPULAR EUROPEAN CINEMA

Edited by

Richard Dyer and *Ginette Vincendeau*

London and New York

First published 1992
by Routledge
11 New Fetter Lane, London EC4P 4EE

Simultaneously published in the USA and Canada
by Routledge
a division of Routledge, Chapman and Hall Inc.
29 West 35th Street, New York, NY 10001

Phototypeset in 10 on 12 point Baskerville by
Intype Ltd, London
Printed in Great Britain by
Butler & Tanner Ltd

British Library Cataloguing-in-Publication Data
Popular European cinema.
I. Dyer, Richard   II. Vincendeau, Ginette
306.485

Library of Congress Cataloging-in-Publication Data
Popular European cinema / edited by Richard Dyer and
Ginette Vincendeau.
p. cm.
Includes bibliographical references.
1. Motion pictures—Europe—Congresses.   2. Europe—Popular
culture—Congresses.   I. Vincendeau, Ginette.
PN1993.5.E8P6   1992
791.43′094—dc20   91–40138

ISBN 0–415–06802–9
0–415–06803–7 pbk

CONTENTS

CONTENTS

LIST OF PLATES

NOTES ON CONTRIBUTORS

Dudley Andrew heads the Institute for Cinema and Culture at the University of Iowa. He has written widely on film theory and film criticism. He has just completed a study of French poetic realism, forthcoming from Princeton University Press.

José Arroyo wrote on Almodóvar for his MA dissertation at the University of East Anglia in 1989. He is presently writing his doctoral dissertation on 'nation and narration in Quebec cinema' at Simon Fraser University.

Christian Bosséno works for *La Revue du cinéma* and *CinémAction*. He guest-edited three issues of the latter, on *Cinémas paysans* ('Rural films'), *Cinémas de l'émigration* ('Emigration films') and *Youssef Chahine l'Alexandrie*. He is the author of *200 téléastes français* ('200 French television directors').

François de la Bretèque teaches film history at the University Paul Valéry in Montpellier. He is at present finishing a thesis on the representation of the medieval in film.

Thomas Elsaesser is Chair of the Department of Film and Television Studies at the University of Amsterdam. Among his recent publications are *New German Cinema: A History* and *Early Cinema: Space Frame Narrative*.

Maria Enzensberger taught film studies at Staffordshire Polytechnic, Stoke-on-Trent, and at Derby College of Higher Education, Derby.

Sue Harper teaches at Portsmouth Polytechnic. She has published a range of articles on British cinema in the 1930s and 1940s. Her book *The Representation of History in British Feature Film 1933–1950* is to be published shortly by the British Film Institute.

Małgorzata Hendrykowska teaches film history and theory at the Adam Mickiewicz University in Poznan. Her recent publications are on early cinema, and her next book is entitled *Film w kulturze polskiej przed rokiem 1914* ('Film in Polish culture before 1914').

Veijo Hietala is Senior Lecturer, **Hanna Kangasniemi, Martti Lahti** and

Kimmo Laine are research students, and **Jukka Sihvonen** is Associate Professor, in Cinema and Television Studies at the University of Turku. **Ari Honka-Hallila** teaches Finnish in Turku.

Jean-Pierre Jeancolas works as a film critic for *Positif*. He is the author of several works on French cinema, including *15 ans d'années trente, le cinéma des Français 1929–44* ('The 1930s lasted fifteen years, the cinema of the French 1929–44'); he has just finished a history of Hungarian cinema.

Carol Jenks's areas of research are horror films and melodrama, and she is particularly interested in political questions of gender and representation.

Michèle Lagny teaches film at the University of Paris III. She is co-author of *Générique des années 30* ('Crediting the 1930s') and has published a study on Visconti. She has just completed a book entitled *Méthode historique et histoire du cinéma* ('Historical method and film history'), and is at present working on cinema and popular culture.

Anne Marit Myrstad is a scholar at the Institute of Drama, Film and Theatre at the University of Trondheim. Her main area of research is Norwegian fiction films of the 1920s.

V. F. Perkins lectures in film studies at the University of Warwick. He is the author of *Film as Film* and one of the editors of the journal *Movie*.

Heide Schlüpmann teaches at the University of Frankfurt and is a member of the editorial board of *Frauen und Film*. She has recently published *Unheimlichkeit des Blicks. Das Drama des frühen deutschen Kinos* ('The eeriness of the look. The drama of early German cinema').

Anita Skwara lectures in the Film History and Theory department of the Silesian University, Katowice, and contributes to weekly and monthly film publications as well as Polish TV programmes. She is currently finishing a PhD thesis on 'The post-modernist image of the body in Peter Greenaway's cinema'.

Tytti Soila is a lecturer in the department of Theatre and Cinema Arts, Stockholm University. She is at present finishing a PhD thesis on Swedish film melodrama of the 1930s. She contributed to an anthology of feminist film theory published in Finland in 1990.

Christopher Wagstaff is a lecturer in the department of Italian Studies at the University of Reading and has published articles on Italian avant-garde literature and Italian cinema.

The editors

Richard Dyer is a senior lecturer in film studies at the University of Warwick. He is the author of *Stars, Heavenly Bodies* and *Now You See It: Studies on Lesbian and Gay Film.* Two collections of his articles are forthcoming. He is at present working on a book on Whiteness.

Ginette Vincendeau is a lecturer in film studies at the University of Warwick. She is co-author and editor of *La Vie est à nous* and *French Film: Texts and Contexts.* Her forthcoming publications are *The Art of Spectacle: French Popular Cinema in the 1930s* and *Anatomie d'un mythe: Jean Gabin.*

ACKNOWLEDGEMENTS

This book was based on a conference organized by the editors at the University of Warwick in September 1989.

We should like to thank the following for making the conference possible: the University of Warwick (the Arts Centre Cinema, the Film Studies department, the European Humanities Research Centre, the Research and Innovation Fund), the British Film Institute, West Midlands Arts, Channel 4, the Grabowski Foundation, British Screen. We are indebted to the British Council offices of Amsterdam, Athens, Belgrade, Budapest, Copenhagen, Frankfurt, Helsinki, London, Madrid, Rome, Oslo, Sofia, Vienna, Warsaw. We also gratefully acknowledge the help of the following embassies: Austria, Denmark, France, Hungary, the Netherlands, Norway, Poland, Spain and Sweden; and of the French Institute and the Goethe Institute in London, as well as the Danish Film Institute, the Ciné- mathèque Universitaire at Paris III, the Amsterdam Film Museum, the Austrian Film Commission, the Swedish Film Institute, the State Film Archive of the German Democratic Republic, the State Film Archive of the Federal Republic of Germany (Koblenz), the German Kinemathek (Berlin) and the German Institute for Film Art (Wiesbaden).

More than sixty scholars gave papers at the conference, and all contri- buted to making it a pleasurable as well as intellectually stimulating event. We wish to acknowledge their participation and express regrets at not being able to include them all in this collection. While the selection process often entailed difficult decisions, we believe the present volume reflects the range of concerns and methodologies that informed the whole conference.

While we were preparing this volume, Maria Enzensberger tragically died. We wish to honour her memory here. In addition to her work on Russian cinema as traditionally conceived, she was one of the pioneers of the kind of study of popular European cinema with which this book is concerned.

INTRODUCTION

Richard Dyer and Ginette Vincendeau

Part of the existing map of cinema is coloured in quite clearly: there is America, which is Hollywood, which is popular entertainment, and there is Europe, which is art. Critics and historians of film have started to put new shades into the picture: the USA has, since the First World War, been massively part of European cinema, above all for audiences; aesthetic developments in European film have time and again found their way into Hollywood production (e.g. expressionism, the horror movie and film noir, the new waves and 'New Hollywood Cinema'). Yet one aspect of the equation has remained stubbornly unacknowledged: popular entertainment cinema made by Europeans for Europeans. This book hopes to inaugurate the business of shading in the map of European cinema with the colours of indigenous popular film.

The popular cinema of any given European country is not always acknowledged even in the general national histories of film in that country. When it is, it is generally marginalized in favour of the often little-seen but critically acclaimed art film traditions, and even this limited awareness rarely extends beyond the study of a nation written in that nation. This is in part because, as Jean-Pierre Jeancolas (Chapter 10) and Veijo Hietala *et al.* (Chapter 9) argue, highly popular European films seldom travel well beyond their national boundaries; when they do, as is the case with the recent French successes based on the novels of Marcel Pagnol (*Jean de Florette, Manon des sources, La Gloire de mon père, Le Château de ma mère*), they are generally repackaged for art cinemas. One of our concerns in this volume is to make the popular in European cinema visible beyond national boundaries. This is not done in the spirit of rescuing great films from critical oblivion (although this may be one of the bonuses). Films are not better for being popular any more than they are worse; as V. F. Perkins argues (Chapter 14), the question, and difficulty, of judgement remains. However, at present, we don't even know the popular cinemas of Europe sufficiently well to start making discriminations.

There is more at stake than adjustments to the map of cinema. To put together 'popular' and 'European' rattles the security with which we use

1

these terms. What do we mean by the popular if we include in it Europe, the *ne plus ultra* of high white culture? And what do we mean by Europe, if its identity is not coterminous with that high white tradition? These are the questions we wish to elaborate in this introduction at a time when the definitions of both popular and European culture are under considerable pressure. Developments in world-wide transnational mass cultural diffusion, by no means exclusively US-led, sharpen further than ever the question of the role, if any, that national media can have in popular culture. At the same time, Europe has never appeared a more contested notion, as the European Community seeks to engineer a new economic and political (and cultural?) unity into place, and as the nature and allegiances of eastern Europe change daily as we write (late summer 1991). We don't know what the prospects for popular European cultures are and we shall not make much headway on that front until we know what those cultures are and have been.

THE POPULAR

The term 'popular' is notoriously slippery or, alternatively, rich. Rather than abandon it because of its resistance to neat definitions and its failure to provide a foolproof guide to categorizing films, we want to use its contradictions and blurred contours to explore a force field of cultural production. The productive messiness of the term may be explored through the supposed opposition between two paradigms, one based on the market, the other drawn from anthropology.

The popular can refer to things that are commercially successful and/ or to things that are produced by, or express the thoughts, values and feelings of, 'the people'. There are various ways of expressing this distinction. One of the most extreme (which virtually excludes film from one pole) would posit 'mass' culture (industrially, centrally produced for wide-scale distribution and consumption) versus 'folk' (artisanally, locally produced and consumed); much less stark would be a distinction between box-office receipts and 'audience preferences'. All these can lay claim to the term 'popular'. For convenience we shall refer to them here as 'market' and 'anthropological' approaches. As a preliminary indication, one might compare Christopher Wagstaff's careful market delineation of who was seeing what where in Italy in the 1950s and 1960s (Chapter 18) and François de la Bretèque's equally careful anthropological tracing of the way French film has drawn on the Provençal tradition of church nativity plays (Chapter 4).

Neither side of the market/anthropology distinction, even taken on its own, is simple. Market approaches seem hard-headed. Records may have been lost, may be hard to gain access to or may be unreliable, but market approaches do offer us plain information about popular cinema. Yet what counts as popular in this approach? Is it the films that made the most money or the films that the largest number of people saw? The two are not necessarily the same thing. A first-run release in a major urban centre may garner greater box-officer receipts from fewer people than a low-profile film that tours every tiny cinema in the land for years on end. Which is more popular? We might be tempted, democratically, to go for the second, but the first-run movie may, by virtue of its higher profile, have had greater impact on the culture as a whole. Large receipts and large numbers of viewers are both indices of popularity, but what exactly they tell us still requires attention to the particularities of each case (see Wagstaff and the comparative discussions in Sorlin 1991.) Moreover, market records are seldom sufficiently complex. They often hide regional or 'sub-cultural' variations in audience and don't take into account something like, for example, the military servicemen targeted by some French films of the 1950s (see Jeancolas).

Anthropological approaches are more obviously complicated, especially with a medium such as film. As Michèle Lagny notes (Chapter 12), whatever else it might mean, 'popular cinema' cannot mean films made by 'the people' – most people will never be in a position to make cinema (even when they can make home movies), the disadvantaged majority have never been the producers of films. One kind of anthropological approach focuses rather on the way film uses cultural practices seen as existing prior to or outside the mass media: nativity plays in Bretèque's example, working-class education or rural stories in Małgorzata Hendrykowska (Chapter 8) and Anne Marit Myrstad (Chapter 13) respectively. One danger of this approach (not encountered in the examples just given) is that of positing a culture 'of the people' which is either not in fact separable from mass (industrially, centrally produced) culture or is not in reality part of the life of the mass of people. Bretèque, for instance, points out that much of the *méridional* iconography in cinema is based on postcards, themselves already an instance of mass cultural production, and on constructions of the Midi in museums, the first of which only opened in 1895, the year in which cinema itself started. Equally Anita Skwara (Chapter 16), in pointing out that the alternative to the alien socialist realism imposed on Polish cinema is a tradition of romanticism expressing a true Polish character, cannot avoid the fact that this is a tradition not in fact meaningful to most Polish people. In Myrstad's account of the images of rural life in silent Norwegian cinema one can see at work the tensions between cultural productions based in peasant language and storytelling traditions, the function of these in urban class cultures and the recycling of them in a mass medium addressing several audiences: the remaining peasantry, the urban classes, Norwegian migrants nostalgic for home, and tourists. There can be no search for a pure folk popularity in a material situation so fundamentally complex.

3

We have so far suggested some productive uncertainties within the market and anthropological approaches, but it is evident that the two approaches are in any case not utterly distinct.

If the notion of a popular culture existing outside mass culture is already problematic, once it comes to the cinema any such 'pure' notion of the popular is wholly untenable. It may even be that there can be no understanding of popular film without reference to the market, because popular cinema has only existed in a market economy. This is Skwara's argument in her discussion of the cinema in communist Poland. She argues that a Marxist-Leninist polity cannot produce popular cinema, not (just) because of its authoritarian fear of what the uncontrolled play of the market might produce, but because Marxism-Leninism, as a theory of labour, has no place for pleasure or leisure (except perhaps as 'recovery', a function of work). Maria Enzensberger's discussion of the Soviet musical *Svetlyĭ put'* (Chapter 6) suggests that this might not be entirely true, but it is significant that her analysis stresses that the Utopia of the film is one of work, as if the communist imagination of pleasure must be in terms of the joy of labour.

The issue of the possibility of a popular cinema within communist societies encapsulates what lies behind the debate about mass versus folk cultures. What is at stake is whether a centrally, industrially produced film is, in fact, able to express something 'of the people'. For many, the market is seen as the bridge linking production that is not 'of the people' with consumption that is; thus the market, through the mechanism of the box-office, can have an effect on what does and does not get produced. On the other hand, the market is an extraordinarily crude device for registering something as complex and various as values and desires.

The market paradigm – the fact that popular cinema is provided by capitalist patterns of distribution and exhibition – entails reference to audiences, but anthropological approaches too have become increasingly interested in these. There has been much work in recent years in the study of what Michel de Certeau (1979: 24) has called 'the production of the consumers'. What has especially been stressed is the differentiation of audiences, moving away from a monolithic concept of 'the popular/mass audience'. This is evident in several of the essays here: gender in Carol Jenks (Chapter 11), Heide Schlüpmann (Chapter 15), Tytti Soila (Chapter 17) (women), and Wagstaff (Chapter 18) (men), sexuality in José Arroyo (Chapter 2), occupation in Jeancolas (Chapter 10) and class in Sue Harper (Chapter 7) and Wagstaff. Similarly Bretèque argues for the importance of distinguishing between kinds of audience responses to *méridional* imagery, according to whether the latter is familiar or exotic to the spectator.

Such work, in stressing the specificity and activity of 'popular response', can reproduce the problem of anthropological approaches suggested above – it can imply that responses are themselves free, untouched by the power of the media (of the films themselves, of control over what films are made and available, over the media industries of which films are but a part). As Geneviève Poujol observes, to recognise the limitations of the mass domination model 'does not so much represent the failure of cultural hegemony as the public's resistance towards such attempts at hegemony' (1979: 38). Resistance is not overthrow any more than it is submission. Several essays here suggest ways in which a text makes an oppositional reading possible (Soila, Jenks) without implying either that all viewers read it so or that one should extrapolate from this that all popular films are subversive.

There is a sense in which 'the popular' is what it is most popularly assumed to be: what people like. The complications arise when we ask questions which underpin both market and anthropological paradigms: which people? how many? and who and what determine what is on offer for them to like? A map of the popular would begin to shade in those complexities. This book can barely begin to do that and even before we can think about how to do it, we have to come to terms with another slippery idea, Europe.

THE EUROPEAN

'Europe', like the 'popular', is both a self-evident term and almost impossible to define. If its map boundaries are relatively determinate to north, west and south, they have never been so to the east, and as a social constituency, Europe resists encapsulation. Since the Second World War, there have been various attempts at making 'Europe' more than the aggregate of nation states, in particular with the Council of Europe (founded in 1949) and the European Community (1957). Since then, several trade agreements have furthered links both between members of the EC (culminating in the abolition of trade barriers in 1992), and between the EC and other European states, including the fast-developing links with eastern European countries. Yet these various economic and political alliances do not necessarily 'make' one Europe. As Benedict Anderson (1991: 53) puts it, '*in themselves* market-zones, "natural"-geographic or politico-administrative, do not create attachments. Who will willingly die for Comecon or the EEC?'

Moves towards unification affect the cultural arena, but stumble over the conundrum: is there a European culture which is more than the sum of the cultures of its nation states? British, French, Hungarian, Portuguese, Swedish cultures are European by virtue of their geographical and historical placements, but what makes them 'European'? Despite the risks of seeming to posit a European essence, this question is worth pursuing if it can alert us to the specificities of the situation within which cultural production takes place in Europe.

5

Typically, European culture has been characterized in two somewhat contradictory ways, one emphasizing the past, the other, modernity.

In the first characterization, the European resides in common, ancient cultural roots. From this perspective, Greek and Roman antiquity, Christianity, the Renaissance and the Enlightenment are the bedrock of intrinsically European values: democracy, freedom, civilization. As Lagny shows, a popular film genre like the Italian peplum recycles elements of classical culture, propagating the myth of a 'European space and time' as the root of democracy. Of course, however genuinely old many of the artefacts making up this tradition of civilization are, it is not in reality an unbroken lineage but a constant process of reconstruction and reperception. Moreover, as Jan Nederveen Pieterse (1991: 3) has argued, it is a view of Europe 'chauvinistic, elitist, pernicious and alienating, [and] wrong' in suppressing regional cultures, in denying popular culture, in being passéist, and in ignoring Europe's contemporary multi-cultural reality.

A less elitist, but still chauvinistic, vision of Europe's venerability sees old peasant stock as containing the seeds of European nationhoods. Myrstad's analysis of the perception of the peasant as the repository of true national values could probably be extended to most of Europe. Such peasant cultures were generally revealed to the nation state at the very moment that it was undergoing rapid urbanization and industrialization: the more peasant economies were destroyed, the more peasant cultures were to be saved. In its search for locatable national essences, this vision easily becomes racist, as Myrstad shows and as debates about the *Heimat* genre in Germany have often highlighted. Recourse to such imagery in contemporary multi-ethnic Europe may be particularly sinister.

Despite the largely illusory nature of European oldness, it would be wrong to underestimate the centrality of this *sense* of oldness to white European identities. The fact of having the corroborating artefacts lying about gives a deceptive but immensely powerful weight to the iconographies of history, landscape and custom at all levels of European cultural production.

This sense of pastness clearly informs the 'heritage' genre of European cinema – *Chariots of Fire* (GB 1981), *Jean de Florette* (France 1986), *Babettes Gaestebud* (*Babette's Feast*, Denmark 1987), *Nuovo Cinema Paradiso* (Italy 1988). Stylistically this does on the face of it seem to be a common European genre (though apparent also in films from other small national industries – Australia, Argentina, Brazil, Canada), easy to see as the film equivalent of Europe-as-a-theme-park (Warwickshire as 'Shakespeare country', the Indre river as the 'Balzac trail' and so on). Yet they are a complex phenomenon. Often big box-office in their country of origin, they generally become art cinema material outside it. In the latter context, however, they are often very successful – a popular middle-class cinema, in societies in which the middle class is increasingly becoming the biggest

class and the mainstay of cinema audiences. They are not a new phenomenon, as the chapters by Bretèque, Harper and Myrstad attest, and their
deployment of the human and geographical landscapes of Europe is what
makes them both evidently European and eminently exportable. There is
a tendency in film studies to deride the whole genre (partly one suspects
out of nostalgia for the toiling masses), whereas it is clearly a subject for
further research and, especially, differentiation. (One might, for instance,
note the use of the genre in a beur film like *Cheb* (1990), where it becomes
a resource for the exploration of Arab-French identity.)

If one characterization of Europe emphasizes history and antiquity, a
second and contradictory vision invokes Europe as originator and site
of modernity, against both vulgar mass culture and 'obscurantist' forces (of
religion, for instance). This reworks themes from Europe's past: Enlightenment scepticism and rationalism, the way nineteenth-century philosophy
and science lent themselves to the justification of racism and imperialism.
Their most vivid contemporary manifestation is the perceived threat
of Islam to European identity, symbolized in the supposed limit case of
Turkey *vis à vis* the EC and the challenge to secularism posed by the
Rushdie affair. Equally, European modernity carries on by other means
the old habit of taste arbitration, in its international pre-eminence in
fashion industries (Swedish design, French couture, Italian menswear) and
especially its invention of 'modern art'. It has been argued that it is in
the latter that, if anywhere, a pan-European culture, able to speak a
common European language, is to be found.

Here we may distinguish two tendencies, both making claims as representatives of the modern and in both of which film, for very different
reasons, has had a privileged place. One is the tradition of 'realism', the
project of 'showing things as they really are' (cf. Lovell 1980). This has
underpinned several key moments in European culture, in each of which
film, by virtue of its supposed special relation to reality, is central: e.g.
Neue Sachlichkeit in Germany in the 1920s, British documentary, French
poetic realism and Soviet socialist realism in the 1930s, Italian neo-realism
in the 1940s and 1950s. On inspection much of this tradition in fact relates
to the past, in both its frequent predilection for the preindustrial or arti-
sanal (*Drifters*, *La terra trema*, *Farrebique*) and in its reliance on popular
forms, notably melodrama (*Kameradschaft*, *Chapayev*, *Toni*, *Roma città aperta*,
Saturday Night and Sunday Morning). As Dudley Andrew discusses (Chapter
1), even a 'classic' realist film at the vanguard of the left alliance of the
French Popular Front such as *Le Crime de Monsieur Lange* draws on sentimental and old-fashioned song and literary genres.

The other approach to the modern breaks with realisms, often with
much sound and fury, and has come to be known as 'modernism'. This
is the most prominent manifestation of the high white tradition, which, it
has been argued, is able to 'speak' a common European language: from

Picasso to the Bauhaus, Yeats to Duras, Meyerhold to Mnouchkine. Film, because of its technological basis and perceived slippery relation to reality, has figured largely, from Eisenstein to Godard, Dulac to Buñuel, Bergman and Wajda to Wertmüller.

Through these various routes from both 'old Europe' and 'Europe the modern', from realism and modernism, a broad category of 'art cinema' has been designated. Useful as the concept is, its Anglo-American origins (e.g. Bordwell 1979, Tudor 1973) have had a tendency to erase stylistic and cultural differences between films within each (continental) European country. Interestingly, in some European countries (France and Italy, for example) critical discourses tend to erect a distinction along the lines of auteur versus mainstream, which can allow for more flexible definitions of each pole of the dichotomy than that of 'art' versus 'entertainment' (i.e. auteur films can be found at all cultural levels of film production). 'Art cinema' or 'auteur cinema' is, however, of considerable importance within each country for reasons part economic, part critical. It is a solution to the problem of the small domestic market for national European films, since 'art films' are shown at film festivals and on international distribution/exhibition circuits dedicated to them (Neale 1981); it is also the cinema that most national European governments have been prepared to subsidize (see Arroyo). To gain this position, art cinema required high cultural prestige. This was achieved by constructing it through the discourses of European culture discussed above, traditions which, for sociohistorical reasons, are accepted as the dominant national cultures in most European countries in a way that is certainly not true in the USA or Australia. Art cinema fed into the resistance to two filmic 'bad others': US cultural influence, including television (though Hollywood, particularly the classical era, has occupied an ambiguous place in this constellation), and the despised indigenous low traditions (cf. Hietala *et al.* on critical attitudes to Finland's supremely popular star and Vincendeau 1992 on attitudes to both Hollywood and indigenous popular film in France in the 1950s).

Despite its success, the 'heritage' film is still a problematic candidate for a unitary popular European cinema based on a 'common' European culture. Moreover, even though individual national industries have flourished, there has never been a pan-European popular cinema, for two suggested reasons: Hollywood and language.

European cinema's struggle to define itself against Hollywood has a long history, going back to the 1920s.[1] There have been various attempts by European film industries, principally Germany, France and Italy, to fight Hollywood domination by creating pan-European alliances – for instance, the Westi company and the 'Film Europe' project in the 1920s, the Franco-Italian coproductions of the 1950s and a number of contemporary initiatives. All have faced considerable obstacles, partly because production and distribution set-ups, as well as levels of state sponsorship, vary enormously. There is a tremendous difference between the dominant industries (France, Germany and Italy) with relatively prosperous cinema and TV markets for their national and coproduced films, and those of other European countries. Recent initiatives (EC schemes such as Media 92 and Eur-images) are trying to revive the 'Film Europe' type of organization, but their avowed aim to 'beat the financial muscle of the US studio system at [its] own game' (BSAC 1991: 8) suggests a defensive strategy rather than a positive attempt at developing a European cultural arena. At the time of writing, the situation in eastern Europe is dramatically changing, from a state-controlled to a deregulated one (with not necessarily welcome consequences, as Skwara suggests). Meanwhile, distribution is as always in US hands.

The coming of sound in 1929/30, by introducing language barriers, was thought for a while to offer a golden opportunity for non-English-speaking film industries. Early 1930s European audiences initially strongly resisted English-speaking films or works hastily adapted to their own language. After the short-lived experiment in multi-language versions, however, dubbing and subtitling settled in Europe. Instead of being barred from non-English-speaking markets, US films strengthened their hold. This was partly because Hollywood had the technology and financial clout to impose US sound patents on most of Europe (thereby deriving extra profits), but also because language made each European country's films less exportable, to each other and the USA. Though acceptance of dubbed and subtitled US films (and English-speaking television) is now part of the European media landscape (with the exceptions of Great Britain and Ireland), patterns for the screening of other foreign language films are far from unified across Europe: where some countries systematically dub (Germany, Italy), others such as Greece, Portugal and the Netherlands show all films in subtitled prints. Others again, like France, use a combination of both formulae. These choices, economically and historically motivated, show there is nothing intrinsic to audiences' acceptance or rejection of foreign voices and that the 'language barrier' could be overcome in the drive to establish pan-European film initiatives.

The question of language is central in another way to the definition of national cinemas, and therefore popular European cinema, and that is by anchoring a sense of local or national identity. For instance, it is an essential part of the construction of *méridional* types (Bretèque) and class differences (Harper) and of the play of French and Arab identities in beur cinema (Bosséno, Chapter 3). In a wider sense, the intertextual connections with language-based entertainment forms (song, music-hall, radio, television), discussed by, among others, Andrew, Arroyo, Jeancolas and Hietala *et al.*, automatically privilege language as a medium for the construction of national identity. There lies, obviously, one of the main reasons

9

for the inexportability of popular European cinema to the rest of the world,[2] *including* Europe, since language is part of the complicity between film and audience characteristic of much of this cinema (see Jeancolas). These films, aiming for the culturally specific (down to the regional or sub-cultural audience) seem more 'foreign' than Hollywood to other countries, because European audiences have been conditioned to receiving Hollywood films in great quantities in subtitled or dubbed versions, which, in their own ways, erase some of the cultural differences. European understanding of US culture is bound to be partial, but the familiarity with Hollywood movies makes it seem less so.[3] (One of the beur films mentioned by Bosséno, *Bâton Rouge*, plays on the gap between the 'reality' of the US and the sense of it derived from Hollywood movies.)

Beyond language in the strictest sense, another aspect of the cultural specificity of European cinema makes it difficult to export: its reliance on a knowledge of the national history by its target audience. This may involve ironic or oblique readings – the peplum (Lagny) or the British historical dramas analysed by Harper – or be more seriously social in aim – the 1930s Soviet musicals discussed by Enzensberger, or the very first film screenings, as much pedagogic as entertainment, as Hendrykowska shows in the Polish context.

All this suggests that even if there is *some* common European identity at the level of high white culture, there is much less beyond it. None the less, European cinemas do have three things in common at the level of their situations: first, the problem of exportability; second, the national standing of high culture, repository of official national identity and the nation's international face; third, not being Hollywood. It is to this last point that we now turn to pinpoint further the character of the popular in Europe.

THE POPULAR EUROPEAN

Europe has a paradoxical place in world culture. The high white tradition is, essentially, European, and many everyday expressions, like 'the east-west divide' or 'down under', unthinkingly perpetuate a European point of view. Yet increasingly Europe is marginalized within popular culture. From Hollywood films like *Pretty Woman* (1990) and *Terminator 2* (1991) to Japanese TV cartoons for children, leisure clothes made in Taiwan or toothbrushes bearing 'Teenage Mutant Ninja Turtle' logos, the common denominators of mass culture visible all over Europe are *not* European. In the face of this, Europe seems able to offer only either heritage movies and itself as theme park, or else a popular culture widely deemed risible. Indeed, European television has increasingly replaced Hollywood as the 'bad other' of high cultural criticism, subsumed under the labels of 'Euro-trash' or 'Euro-puddings', be it the Eurovision song contest, the 'housewife striptease' syndrome (Nowell-Smith 1989: 1), non-British European rock and pop, or TV soaps like *Riviera*.

This attitude towards popular European culture has always been held towards popular European cinemas. When not despised through a comparison with art cinema, they have often been judged in relation to Hollywood and found wanting. Both views of popular European cinema's inferiority (to art cinema *and* to Hollywood) are generally based on ignorance. For instance, popular European cinema may be differentiated from art cinema by having no great auteur directors. However, first, this is to fail to recognize, as Perkins points out, that directors in the art cinema pantheon, like Jean Renoir or Luchino Visconti, in fact worked in popular cinema; and second, it seems altogether probable that a table of auteur directors (*à la* Sarris 1968) working exclusively within popular European cinema could easily be drawn up (e.g. very randomly, Claude Autant-Lara, Mario Bava, Muriel Box, Christian-Jacque (see Andrew), Doris Dörrie, Gustaf Edgren (see Soila), Alice Guy, Raffaello Matarazzo, Spede Pasanen (see Hietala *et al.*), Reinhold Schünzel (see Elsaesser, Chapter 5), to say nothing of cases such as Alfred Hitchcock and Pedro Almodóvar (see Arroyo)).

At one level the comparison with Hollywood is nonetheless fair enough. Popular European cinema was and is produced in the context of Hollywood's massive presence in Europe (a market approach to popular European cinema would in many countries have to conclude that popular European cinema is US cinema). Yet undeniable as its importance is, we need to investigate two assumptions further: that popular European cinema is the same as Hollywood and that it is therefore historically a copy of it.

The assumption of sameness is suggested by formulations to the effect that popular European cinema is 'Hollywood in foreign dress'. There are two problems with such formulations. One is the implication that, even were it true, 'foreign dress' would be so superficial a difference. This entails a model of film in which only the specifically filmic (e.g. cinematography, editing) is decisive, whereas of course 'dress' (e.g. *mise-en-scène*, performance, dialogue) is as fully significant an aspect of film semiotics. Moreover, 'dress' covers such cultural signs as landscapes, language, gestures, clothing, kinds of heroes and heroines, the kinds of thing people find funny, the kinds of stories they tell and are used to having told and so on; in short, whole and distinctive ways of thinking and feeling. It would be enough that popular European cinema wears such European 'dress' for it to be at the very least not self-evidently the same as Hollywood.

Second, however, the work simply has not yet been done on finding out how popular European cinema compares with Hollywood. We may consider two avenues of research here. One is into that kind of cinema which most apparently conforms to the model (often invoked in these pages) of classical narrative cinema, assumed to be supremely represented by Hollywood. Areas such as the *cinéma de qualité* in France, for example, or in Britain the Rank challenge to Hollywood in the 1950s, might repay a strict formal scrutiny of their textual workings in terms of determining what forms European popular classicisms take.

A second avenue of research is into forms that derive from the most 'low-brow' types of popular entertainment (a criterion with an extra edge in most European contexts (cf. Hietala *et al.*)). These are often discussed in terms of their formal differences from classical narrative cinema: their emphasis on the 'spectacular', their hybrid, disunified, aesthetically as well as ideologically contradictory nature. Both Harper and Lagny use the term 'patchwork' to characterize popular cinema, embodied for the latter in the endless exuberant transformations and combinations of elements in the peplum cycle. The implication may be that, compared with classical narrative cinema, such popular European cinema is less subjected to the disciplines of verisimilitude, generic unity and a rigorous regard for coherence, relating it to the aesthetics of 'primitive' cinema (Burch 1990; Gunning 1986). Again, the economics of film production in Europe, above all in the smaller or less wealthy countries, can lead to a relative poverty at the level of production values that may imply a different aesthetic (rather than the dismissive judgement 'failed Hollywood'). The specificities of such 'low-brow' or 'poor' European cinemas await examination.

The assumption of sameness to Hollywood and the hitherto US-centrism of film history have entailed a historical model of popular European cinema as derivative of it. The study of genre – clearly central to popular European cinema, as this book demonstrates – is instructive. In his account of *Hallo Caesar!*, Elsaesser traces the way that the film's director/star, Reinhold Schünzel, adopted Hollywood models to German needs, so that the result is distinctively European (that is, German). This notion of a European version of the Hollywood model informs – haunts – several other chapters here. In some cases the borrowings are indisputable – in the exploitation of genres in Italian cinema (Jenks (Chapter 11), Wagstaff), in their camp appropriation in Almodóvar (Arroyo); but elsewhere there is a real historical difficulty in giving Hollywood priority. On the one hand, the overwhelming presence of Hollywood in Europe cannot have functioned other than as a reference point, for both filmmakers and audiences. On the other hand, certain genres either (the epic in Italy) predate, or (melodrama everywhere) cannot be given historical precedence over, their adoption by Hollywood. Furthermore, is there any clear evidence that the very notion of organizing films around genres, stars, narrative, spectacle and the goal of entertainment was pioneered by Hollywood? The discussions of epic by Lagny, of melodrama by Soila and Schlüpmann and of the historical film by Harper are especially pertinent here, since each suggests both differences from *and* similarities between Hollywood and Europe without ascribing historical precedence to either.

The search for a European specificity or precedence in popular cinema runs the risk of reproducing the problematic searches for the essence of Europe that have been triggered by the possibilities of European integration. Yet there is a common specificity to the material situation within which popular cinema has to be produced in Europe. A survey of the material situation of contemporary European cinema shows the depressing uniformity (with a few rare exceptions) of the hold of Hollywood on European markets, and of declining cinema audiences (*European Market and Media Fact* 1990). At the same time, the inheritance of traditions of pre-cinematic popular forms; the problems, at once economic and cultural/aesthetic, posed by working in an expensive medium for a small language pool; the varying status of the high white tradition as the emblem of national identity (particularly in its exportable form); the iconographies and languages of different national histories and landscapes – all these are nationally specific. The following chapters rescue from oblivion and explore aspects of this rich European history. This book alone cannot begin to encompass such diversities, but at least we hope to show that, if there is no such thing as popular European cinema, there certainly are popular European cinemas.

NOTES

1 Here it is important to mention a further problem of definition, because it is one that has had a strong influence on the place of European cinema within British or British-inspired film studies. From a British perspective, Europe is still generally understood in the sense of 'continental', excluding Britain. Thus European cinema comes to mean the cinema in European countries *other than* Britain. At the basis of this distinction is the ambiguous place occupied by British cinema in relation to Hollywood (because of the linguistic receptivity to US products in Britain, though not vice versa) and in relation to the continent (because of the history of Britain's relation to the EC and its geographical location).

2 In the case of Britain and Ireland it is accent rather than language that has been the barrier to export, caught between the incomprehensibility of regional dialects and the ineffably snobbish sound of English received pronunciation.

3 How one should conceptualize European audiences' apparent ready understanding of Hollywood cinema is moot. On the one hand, one can ascribe it to market forces: Hollywood is what people get and therefore what they get to like. On the other hand (or rather, in addition), one can look for aesthetic criteria: the necessity for Hollywood to address a mixed, immigrant domestic market enabled it to develop a form of storytelling less bound up with local specificities and therefore more able to transcend national boundaries.

REFERENCES

Anderson, Benedict (1991) *Imagined Communities*, London/NewYork: Verso.
Bordwell, David (1979) 'The art cinema as a mode of film practice', *Film Criticism* 4 (1): 56–64.

BSAC (British Screen Advisory Council) (1991) *The European Initiative: the Business of Television and Film in the 1990s* (internal report).

Burch, Noël (1990) *Life to those Shadows*, London: British Film Institute.

de Certeau, Michel (1979) 'Pratiques quotidiennes', in Geneviève Poujol and Raymond Labourie (eds) *Les Cultures populaires*, Paris: Privat.

European Market and Media Fact (1990) Zenith, Media Worldwide.

Gunning, Tom (1986) 'The cinema of attraction: early film, its spectator and the avant-garde', *Wide Angle* 8(3/4): 63–70.

Lovell, Terry (1980) *Pictures of Reality*, London: British Film Institute.

Neale, Stephen (1981) 'Art cinema as institution', *Screen* 22(1).

Nowell-Smith, Geoffrey (1989) *The European Experience*, London: British Film Institute.

Pieterse, Jan Nederveen (1991) 'Fictions of Europe', *Race and Class* 32(3) (*Europe, Variations on a Theme of Racism*): 3–10.

Poujol, Geneviève (1979) 'La résistance à l'inculcation: résistants ou handicapés?', in Geneviève Poujol and Raymond Labourie (eds) *Les Cultures populaires*, Paris: Privat.

Sarris, Andrew (1968) *The American Cinema*, New York: Dutton.

Sorlin, Pierre (1991) *European Cinemas, European Societies*, London: Routledge.

Tudor, Andrew (1973) *Theories of Film*, London: Secker & Warburg.

Vincendeau, Ginette (1992) 'France–Hollywood 1945–1960: the *policier* as international text', *Screen* 33(1).

1

FAMILY DIVERSIONS

French popular cinema and the music-hall

Dudley Andrew

Jean Renoir's *Le Crime de Monsieur Lange* (*The Crime of Monsieur Lange*, 1935) always rises into focus as an eloquent image helping us sort out that *mélange* of competing values that defined French culture at the moment of the Popular Front. While its allegory of urban labourers who succeed in a struggle against exploitation and corruption might seem naïve today, the fact that the outcome of its social drama turns on the power of popular art makes it quite sophisticated and perennially interesting. Film historians are naturally taken with a film in which the downfall of evil management by a workers' co-operative in a publishing house is modelled on the exploits of 'Arizona Jim', a legendary cowboy whose tale, read by everyone in Paris, keeps the enterprise thriving.

Because of the lightness of Jacques Prévert's script, its serious political issues (including the legitimate use of violence, even assassination, in the formation of a just society) bubble up in laughter. The film's hero, Amédée Lange, is a creative writer whose work inspires his confrères at the publishing house and soon an entire class (the workers of Paris) who await each weekly instalment of 'Arizona Jim'. Through Lange's growing social awareness and responsibility, art and life converge in a directly political act, the killing of the corrupt Batala. Thus everyday life becomes mythologized through fiction until fiction provides the model for political behaviour. *Le Crime de Monsieur Lange* is an unpretentious film about an unpretentious hero, a popular representation replete with popular images (dime novels, posters, a low-budget movie in the works). It deserves to be in the foreground of anything deserving the name, 'The Popular Front', the movement whose official programme was published just days before the film's première in January 1936 (Sesonske 1980: 185–6).

The exceptional achievement of *Le Crime de Monsieur Lange* can best be felt by setting it alongside any of the innumerable other French films of the day that purport to treat the life of the underdogs of society. One such film, Christian-Jaque's *Rigolboche* (1936), premièred six months later in September 1936, might well be thought of as a twin of Renoir's film because it too concerns the rise to popular success of an exploited artist

15

of the people. The most noticeable link between the two films is surely Jules Berry, who portrays a cardsharp named Mr Bobby, in *Rigolboche*, using the same inimitable hand gestures, improvised dialogue and unconcealed cunning that gave such verve to the magnificently impeccable swindler Batala, editor of the publishing house, in *Le Crime de Monsieur Lange*. In both films that cunning snares whatever women come in sight as well as the unsuspecting *ingénues*, Amédée Lange (who is but a closet novelist until Batala gives him a chance) and the naïve cabaret singer just arrived from Dakar, whom Mr Bobby christens 'Rigolboche'.

Managing their careers, Jules Berry in fact uses both grateful artists as shields to interpose between himself and the irate victims of his failed scams. In what can readily be seen as a reference to the Stavisky scandal two years previous,[1] financial misdealings and illegality ultimately put the Berry character to flight, a disappearance balanced by the unprecedented rise of Lange's serial novels and Rigolboche's nightclub act until in each case the artist takes over the means of production. Ultimately Mr Bobby and his pals are edged to the side of an enterprise that has outgrown them, and Batala, in trying to reclaim command of the co-operative, is dropped by Lange's bullet amid the garbage cans of the courtyard.

For our purposes, the differences between Berry's Batala and his Mr Bobby outweigh these remarkable similarities. Because Renoir and Prévert provide no authority figure able to sort out the authentic from the sham, Batala's charm, delightful as it may be, proves genuinely dangerous and evil. Against his wiles and\his power the people must become their own saviours. And they do so first by banding together and second by risking violence to protect themselves. In *Rigolboche*, the presence of police, detectives and a powerful nobleman keep Mr Bobby in check and ultimately form a reassuring umbrella over Rigolboche herself, even though for a time she, like Mr Bobby, must live in hiding. Having learned to survive in the murky milieu of nightclubs, he becomes a street-wise big brother to Rigolboche rather than her evil seducer.

More important is the fact that Rigolboche, unlike Lange, cannot really protect herself; she would be ruined financially were it not for her adoring Count, the man who ultimately buys her the music-hall that crowns her success. In contrast, Lange's fate falls to his peers, a hastily constituted jury at the border, that can aid or prevent his escape. Nothing like a marriage of classes lets everyone live happily ever after, for urban society in Prévert's view is a new wild west where violence may be a tool of justice in the hands of the people. A lone ranger, Lange understands that he must retire from the fledgling community he has audaciously protected with his gun. Presumably it can now govern itself.

Rigolboche on the other hand understands nothing about community, understands very little at all. A survivor, she is at the mercy of forces both above and beneath her (the Count and a blackmailer from Dakar). Her success depends upon her winning ways, her smile and open goodness of heart. Even if she is exploited by Mr Bobby and others, such is the message of the film that this smile and goodheartedness will protect her in a world where traps are too numerous to avoid but where faith in humanity, especially when infectiously expressed in song, will ultimately extricate you. Taken under the wing of smitten father figures, Rigolboche feels no allegiance to her class or its culture. Rather, she treads unfalteringly up the ramp of money and power that extends from club to cabaret to magnificent music-hall. Compared to the vibrant courtyard that Amédée Lange shares with the laundresses, labourers and even the cranky concierge, a courtyard that no amount of financial success can make him abandon, the increasingly glitzy entertainment sites in *Rigolboche* harbour a depressingly bourgeois view of society, a 'social climber's' view no doubt held by the majority of the film's spectators.

A comparison of these films shows something at stake more subtle than the obvious contention between regressive and progressive social visions; it points to a competition between modes and technologies of entertainment that in themselves carry (and engender) their own versions of Utopia. Counterpoised to pulp fiction and to the modest scribbler Lange (played by the mild, winsome René Lefèvre) is highlife spectacle and the extroverted Rigolboche who is portrayed by the most famous music-hall performer of the era: Mistinguett.

Yet Mistinguett understood the film medium well enough not to overwhelm the audience immediately with the extraordinary pyrotechnics of her art. Instead, with calculated intimacy she sets out to seduce us into identifying with her as an ordinary and very vulnerable young woman. Thus when she sings her son to sleep behind the curtains of their modest home, she delivers the kind of song all of us have sung. In this way the stunning décor and intricate technological precision of the music-hall scene on which the film concludes serve to amplify her humanity and the natural human voice that made it special. And so the film justifies power and money through a story of the 'natural origins' of its heroine (and of Mistinguett).

In fact the film tells its rags-to-riches tale on more than one level, building a myth, as we shall see, of the music-hall itself. A key to this process is the hidden story of the title of the film and its heroine. Here is how it works: pressed by a nightclub owner to introduce his latest 'discovery', Mr Bobby, who has picked up Mistinguett, scans the walls of the office and lights on an antique poster with the curious name 'Rigolboche' displayed; thus is the heroine baptized. Although the film does not gloss this reference, the original Rigolboche was a beggar named Marguerite, who became a symbol of the rise of the people. In 1841 she found her way onto the stage of the Chartreuse, later to become the Closerie des

Lilas. Just prior to the great age of the café-concerts, this coffee house, according to a contemporary habitué,

> allowed on stage whoever wanted to sing or recite, especially students who felt they had musical or poetic genius. They would execute their compositions to great effect on a crowd sensitive to freedom and instinct. I heard things there that were amusing and of an unusual and bizarre originality.
>
> (de Banville 1933: 307)

The most remarkable performance this man heard there was that of Rigolboche before she gained her fame.

> Hardly beautiful, thin and pale, she spent the day sitting on the floor in a corner of the attic. You could see her mending secondhand clothes she had found. In the evening, having thrown together some kind of dress with her fairy's needle, she sang at the Chartreuse! She hadn't learned composition or verse, but she understood them instinctively, and her couplets often had the ingenious and primitive grace of popular songs.
>
> (de Banville 1933: 307)

In its very title, then, the film calls on the central myth of the music-hall, that it grew from the unschooled and 'natural expressiveness' of Parisians singing in local cafés. This is doubly a myth, for it is a tale of origins and it also masks the truth. Specifically, the film displays Mistinguett who adopts the name and role of an early singer whose authentic popular origins and appeal are distinctly opposed to this twentieth-century star. For Mistinguett was known not for rags magically stitched together but for costumes weighing kilos, full of feathers and jewels. In this film, such sumptuousness is represented as a mere amplification of a natural style visible in the character's humble origins and private lullabies just as the music-hall itself is presented as simply enlarged space for intimate and personal expression.

In fact there was nothing ordinary or personal in the spectacular career of Mistinguett which parallels that of the music-hall itself. She made her debut at 12 years old in 1885, blossomed at the Eldorado in the first years of this century, and was the mainstay of the Folies-Bergère during its heyday; she could still be seen on the stage after the Second World War. From 1910 to 1940 she was unquestionably France's dominant performing artist, 'a national treasure', as Colette called her. A host of younger stars from Maurice Chevalier in 1912 to Fernandel in 1933 would be graced to trail behind her into the stage lights. One virtually needed her blessing to succeed.

Mistinguett was destined to run smack into the cinema. A woman of extraordinary 'presence', whose personal vibrancy counted far more towards her success than her mediocre voice and dancing, or her fabled legs and costumes, she was lured to the silent cinema where she played in nearly a dozen features. But the sound film troubled her deeply, as it did the entertainment form of which she was the queen. For here a recording was meant to replace a living encounter. In 1932 when her colleague Georges Tabet began making records, she scolded him for bartering away the spontaneity of performance (Tabet 1979: 155). She knew instinctively that her own success depended on the way she could measure and play an audience, seducing them anew each night, but she did not know how to seduce the camera and the microphone, and so she literally refused to play to them, at least until 1936 and *Rigolboche*.

For her sound film première Mistinguett demanded a script in which cinema is made to show off the particular possibilities of music-hall. She insisted that the story be such as to allow her to change station (and costume) over and over; this way audiences could ride with her from poverty and anonymity to the heights of wealth and glory. She demanded a melodrama in which she could be both a doting mother and a seductive woman of the cabarets. Naturally her shifts in fortune would be marked by the *mise-en-scène* of the production numbers that were the real reason for the film in the first place. For three weeks she worked on the script with Christian-Jaque until she was satisfied that she could dominate the film and its audience.

And she succeeded, by achieving a moral superiority founded on her status as faithful but indigent mother alone in Paris with a young son. Her tender lullaby to him guarantees the authenticity of singing as the medium of pure communication while it establishes the family unit as its original source. Mistinguett, we may now go on to believe, has us in mind, tucks us in our seats in the cinema, as she performs at her nightclub and eventually on the ornate staircase of her very own music-hall.

Le Crime de Monsieur Lange treats spectatorship very differently. When his writing attains the summit of popularity, Amédée Lange agrees to a movie version of 'Arizona Jim', effectively inviting his diegetic reading public to shift attention, but not allegiance, to the medium that we, the actual public, have already chosen, the cinema. In fact the 'Arizona Jim' film permits all the members of the courtyard to participate in their own allegory, dressing in western costumes and acting out the moral dramas of their everyday life. This amounts to a playful, satirical cinema, close to the skits Prévert wrote for the Groupe Octobre, like *L'Affaire est dans le sac* (*It's in the Bag*, 1933). As in Brecht's theatre, the audience for such films is meant to sense themselves as a community that applauds or shouts down characters and actions. The crude filmic technique, like Lange's unsophisticated prose, addresses the public as an extended community of equals and gains its assent through the modesty and justness of what it shows.

19

Plate 1 Glitzy sexual display: Mistinguett in the 1930s. By courtesy of the British Film Institute, London.

This democratic openness is expressed best of all by Valentine, the toughminded laundress, who will not be duped by Batala. She is Lange's best reader but her practicality brings his wonderful dreams down to earth. Most important, she represents a public that has a voice of its own, that can sing its life in its own style. In this context, how appropriate that Valentine be played by Florelle, the singer who moved from the café-concert to the music-hall after the First World War, and who replaced Mistinguett at the Casino de Paris and Moulin Rouge in 1928. Her lone song in the film, written by Prévert and Joseph Kosma, 'Au jour le jour' ('Day after day'), rhapsodizes the hard urban life of a woman of the world. In the courtyard Florelle expresses her sexuality freely but without ostentation.

In contrasting these films I have meant to locate the possibilities held out by the various popular arts of the time: cinema, pulp fiction, the café-concert and the music-hall. Critics of the time argued about the explicit rivalries that grew up among these forms. Some projected a unified entertainment field in which all modes could be said to coexist in relatively happy collaboration, using one another as intertexts, sharing actors, writers and an audience (Vincendeau 1985: 117–25). And indeed after a grave initial defection of spectators from live performance to cinema in the first years of sound (Paris nearly doubled its number of cinemas from 1928 to 1935), a stable bourgeois clientele allowed the boulevard theatres and the remaining music-halls to function at full capacity right up to the war. An effect of audience 'accumulation' benefited both cinema and theatre, including major music-halls (Vincendeau 1985: 119).

This helps to explain the dominant look and themes of French cinema in the 1930s and their conservative aesthetic. Performance values lorded it over every other concern; French audiences were more attuned to acting, including song and dance, than to story and certainly to so-called 'cinematic' values like camerawork and editing. Nearly everyone concerned with filmmaking in France around 1930 was engaged, consciously or not, in reshaping known and popular entertainment forms to the exigencies of the movies. Sacha Guitry and Marcel Pagnol are only the most distinguished traffickers in such mixed forms.

Films about performers like *Rigolboche* preach the ideology of the unity of entertainment and of audiences. And it is true that *Rigolboche* did command an important reception, premièring at the Salle Pleyel in front of 'le tout Paris'. News cameras filmed this opening night to court the broader public who would flock to it in its first run (see *Cinémonde*, 2 October 1936). No such attention was accorded to *Le Crime de Monsieur Lange*. *Rigolboche* garnered the audience that Amédée Lange (and Renoir) could only dream of.

And yet then as now most film scholars treated theatricality as the inert dross that a refined cinema needed to shed. They observed (and often exacerbated) a brutal struggle between theatre and film, assuming that competition among media and texts is the norm, even in the realm of the purely popular.[2] It takes only a modicum of suspicion to look past the agreeable face that entertainers always turn towards the public in order to recognize their often frantic search for a secure footing. Such suspicion must mock the sappy ending of *Rigolboche* in which a diegetic music-hall audience as well as an actual film audience melds into a single chorus of bravos in front of a stunning entertainer. The Popular Front message of Renoir and Prévert may have preached unity, but it preached vigilance, first of all,[3] and then class unity in a struggle against fascism, in a struggle in fact against blind adulation of any person on stage, be it an entertainer or a politician.

To the 'vigilant' observer of French culture in the 1930s, the so-called system of entertainment maintains itself not as a co-ordinated industry but as a precarious network of counterbalanced forces pushing against one another. For example, the virtual extinction of the neighbourhood café-concert may have spelled the ascendancy of the large music-halls, but a general public was thereby lost to live entertainment as music-halls became increasingly the domain of the middle class and the bourgeoisie. The cinema now was alone in attracting a general public.[4]

Far from guaranteeing a homogeneous culture, the multi-layered cinema audience suggests to me the possibility of diverse appeals for any given film and even of diverse genres targeting one or another audience sector. While the bulk of French 1930s cinema certainly followed an old-fashioned entertainment formula, one can see tensions and alternatives within many standard films. From this vantage point the amiable *Rigolboche* can take on a crafty demeanour. Contemporary interviews with Mistinguett do not reveal why it was that she agreed to make a film in 1936. Shall we consider it accommodation to reality, a realization that the end of the 'golden age of the music-hall' had come (Castle 1985: 197)? After all, she could hardly avoid certain facts: just a year earlier she concluded her sumptuous return to the Folies-Bergère in a revue that was hailed as remarkable, given her age, but no longer magical. She also had watched the conversion of one music-hall after another into a movie palace. And in a telling reversal of the usual pattern, her newest partner, Fernandel, had gained his fame on the screen before moving to the Folies-Bergère. Even her greatest rival for popularity, Josephine Baker, was expanding her name and her wealth through the cinema with *Zouzou* (1934) and *Princesse Tam-Tam* (1935).

Mistinguett may have decided to use *Rigolboche* as a kind of Trojan horse, a last-ditch tactic in a war that her side was clearly losing. She could appear to capitulate to an overconfident cinema industry that had no qualms about serving up ersatz music-hall fare as long as it brought patrons to the box-office. But Mistinguett would rise from this film to seize the spectators in the cinema through her alluring performance and hope to draw them to defect to live entertainment thereafter. As the 'Chantons' ('Let's sing') number that launches her career in *Rigolboche* tries to make plain, Mistinguett believed she had nearly supernatural abilities to sway any audience. There, under the eye of an incredulous Mr Bobby and the café-concert owner, she infects a small, tough audience until they join her song. How could the cinema spectator hope to resist her? After all, dazzled by the fabled smile her carefully designed clothes set off so perfectly, she had often conquered audiences at immense distances in music-halls seating 4,000; somehow each and every seat was within range of her charisma. At the climax of her routine, she was always able to make the crowd join in her song . . . a duet performed with 4,000 partners at the same time.

A rhetoric of 'intimacy' and 'contact' has always fashioned the manner in which theatrical personalities speak of themselves as performers. Actors tell of experiencing a different feeling with each successive audience for the same play. Dancers and singers go further since it is their very person (their voice and body) that is the site of attention, rather than a drama played through them. Over and over again, music-hall singers regret the impersonality of the cinema. Just a year before *Rigolboche*, Maurice Chevalier declared that performing live was 'the best *métier* in the world' because of the real contact with the public he loved so overwhelmingly, a contact he could not feel before the camera (Chevalier 1935).

Yet how much contact can one imagine in a music-hall the size of the Eldorado or the Alhambra? Just as the cinema invented stories like *Rigolboche* to incorporate music-hall values under its umbrella, so the music-hall likewise played up its homey origins in the very café-concerts it had run out of business. One revue that the Alhambra featured in September 1935 was titled 'Boites de nuits'. Four separate acts at nightclubs around the world (including 'The Collegiate American Bar') illustrate the social need for places where individuals can gather, drawn by the lights, the people, and the food and drink. The act progressively integrated the diverse attractions of these bars in an overriding musical rhythm that grew slightly demonic. The music-hall here represented itself as satisfying a universal need for community, conviviality and partially controlled emotional release (see *Le Music-Hall*, 2, 27 September 1935).

In its advertising, the Alhambra, like other music-halls, proclaimed both its opulence (colour, live music, impressive acts) and its homey atmosphere. Trading on its origins in the local café-concert, the Alhambra proudly announced that its beverage service would make you think you were in your local bar. They even promised to have patrons paged to their phone for emergency messages from babysitters or business partners. Such personal attention one could never find at the cinema, where anonymity ruled.

A general panic seems to have struck the music-hall world around 1935 after the conversion of so many opulent establishments to cinemas and the even more discouraging conversion to the silver screen of some of its finest entertainers (dare we mention Jean Gabin?), stars who took with them an enormous public. Thus we find the music-hall attempting simultaneously to appeal both to those in search of the exotic (via acts and dances that bordered on the lascivious) and to those hungering for a more personal, domestic quality in their entertainment. This latter impulse is most notice-able in the increasing dependence of the music-hall on nostalgia, always an unhealthy sign as a form rummages in its past glories for reasons people might want to attend to it today.

In promulgating the myth that its live performances fostered neighbour-hood values as opposed to the homogenized, international appeal of the cinema, the music-hall tried to erase its link to the cinema as part of mass entertainment. Comforting as it is to imagine performers sitting down with local patrons as in the early days of the café-concert (or, even, as at the Chartreuse in the days of Rigolboche, patrons themselves getting up to take a turn on the ramp), the music-hall could only fabricate this homey atmosphere as one of its many illusions. For the economics of entertainment had been transformed just before and after the First World War, when the Moulin Rouge, the Folies-Bergère and the Eldorado dominated night-life. This was the era of the cigar-smoking entrepreneur, who, though tied to a single house, had little in common with the café-concert owner of years past. Cutting deals with stars, or rather with agents, the Hollywood producer would soon be the model of such potentates.

Entertainment in the era of high capitalism became a regular war, the first casualties of which were those institutions holding on to traditional values. The music-hall survived the café-concert because its scale and business methods were commensurate with the cinema's. For the same reasons it overtook the circus, which, old-fashioned in both its institutional structure and its fare, was bound to fall. Circuses were organized as family enterprises in which only rarely did a key performer dominate the ensem-ble. The circus was truly a combined form, symbolized by the concept of multiple rings that came into vogue at just this moment. One cannot imagine Mistinguett or Maurice Chevalier strutting before an audience whose eyes were encouraged to stray to other focuses of attention.

The image of the ring also helps us to recognize the way circus fare differed from, and ultimately lost out to, that of the music-hall. The circus dares to expose whatever artifice it relies upon. Clowns break from the ellipse of the arena and enter the space of the audience. Performers assist in rigging their own equipment. Everything remains in view. The music-hall, on the other hand, takes its cue from the modern theatre, masking its performers behind curtains so as to present them dramatically or mys-teriously. A hidden technology of lighting, décor and music assists the performers from a world beyond, and suffuses the spectator in an ambience of the marvellous or uncanny.

The modern circus developed from the Renaissance fair, and specifically in France from what is called the *fête foraine*. Performers could be thought to have emerged from the community they entertained, and the audience for its part participated by walking through the fair. Pierre Bost, who later became well known as a novelist and scriptwriter, stressed this point in his clairvoyant monograph, *Le Cirque et le music-hall* (Bost 1931: 28–33). He regrets the defection of the circus public to the music-hall (and implicitly to the cinema) not out of nostalgia but out of an awareness of the loss of authenticity in entertainment. The circus acrobat relates casually to those he or she entertains, relates almost like a neighbour. And we cheer on the acrobat to greater feats as a way of congratulating ourselves on what the human body, our body, is capable of. But the star on the big screen or the music-hall stage has risen far above us, transcending the world we toil in. Stars are distant; they only make us dream.

Although the music-hall made use of circus acts in its bid for universal appeal,[5] it had clearly thrown in its lot with more modern practices of entertainment, practices the cinema knew best how to exploit. These included a reliance on hidden technology, on continual novelty, on illusionism, on the female body, on scale and increasingly on narrative. By the late 1920s when the music-hall turned to the thematically unified 'Revue de grand spectacle', the impact of Hollywood cinema was unmistakable. Acts that had previously been staged, as in the circus, for their variety, were now connected by a plot or theme (Bost 1931: 21).

Victorious over its rivals in live entertainment, the music-hall would in turn be conquered by the very cinema whose methods it had so cleverly learned to deploy. Hence the bad faith one should sense in the nostalgia promoted by the music-hall, for it had made obsolete the community values of live entertainment, yet still dared to pretend to thrive on intimacy and audience contact. One senses this doubly in *Rigolboche* precisely because it is a film about the music-hall and about intimacy. In each of the four numbers carefully punctuating the plot of this movie, Mistinguett gives personal and social experience value simply by putting it into song. Isolation, exploitation and tragedy find their fulfilment and justification when they become the subject of the music-hall, and especially when they are set to tune by a star for a worldwide audience. The sins of society, including the small privations of daily life, are thus expiated on stage by a heroine whose fitness for her role is registered by the distance she has put between herself and her audience in terms of personal success and wealth. No wonder Mistinguett celebrates the act of singing so jauntily and with such sincerity; song has literally transformed her life into glitter. There is no 'outside' once the music-hall has grown to the size of the egos of its producers and performers. The audience is rather invited inside the partake of their glory.

Florelle in *Le Crime de Monsieur Lange* sings otherwise. With only Lange

to listen, and us to overhear, she invokes the 'outside' of the streets of
Paris:

> Boulevard de la Chapelle where the métro soars by
> there are some pretty girls and boys who aren't shy
> starving bums soak up canned heat
> and dolls at sixty-five
> still walk the street.
> Day to day
> night to night
> under the stars
> that's how it is.
> But where are the stars?
> I've never seen them
> though I roam forgotten streets at night.
> Day after day
> night after night
> under the stars
> that's how I live
> and never a lucky star.
> That's how I live.

This *chanson réaliste* harks back to a style of singing that had dominated
the café-concerts of the nineteenth century but which, with a few exceptions, was definitely out of favour at the music-halls in the sophisticated
1930s.[6] Those exceptions include Damia, Fréhel and a rising talent, Edith
Piaf.

While a great many French films of the 1930s incorporated popular song
into their dramas, the specifically tawdry quality of the *chanteuse réaliste*
makes her an index to the stylistic labour and ideological difference of a
style of film for which *Le Crime de Monsieur Lange* could be called a harbin-
ger. Moreover, just after writing these lyrics about a seamy urban landscape, Prévert scripted *Quai des brumes* (*Port of Shadows*, 1938) and *Le Jour
se lève* (*Daybreak*, 1939).

The appearance of a *chanson réaliste* dead centre in *Le Crime de Monsieur
Lange* pays homage to the milieu of the small cafés where such songs
originated and to the milieu (the underworld) of which its lyrics invariably
spoke. Here, in the complex biology of textual borrowings and influences,
we find the cinema propelled forward stylistically by songs that were out
of fashion if heard at a theatre or on the radio. Damia sings a similar song
in *La Tête d'un homme* (*A Man's Head*, 1932) and so does Fréhel in several
of the half-dozen key films in which she played a part, *Pépé le Moko* (1936)
being the most famous. One might imagine that the music-hall milieu had
grown too elaborate to serve as appropriate *mise-en-scène* for the pathos of
such lyrics whereas the cinema, at least that cinema known as naturalist,

26

realist or, later, 'poetic realist' was eager to spread such sentiment across the screen.[7] And so if the *chanson réaliste* was nearly an anachronism in the music-halls of 1936, it helped to establish the most daring sensibility produced by the cinema of the time.

In fact Prévert's 'realist' tack in song and cinema can be taken as an angry reaction against the brilliant artifice of both the music-hall and the conventional cinema that he so loathed. Like many disaffected intellectuals of his day he was infected with a radical nostalgia for the small café-concert which had been displaced by the music-hall, for the street singers displaced by the radio, and for the crude serials of Louis Feuillade displaced by extravagant sound films.

What his generation of malcontents approved, and determined to sample, was the down-and-out world of social marginals with whom they could unashamedly identify. With this in mind, Florelle's song is not a homage to music-hall performance at all but rather to life on the Boulevard de la Chapelle, the same area of Paris singled out in the litany of métro stops recited by Jean Gabin in *Pépé le Moko*. These films actually celebrate one of the last Parisian neighbourhoods untouched by modernization and sanitation. Moreover, they call up the indigenous entertainment form at the edges of Montmartre (the entertainment form of these marginals, not of tourists dropping piles of money at the Moulin Rouge),[8] the *bal populaire*.

It may seem odd to conclude my discussion of French entertainment with something so quaint as the *bal* but in fact this was the only live form to register dramatic gains in revenue during the 1930s.[9] And it suits my purposes exactly, for the *bal* stands opposite the music-hall in every respect. It rejects illusion, technology, grandeur and passive spectacle in favour of modesty and participation (the clients dance, talk and even sing). Moreover, like the café-concert of the nineteenth century, it fostered a family atmosphere, only this time the 'family' was the Mafia, or their Marseillais and Corsican counterparts (Chevalier 1980: 344). Prévert claims to have felt authentically alive there, and so did artists like Utrillo, photographers like Brassai, and (most important for the cinema) writers like Francis Carco and Pierre Mac Orlan.[10]

Although *Le Crime de Monsieur Lange* was a studio-made film, it did take for its subject the working-class milieu which it then consciously mythologized as a new kind of family. Perhaps more important, it was produced by just such a family, by an *équipe* (a team) of artisans whose mutual respect and dedication lifted their labour out of the alienating conditions that technology and contemporary business practices enforced. Thus, the ideology of domesticity returns here on the other side of the music-hall which had bartered it away in the search for mass entertainment and profit. The family celebrated in the poetic realist cinema, however, is not the productive and reproductive social cell but the 'band', tied together by respect and honour, against the odds that modernity has stacked against

27

Plate 2 Community entertainment: Florelle (left), Maurice Baquet (centre) and René Lefèvre (right) in *Le Crime de Monsieur Lange*. By courtesy of the British Film Institute, London.

everyone. Its place of relaxation and togetherness is the *bal*, not the gaudy music-hall.

Let me conclude by looping back to Mistinguett. In 1918, while in search of a showcase number to tie down her act, she fell upon an early novel written by Carco. Working with his images and prose, she and her writers came up with what would ever after be her signature song, 'Mon homme' ('My man'). And so Carco, who, before the First World War, had played cultural hooky, to take in life at the café-concerts, inspired their greatest star at just the moment when she would take the music-hall into the realm of mass art and he would desert her for the back alley *bals* of Montmartre. One finds neither Carco's name nor Mistinguett's in the credits of more than a couple of films of the time, but I hope to have shown that their presence, their competitive presence, helped to define and animate the French cinema of the 1930s as part of a very unsystematic entertainment milieu.

NOTES

1 We might also mention the sensational murder of the music-hall king Oscar Dufrenne, director of the Casino de Paris and a municipal councillor, that rocked the entertainment world a few months before the Stavisky revelations. See Louis Chevalier, *Montmartre du plaisir et du crime*, Paris, Laffont, 1980, p. 420).

2 A most thorough treatment of the competitive relationship between media and texts can be found in Jim Collins, *Uncommon Cultures: Popular Culture and Post-Modernism*, New York, Routledge, 1989.

3 The Popular Front is commonly said to have organized itself with regard precisely to 'vigilance', and specifically to have arisen from the 1934 CVIA (Comité de Vigilance des Intellectuals Anti-fascistes).

4 The fluctuation of audience types at various forms of entertainments has been documented for one region by René Noëll, 'Histoire du spectacle cinématographique à Perpignan, 1896–1944', *Cahiers de la cinémathèque*, special number, 1973.

5 In the 1930s the music-hall recruited ballerinas, opera singers and even the poet Maurice Rostand as bait for the educated public while clowns, animals and chorus lines were targeted for a different part of the audience spectrum. This apparent schizophrenia was justified by the term 'variety'.

6 In fact the melodramatic style that fanned the growth of the café-concert fifty years earlier had been derailed by the joyous, often irreverent, and scintillating songs of Mistinguett among many others. The music-hall's fabulous growth just after the First World War coincided with the arrival of American jazz. Josephine Baker, Mireille, Charles Trenet and many others recruited the energy of jazz for their own purposes.

7 This link between the *chanson réaliste* and poetic realist cinema was already made in Pascal Sevran, 'Fréhel', in *Le Music-hall français de Mayol à Julien Clerc*, Paris, Orban, 1978. See also Ginette Vincendeau, 'The mise-en-scène of suffering: French chanteuses réalistes', *New Formations* 3, 1987.

8 As early as 1923 Maurice Sachs complained that Montmartre music-halls existed solely for tourists, primarily American. For a thorough history of the entire Montmartre scene, see Chevalier 1980: 343–6.

9 To picture these sites, call to mind images from scores of films of the 1930s, the 'Bal de Quatre Saisons', for example, in Jean Vigo's *L'Atalante* (1934). Jacques Becker would set the major action of his homage to poetic realism *Casque d'Or (Golden Marie*, 1952) in such a bar-room.

10 For a discussion of these writers in relation to the cinema, see Dudley Andrew, 'French film and fiction in the 1930s', *L'Esprit Créateur* 30 (2), 1990.

REFERENCES

Andrew, Dudley (1990) 'French film and fiction in the 1930s', *L'Esprit Créateur* 30 (2).

Bost, Pierre (1931) *Le Cirque et le music-hall*, Paris: Au Sans-Pareil.

Castle, Charles (1985) *The Folies-Bergère*, New York: Watts Publishers.

Chevalier, Louis (1980) *Montmartre du plaisir et du crime*, Paris: Robert Laffont.

Chevalier, Maurice (1935) *Le Music-hall* 3, 11 October.

Collins, Jim (1989) *Uncommon Cultures: Popular Culture and Post-Modernism*, New York: Routledge.

de Banville, Théodore (1933) *Souvenirs*, quoted in Pierre Dufay, 'De l'Alcazar au cinéma', *Mercure de France*, 1 September.

Noëll, René (1973) 'Histoire du spectacle cinématographique à Perpignan, 1896–1944', *Cahiers de la cinémathèque*, special number.

Sesonske, Alexander (1980) *Jean Renoir: the French Films 1924–1939*, Cambridge, Mass.: Harvard University Press.

Sevran, Pascal (1978) 'Fréhel', in *Le Music-hall français de Mayol à Julien Clerc*, Paris: Orban.

Tabet, Georges (1979) *Vivre deux fois*, Paris: Robert Laffont.

Vincendeau, Ginette (1985) 'French cinema in the 1930s, social text and context of a popular entertainment medium', unpublished PhD dissertation, University of East Anglia.

—— (1987) 'The mise-en-scène of suffering: French chanteuses réalistes', *New Formations* 3.

2

LA LEY DEL DESEO

A gay seduction

José Arroyo

INTRODUCTION

Pedro Almodóvar's *La ley del deseo* (*The Law of Desire*, 1987) is a deliriously romantic, relatively sexually explicit, gay melodrama. The narrative has two plot lines: the relationship between Pablo (Eusebio Poncela) and his transsexual sister Tina (Carmen Maura) and a gay romantic triangle – Pablo is loved by Antonio (Antonio Banderas) but loves Juan (Miguel Molina) who is straight. The film's exploration of the protagonists' relationships is very tender, giving full due to their emotional dimension while revealing joyful and sensual sex lives. The characters are easy to identify with, their emotions operatic, their actions mythic. And it is erotic. In the age of AIDS, it is the last thing I expected to see in a relatively big-budget mainstream film, especially a Spanish one.

The Spanish cinema I remembered from my childhood in Spain was a series of historical pageants and folkloric tales in which the state, the church and the family were idealized; poverty was a state of grace that speeded one's entry into heaven; the foreign was depicted only to reveal its inherent inferiority; and Immaculate Conception was experienced by all Spanish women. For me, this period is best represented by Ladislao Vajda's *Marcelino, pan y vino* (*Marcelino, Bread and Wine*, 1954) in which an orphan is left to live with monks. I saw it in the late 1960s (it circulated around rural Spain for years after it was first released in Madrid) and I have never forgotten the ending in which Jesus sweeps the little boy off to heaven.

Under Franco's regime, Spanish filmmakers were culturally isolated and their work heavily censored. According to Virginia Higginbotham, 'censorship was the central fact of cultural life in Spain for thirty-eight years' (Higginbotham 1988: 17). Censorship was changed in Frankist Spain in 1963 when new norms were introduced. Ce'sar Santos Fontenla writes that they were 'received with joy . . . under them, one could speak of liberty of expression for new filmmakers' (1986: 180). Yet still prohibited were an endless list of subjects: the justification of suicide, homicide, revenge,

31

divorce, adultery, illicit sexual relations, prostitution, abortion and contraception. Homosexuality, whether the film justified it or not, was forbidden representation as a central part of the plot or 'even with a secondary character, except if in this last case it is required in order to develop the action and has a clear and predominant moral consequence' (Molina-Foix 1977: 48). Even after censorship was formally abolished in 1977, two years after Franco's death, 'there were still certain unwritten taboos, the main ones relating to criticism of the monarchy, the armed forces, and perhaps the police, or more pointedly the almost sacrosanct and feared Civil Guard' (Besas 1985: 185). In *La ley* not only is a gay triangle a central part of the plot, but a Civil Guard is depicted as gay and the police are satirized as lazy and buffoonish.

I continued to see Spanish cinema as a teenager growing up in Montreal but *La ley* seemed to bear little relation to it. Franco's death in 1975 did not immediately bring the radical changes to Spanish cinema many expected. Since the only personal expression an authoritarian state condones is that which coincides with its own ideology, some of the best Spanish filmmakers had to create a covert film style to communicate and survive, one the censors didn't understand. In an interview director Carlos Saura noted that, 'For me and my compatriots, to make the stories we wanted to make, we had to use indirect methods. For example, we couldn't use a linear structure or the ideas would be too clear' (Kinder 1979: 16). Filmmakers who had relied on metaphor, symbol and ellipsis for many years continued working in such a style even after censorship was abolished in 1977.

When I saw *La ley del deseo*, the other Spanish films showing at the Montreal World Film Festival that year, 1987, were concerned with the past. Mario Camus's *La casa de Bernarda Alba* (*The House of Bernarda Alba*, 1987) was an adaptation of Lorca's play; Fernando Trueba's *El año de las luces* (*The Year of the Lights*, 1987) was about adolescents growing up during the civil war; and Manuel Gutierrez Aragon's *La mitad del cielo* (*Half the Sky*, 1986) spanned thirty years in the life of a woman and ended in the 1960s. Films such as Jaimen de Armiñan's *Mi general* (*My General*, 1987) were meant to be contemporary but could just as easily have been set in the past. *La ley del deseo* was set in contemporary Spain, it acknowledged no taboos, and it was refreshingly direct. It was the only film I saw at the Festival which seemed not to be burdened by the *estética Frankista*.

As a Spanish-Canadian who had not returned to Spain for many years, the very existence of *La ley* was unexpected. Spanish society remains mostly homophobic. A recent poll in *El Pais*, a popular daily, reveals that 50 per cent of Spaniards still believe homosexuality should be condemned (cited in Garcia de Leon and Maldonado 1989: 63n.37). The assumption that relatively explicit gay romantic love would normally be a barrier to a film's box-office success in Spain is not unreasonable. Yet *La ley* was the most popular Spanish film in Spain in the first quarter of 1987 (Besas 1987: 37) and was still playing in Madrid close to three years after its initial release (*La guia del ocio*, June 1989: 28–32). Moreover, the film was funded by the Ministry of Culture.

In this chapter I will try to fill in the gaps between expectations and outcomes that resulted in the above surprises. I propose to show some of the ways in which the film overcame the barrier to mainstream acceptance which its explicit depictions of homosexual romance represent. In order to do so I will briefly sketch a context for the production and consumption of *La ley del deseo* in Spain. I will then examine aspects of the film's narrative in order to demonstrate some of the strategies by which the film tried to avoid alienating its audience.

DELINEATING A CONTEXT

In the early 1980s, Almodóvar's persona, a diverse group of young Madrid artists – labelled *la movida* (the upsurge) by the press and post-Franco Spanish society were engaged in a dynamic interaction. To different extents, each element influenced the construction or the development of the other. Underlying all of them was the concept of the new: the cinema of a new filmmaker produced by a new culture in a new society. The linchpin to these mutually reinforcing structures can be found in Almodóvar's first films.

Pepi, Luci, Bom y otras chicas del montón (*Pepi, Luci, Bom and All the Other Girls*, 1980), Almodóvar's first film, is a cartoonish punk movie. Roughly shot, episodic in structure and anarchic in sensibility, it was privately financed on a minuscule budget of 5–6 million pesetas (Vidal 1988: 25) and released in a repertory cinema. The critics immediately praised it. José Luis Rubio wrote, 'it is one of the most diverting, free, audacious and imaginative films ever made in Spain' (cited in Garcia de Leon and Maldonado 1987: 242). It grossed 18.5 million in its first year (*Boletin Informativo de Control de Taquilla, Datos '87*: 125). *Laberinto de pasiones* (*Labyrinth of Passions*, 1982), a farce about two nymphos who meet each other and turn monogamous, was financed, distributed and exhibited by the same cinema in which *Pepi* had been shown. When it was released, Antonio Lara (1982) wrote, 'A new aesthetic inevitably requires new spectators gifted with a new sensibility . . . *Laberinto* unquestioningly belongs to this new form of making and seeing.' It cost 20 million (Para 1982) and grossed 67.5 million (*Boletin Informativo de Control de Taquilla, Datos '87*: 93).

Pepi and *Laberinto* represented a kind of guerrilla cinema, produced and consumed outside the mainstream. It was a cinema targeted at a youth audience ignored by both commercial and 'art film' directors in Spain. The two films aimed to *épater* not only *les bourgeois* but everybody. Neither audiences nor critics were used to raw, sometimes technically imperfect, chaotic narratives depicting cartoonish characters eating snot, participating in 'General Erections' contests, or enjoying their nymphomania.

Members of *la movida* participated in the first films. Alaska, who played Bom, the sadistic lesbian punk in *Pepi*, became one of the biggest pop stars in Spain after its release. Others included the Pegamoides who sang in *Pepi* and *Laberinto*; painter Guillermo Pérez Villalta and Costus who helped design the sets; fashion designers like Ouka Lele and Montesinos contributed costumes, and director Ivan Zulueta and cartoonist Ceesepe created the posters.

All these diverse artists gained celebrity around the late 1970s or early 1980s. Their contributions helped to focus attention on *Pepi* and *Laberinto*. Their fame was in turn augmented by the subsequent success of the films. Members of *la movida* also attended the scandalous premières (Garcia de Leon and Maldonado 1989: 57); there were bomb threats (ibid.: 61) and, in the case of *Laberinto*, the distributor withdrew at the last moment claiming the film would incite public unrest (Ferrando and Echeverria 1982: 34).

At the same time Almodóvar had also gained a small measure of celebrity in several other fields. He acted with an avant-garde theatre group, wrote for underground magazines and national newspapers and weeklies, created several porn *fotonovelas*, published a short novel and founded his own punk band, Almodóvar y McNamara. According to Méndez-Leite, during this time, 'Almodóvar devoted himself to shock in all fields: press, television, rock' (cited in Bayón 1989: 58). His shock tactics paid off. Almodóvar's celebrity quickly surpassed that normally due to a successful film director and became more like that of a movie star. What he wore, whether he had gained weight, his love life, his origins, all were of interest to the media (Garcia Leon and Maldonado 1989: 70–1). Almodóvar's celebrity in the fields of comics, music and literature also helped publicize his films and his films in turn increased his fame.

'As a child [Almodóvar] was poor and Manchego; as an adult he is a shining star', wrote Rosa Montero (cited in Garcia de Leon and Maldonado 1989: 30). The comment is typical. A few years before, Almodóvar had been a lowly clerk in the national telephone company and now he was a celebrated filmmaker; he was born poor and was now rich; he had been rural and now personified urban chic; from the backwater of La Mancha he travelled to distant parts of the world to receive acclaim for his films. He embodied the promise of post-Franco Spain: equal opportunity to all for the expected new wealth; industrialization and urbanization; international markets and international acceptance. According to Garcia de Leon, 'Today [1988], Almodóvar has become a type of social institution that defines what's new in Spanish society' (Garcia de Leon and Maldonado 1989: 71).

In 1982 Francisco Umbral wrote that,

Themes that another cinema (like the society it reflects) would circle and circumvent via the old psychological approach . . . themes that in the culture of the cultured are totem and taboo (so that they may last rather than so that they may be resolved), [Almodóvar's] cinema treats directly, it turns them upside-down.

(quoted in Garcia de Leon and Maldonado 1989: 65)

The first films derived their uniqueness, at least in part, from being released at a time when literary adaptations reigned. Jorge Berlanga (1984) noted that Almodóvar's films were seen as shocking because the rest of Spanish cinema was 'obsessed with the obtuse existentialism of lefty academics, the dryness of rural drama, the reliving of the civil war or stupidly dense poetic dreams'.

Pepi and *Laberinto* could not have been made during the Franco years. Their existence and circulation in turn publicized the difference of the new government and the changes in society. It is no surprise that the government supported Almodóvar's filmmaking from the beginning:[1] his cinema was personal; the foreign critics said it was good; and, as an unexpected bonus, it was even popular in Spain. The interface between the Almodóvar *œuvre*/persona, *la movida* and the new society (especially its morality), and the wide publicity given to all of these factors, enabled the films to be made and put into circulation, and created a context for their consumption.

In December 1983, the Partido Socialista Obrero Español, elected in 1982, introduced new film legislation. The law is popularly known as the 'Miró decree' after Pilar Miró, the director of *El crimen de Cuenca* (*The Crime of Cuenca*, 1979), who was then Minister of Culture. The Miró decree explicitly stated that 'we are looking to facilitate production of quality films, projects for new filmmakers, those aimed at children and those of an experimental nature' (LLinás 1987: 36).

Quality cinema was to be bought by pouring money into production. Following the French system of *avances sur recettes*, a film could now receive a grant of up to 65 per cent of its budget, on the strength of the quality of the project or the grosses of the director's previous films. Once the film was made, the Protection Fund could award it a further subsidy of up to another 65 per cent of its box-office gross also on the strength of its quality. Whether a film qualified as 'quality' or not was judged by a committee. Almodóvar was to benefit greatly from this system.

Thomas Elsaesser has written that, 'what is valued by a government financing its filmmakers is not a particular use-value or even propaganda function, but, precisely, a relentless commitment to self-expression' (Elsaesser 1989: 44). Spanish film financing also encourages personal expression, but precisely because it sees 'art' as its by-product and thus derives both a use-value and propaganda function (though sometimes its use-value may only be its propaganda function). Almodóvar's cinema

35

became the perfect raw material for a country which wanted to present a new image at home and abroad.

According to Marvin D'Lugo (1986: 53), 'The implicit message of the dominant narrative genres of the Franco years – particularly the novel and film as they exploited national historical themes – was, as Frankist apologists like to put it, "Spain is different".' The interaction between Almodóvar's persona, his films, *la movida* and the new Spanish society also emphasized difference. But it was not the difference from the rest of Europe so energetically cultivated by the previous regime. Rather, the dynamic interaction reinforced an image of difference from Frankism itself. And one of the ways it did this was through the creation of an image of Spain in successful pursuit of similarity with the rest of Europe. Writing about *Entre tinieblas* (*Dark Habits*),[2] Almodóvar's 1983 film which featured a lesbian nun as one of its protagonists, Julian Peiro (1983) opined that, 'the acceptance of such a film is evidence that Spanish society has changed much more than part of this society would have us believe. Its development has produced filmmakers like Almodóvar and has made possible films like this one.'

By 1987, most people knew what kind of cinema they were getting when they went to see an Almodóvar film. After the sadomasochistic punks and bisexual nymphos of his first films, he wrote and directed *¿Qué he hecho yo para merecer esto!* (*What Have I Done to Deserve This?*, 1984) in which an oppressed working-class housewife kills her husband with a hambone and sells her gay son to a dentist, and *Matador* (1986) in which a man and a woman who both kill their sexual partners in the midst of orgasm get together for an ultimate thrill.

Spanish audiences knew they were going to see something original and shocking when they went to see *La ley del deseo*, but this was because the film was Almodóvar's rather than because it was about gays. Spanish audiences had had plenty of opportunities to see gays in film before Almodóvar had even begun making features. According to Román Gubern (1983: 20),

> the most significant aspect of this chapter [the mid to late 1970s] in the history of Spanish film is that in a number of movies, one finds serious treatment of male homosexuality and transvestism for the first time. Among these films are Vicente Aranda's *Cambio de sexo* ([*Change of Sex*] 1976), Eloy de la Iglesas' *Los placeres ocultos* ([*Hidden Pleasures*] 1976) and *El diputado* ([*The Deputy*] 1978), Jaime Chavarri's *A un dios desconocido* ([*To an Unknown God*] 1977), Pedro Olea's *Un hombre llamado 'Flor de Otoño'* ([*A Man Called 'Autumn Flower'*] 1978), and Ventura Pons's *Ocaña, retrato intermitente* ([*Ocaña, Intermittent Portrait*] 1978).

Moreover, the press had long recognized a gay sensibility in Almodóvar's films, even taunting him about not giving it full expression. 'In the end he's not prepared to reveal more . . . directly through [his] sexuality', wrote Carlos Benitez Gonzalez (1982). The fact that Almodóvar would not put homosexuality at the centre of his films was seen as a block to his self-expression. In turn, this was interpreted as a reason why his films were not those of a true auteur. When *La ley* was released Pedro Crespo (1987) titled his review, '*La ley del deseo* unblocks the career of Pedro Almodóvar'. In the text he added that the world depicted in *La ley* was 'relatively similar to [Almodóvar's] own'. Not only had the scene been set for the positive acceptance of *La ley* on various levels, but there was even a desire for the film.

THE TEXT

La ley del deseo was made in a country where US films have long dominated the box-office and where classic Hollywood films, dubbed into Spanish, are a perennial fixture of prime-time television. It should be no surprise that *La ley* differs from and defers to classic Hollywood cinema. *La ley* addresses a spectator familiar with the conventions of classic cinema even as it confounds them. Part of the viewer's pleasure lies in the recognition of misrecognition. Yet *La ley* transgresses some of the classic mode's central tenets: if in the latter, 'the male figure cannot bear the burden of sexual objectification' (Mulvey 1988: 63), in *La ley* he has become Olympian at it; instead of the formation of the heterosexual couple (Bordwell 1986: 19), it is the formation of the homosexual couple that is a central structuring element in *La ley*'s narrative; and whereas 'the Hollywood film strives to conceal its artifice' (Bordwell *et al.* 1985: 3), *La ley* delights in showing it off, yet still manages to create an effect of verisimilitude. All this begs the question of whether and how *La ley* regulates and/or contains these differences.

La ley's beginning is a preamble. None of the characters in it will reappear throughout the rest of the film. The bulk of the exposition occurs in the next scene. The central problematic of the film, the desire to possess another, is evident here, but in a different way. The rest of the film will emphasize love; the beginning emphasizes raw sex – having it, watching it, depicting it, buying it. This opening sets a tone and is a treatment of male homosexuality that makes great demands on the viewer who is not a gay male.

According to David Bordwell (1985: 38), 'The sequential nature of narrative makes the initial portion of a text crucial for the establishment of hypotheses.' The beginning of the film creates strong first impressions which 'become the basis for our expectations across the entire film' (Bordwell *et al.* 1985: 37). Bordwell calls this process 'the primacy effect'. *La ley*'s beginning leaves the viewer few options: s/he can watch or s/he can leave. And if s/he passes that first hurdle, and if we assume that there is indeed a 'primacy effect' in operation, nothing in the rest of the film will be as problematic.

La ley begins with an unnamed man walking into the frame. A male off-screen voice directs him: 'start undressing . . . look at yourself in the mirror. Kiss yourself . . . think it is me you are kissing and you like it. Touch yourself between your bum . . . you're getting more and more turned on . . . ask me to fuck you.' As this is going on the man's body is displayed as spectacle. The camera moves in to get a good view and different shots emphasize different parts of his body. New characters are then unexpectedly introduced, we realize that they are dubbers and that the initial part of the scene was just a movie within a movie.

The scene has two points of intensity. The first is when the sexual object is ordered to ask to be penetrated. The second is when he has his orgasm. After the first, the film begins a denouement. The subsequent shots gets shorter in length. The narration is much more knowledgeable than the spectator. Each new revelation is incongruent and results in laughter (throughout the film every sexual situation that could result in discomforting a heterosexual audience is defused by humour). The second point of intensity, the sexual object's orgasm, is accompanied by the laughter that results in showing a bald, fat, short man dubbing the orgasm, and the audience's knowledge that there is going to be no penetration.

The introduction to the film is disturbing in both what it depicts and how it is depicted. It breaks all the rules. There are no establishing shots. The narrative travels through four different spaces: the bedroom, the dubbing studio, the lab of the dubbing studio and then the cinema. The narration is highly uncommunicative, as we become conscious of these differences in diegetic space only near the end. Nor does the narration respect the rules of continuity editing. But at the end of the scene we are made to laugh, and then the knowledge that it is just a movie is brought to the fore. So is the reason for the two climaxes. The first indicated what the film threatened to become. The second reassured us as to what the film would in fact be like.

Roland Barthes has written of the distinction between what he calls a 'text of bliss' and a 'text of pleasure'. The first is the 'text that imposes a state of loss, the text that discomforts . . . unsettles the reader's historical, cultural, psychological assumptions' (Barthes 1977: 14); the second is 'the text that contents, fills, grants euphoria; the text that comes from culture and does not break with it, is linked to a comfortable practice of reading' (ibid.). In the first shot of the next scene there is a freeze-frame of *La ley del deseo*'s three main protagonists as the title of the film is superimposed over them. We have been taken from the shocking movie-within-a-movie to the comforting 'reality' of the 'real' movie in a burst of applause. If the first scene could be said to lean towards a text of bliss, then the first shot signals that the rest of the film will be more of a text of pleasure. And in

fact nothing in the rest of the film will challenge our old viewing habits
or our new expectations to the same extent.

LIFE IS A BOLERO

> Love like ours is a punishment
> that one carries in one's heart until death.
> My fate needs your fate,
> and you need me so much more.
>
> That is why there will never be a goodbye,
> and there will be no peace that will console us.
> And the pace of pain will find us
> going through life on our knees
> face to face and nothing more.
>
> Carlos Arturo Briz, 'Encadenados' ('Chained')

'Love is not a joke,' says Antonio to Pablo in *La ley del deseo*. But as the
above lyrics to Lucho Gatica's bolero prove, it could be funny. Yet, when
I listen to 'Encadenados', I find it very moving. The bolero is the mode
par excellence of Hispanic sentimental music. In a bolero, a dialectic interaction of lyrics, music and performance can make the most delirious
emotions seem the essence of verisimilitude. In Almodóvar's *Entre tinieblas*,
Yolanda, the protagonist, sings 'Encadenados' and then says, 'It's music
that speaks of, that tells the truth about life. Because rich or poor, everyone's been in love or suffered a disappointment.' The bolero can not only
'contain' excess, it demands it.

The freeze-frame that introduces the title in the second scene plants
the protagonists. The man and the woman embracing in the centre of the
frame are Tina and Pablo. Tina used to be Tino. But he fell in love with
his father. They were caught by the mother. And they left the family to go
to Morocco to consume their passion. Tino loved his father so much that
he decided to become a she for him. There have only been two men in
Tina's life: her father and her spiritual director. Both left her and she's
never been able to give herself to another since.

Pablo is a famous film director. It was his film that we saw at the
beginning of *La ley*. Pablo is in love with Juan. Juan loves him too, but
without passion. By the time Juan is ready to reciprocate Pablo's passion,
it will be too late. Antonio, the man who came out of nowhere to be frozen
on the left of the frame during the title sequence, will kill Juan before that
passion can be consummated.

As the story develops, there will be a lot of letter writing, many misunderstandings, and Pablo will develop amnesia. Like the lyrics to the bolero, it
all sounds a bit absurd. But like the bolero, which will itself play an

Plate 3 Desire: Eusebio Poncela and Antonio Banderas in *La ley del deseo*. By courtesy of the British Film Institute, London.

important role in the narration, it is not absurd because the mode of narration chosen to tell this story is the melodrama.

LINEARITY AS CONTAINMENT

One of the ways *La ley* attempts to regulate its excesses is through a quasi-classical narrative structure. *La ley* has three, rather than one, psychologically motivated protagonists – Pablo, Antonio and Tina. But Pablo is the one whose presence or absence is the key structuring element. When he's not on-screen, the other characters talk about him, act so as to meet him, block his desires, or plot to have him fulfil theirs. He's the one who writes the letters, makes the film, writes the screenplay and gives the interview that links all the other characters. His typewriter, screenplay and letters also play important roles in driving the narrative forward.

David Bordwell has written that, 'The classical film has at least two lines of action both causally linking the same group of characters. And almost invariably, one of these lines of action involves heterosexual romantic love' (Bordwell *et al.* 1985: 17). In such films the line involving love often simultaneously signals a passage from the conjugal into the familial. According to Raymond Bellour, classic film narrative can be seen as an Oedipal trajectory in which the hero has 'to accept as his own a positive relationship between desire and the law' (Bergstrom 1979: 93). He must 'accept the symbolization of the death of the father, the displacement from the attachment to the mother to the attachment to another woman' (ibid.: 90).

In *La ley*, Pablo must also reconcile his desire with a symbolic law of the father. Except that in *La ley* the desire, the first line of action, is not for socially acceptable heterosexual coupling but for homosexual love. Pablo has no problems with sex. He fucks often and he fucks fine. Sexual desire arises continuously in Pablo but it is often, even if only momentarily, fulfilled: 'You're so promiscuous', Antonio tells him. The desire of Pablo's that continuously gets blocked is what Steve Neale has called the 'key to the melodramatic fantasy' (Neale 1986: 13), the union of a couple through love. And the major blockage to the fulfilment of that fantasy is heterosexuality: Juan is straight. However, in *La ley*, the formation of a family, rather than being subsumed into the formation of the couple, is a separate, secondary, line of action. It will naturally bypass the conjugal.

As the narrative unfolds, these two lines of action balance each other. The formation of the homosexual couple is juxtaposed to the formation of a non-nuclear family. When things in one line get worse, the other compensates for it. For example, at the beginning of the film, when Pablo's relationship with Juan is in crisis, Ada, Tina and Pablo are shown as a happy family. After Pablo receives the letter saying that Juan loves him, he has a big fight with Tina. And after Tina and Pablo patch things up,

Antonio will kill Juan. At the end of the film, when Antonio and Pablo are finally joined for a last hour of love, Tina and Ada are ejected from the apartment. If one could read the formation of the homosexual couple as a transgression of patriarchy, and the formation of the family as an affirmation of it (the family depicted in *La ley* is non-nuclear rather than anti-nuclear), it's almost as if the struggle between the two lines of action which interact dialectically and help push the narrative forward is involved in a process similar to that of myth – *La ley*'s narrative attempts an imaginary resolution of real contradictions (Lévi-Strauss 1968: 229). It is quite characteristic of the film to subvert even as it satisfies.

Heterosexuality is a metaphoric, and sometimes literal, block to the fulfilment of the protagonist's desires. In *La ley*, Juan's love for Pablo is more philia than eros. Even when Juan tells him over the phone that he loves him, or when he submits to him and signs the letter which Pablo wrote and wants to receive, it's due merely to a desire to desire. Pablo and Juan's desires are incompatible. This is made clear when at the beginning of the film Juan asks him, 'What are we doing together Pablo?' And Pablo answers, 'It's not your fault that you're not in love with me. And it's not my fault that I'm in love with you. That's why it's good that you're leaving. If I don't see you, I'll get over it.'

Antonio also sees Juan as a block to his desire. But it is his socialization as a heterosexual man that is his worst enemy. The scene at the lighthouse, where Antonio kills Juan, is illuminating. The phallic imagery is overdetermined: the scene begins with a long shot of the lighthouse itself towering over them and seemingly touching the stars ('Pablo needs something more', says Juan); Antonio carries a flashlight which lights the way ('Why don't you stop playing with the flashlight?' Juan asks him); Antonio holds a bottle of whisky for Juan to drink from and then takes it back; after which Antonio will try to kiss Juan and then, in the shot which follows, will say, 'I want to possess you.' This scene could be read as a suicidal struggle between heterosexuality (Juan) and patriarchy (Antonio), where the former is the latter's victim. For the same characteristics that oppress Antonio socially as a gay man are here attributed to him personally: competitiveness, power, domination, violence, the need to control, and the need to possess. But they both lose – in killing Juan, Antonio seals his own doom.

Heterosexuality is also a problem for Tina. Her sex change was an attempt to mould herself into what her father desired. Her father's leaving her is part of the reason she doesn't want to get emotionally involved again: 'All that is over for me and I don't want to talk about it', she says. The other reason is that she has problems accepting her changeover into heterosexuality. 'I know I'm ridiculous', she tells Pablo. Even Ada's desire for a family is blocked by heterosexuality – her mother always leaves her as a result of getting involved with men. Moreover, all the figures of authority in the film (Antonio's mother, the policemen, the detectives, the absent fathers, the doctor) are all straight. Yet one of the interesting things about *La ley* is that even as heterosexuality is presented as a block, it is not depicted negatively. The figures of authority are not all repressive and some (the young policeman, the old detective and the doctor) are very helpful and sympathetic. It is only the homophobic characters that the film makes villainous, by inviting us to identify with the protagonists.

The narrative's presentation of the family is also very contradictory. The nuclear family is depicted as oppressive. Antonio makes Pablo sign his letters with a woman's name so that his mother won't find out he's homosexual. The family never delivers the love and security it promises. Fathers (Tina and Pablo's, Ada's and Antonio's) are always absent. Antonio's mother snoops on him even as she smothers him with attention. And fathers leave, families dissolve and one is left alone (Tina and Ada). Yet, the support and the affection that are traditionally provided by the family is valued.

La ley depicts a 1980s version of the 'family romance' at various levels of the narrative. The story of Ada is almost a literal re-enactment of the sexual stage of the family romance as described by Freud: Ada knows who her real mother is but she wishes that Pablo, who she's in love with, were her father. For Freud, the child's fantasies are a 'means through which the child, in its own mind, may oppose its parents and challenge their position of authority' (De Cordova 1987: 256). Ada feels slighted by her mother. And she retaliates, and gains her independence, by adopting Pablo and Tina as her new parents. Metaphorically, *La ley* also recounts Antonio's and Tina's growth into sexual identity within the family and their attempts to resolve the Oedipus complex.

The second line of action gets resolved when Tina fills Pablo in on her past with their father and they finally clinch their bonding through an embrace. The film's imaginary resolution to this contradiction is to create an alternative family that delivers the promises of the nuclear one: the gay brother and the transsexual sister will provide the love and security Ada's real parents deny her.

At the end of the film both lines of action converge. Pablo saves his family by giving himself to Antonio. (Antonio's threat was foreshadowed earlier: Ada, Pablo and Tina are laughing together after the success of their play. Antonio, the outsider, is shooting at a video machine, spying on them. His image is reflected on the glass that separates him from this happy family. They are clustered on the right side of the frame. He is on the left pointing to them with a gun.) Pablo's family and all the heterosexual figures of authority who've tried to prevent this union are downstairs on the street, gazing upwards in awe, seemingly astounded by the power of what they imagine is taking place. But then Antonio kills himself. Pablo, who thinks it was his writing the letters and the screenplay that caused all the problems, throws his typewriter out of the window. There's an unexplained explosion and, irrationally, all the people who had been waiting outside start climbing up the fire-escape as if they were the Keystone Cops. In order to satisfy, the end, which could have been tragic, is made humorous. It is only when this image has been frozen and the credits begin that Bola Negra's 'Dejame recordar', the bolero which had accompanied the image of Pablo embracing Antonio's dead body, re-emerges on the soundtrack:

> Who of your life would you erase
> who in reminding you, will make you forget
> this love, made of blood and pain,
> poor love which saw us both cry
> and also made us dream and live
> when did it cease to exist
> today that it's lost
> let me remember
> the strong beating
> of the departing heart's goodbye.

So the end has itself been subverted. The freeze-frame of the crowd in mid-motion is forgotten and the soundtrack provides full narrative closure. Before that there had been a linear progression of events that led to the end and made it understandable. The two wants of narrative, process and closure, have been satisfied.

CONCLUSION

La ley is a locus of contradictions. But the text also offers imaginary resolutions. It overcomes such blocks as the objectification of the male body, the formation of the homosexual couple and its own self-consciousness by effacing them with the pleasures traditionally associated with narrative. The 'primacy effect' creates a new set of expectations; the struggle between the two narrative lines disguises the shock of the 'new' subject matter by making it compatible with the affirmation of traditional values such as the family; and various aspects of the narration siphon off excesses so that the 'outrageous' conforms with verisimilitude. All of these elements together interact so as to regulate the film's transgressions. They create, and make believable, a fantasy of love and caring between people, and subvert a mainstream audience's regular reactions to the kind of people being depicted. The film is then able to invite the spectator to identify with the protagonists through point-of-view structure, through the narration itself, and through the fantasy scenario, just as with any other melodrama. And the narration's regulation of knowledge generates its own brand of affects – laughter and tears. *La ley* regulates its differences so that the spectator is drawn into the world of the diegesis, and through the unfolding of various desires, kept there until the end. In containing its difference, while flaunting others, *La ley* offers many audiences various pleasures including that of sameness and that of singularity.

The film had been produced in a context in which the funding bodies encouraged its differences. The explicit depictions of gay romance, what I had initially thought of as a barrier to the film's box-office success, were eagerly awaited by important critics. And the 'shock' which is one of the effects of such depictions is a characteristic of Almodóvar's authorial persona and was one of the pleasures Spanish audiences expected when they went to see one of his films.

It is significant, however, that *La ley* was made and consumed in a context in which cinema had ceased to be a popular medium. In 1986 a poll commissioned by the Instituto de Cinematografia revealed that 60 per cent of Spaniards never go to the cinema at all (Guarner 1988: 309); cinema attendance had dropped from 220 million spectators in 1978 to 85.7 million in 1987 (Guarner 1989: 294) and in 1987, the year in which *La ley* was released, Spanish films accounted for only 14.7 per cent of the cinema audiences (ibid.) compared to 30 per cent in 1975 (*Boletin Informativo de Control de Taquilla, Datos '87*: 38). Could it be that films like *La ley del deseo* are only possible when cinema becomes relatively insignificant as a social institution?

NOTES

1 The government awarded Almodóvar a 5 million-peseta prize for best new director for *Laberinto*. See 'Premios', *Dirigido Por* 11 (101): 12.
2 Roughly, 'In The Dark'; also known as *Dark Hideout* and *Sisters of the Night*.

ACKNOWLEDGEMENTS

I am indebted to Thomas Elsaesser for his advice and help while formulating some of the ideas expressed in this chapter. I would also like to thank Andy Medhurst and Jamie Gaetz for their feedback.

REFERENCES

Part of the research for this chapter was done at the Filmoteteca Española in Madrid. They graciously provided me with voluminous clipping files on Almodóvar and his films. However, the newspaper clippings often did not list page numbers and I did not have the means to trace them.

Barthes, Roland (1977) *Image-Music-Text*, London: Fontana.
Bayón, Miguel (1989) 'El Hombre del año: Pedro Almodóvar, el ingenioso manchego', *Cambio 16* 895: 56–9.
Benitez Gonzalez, Carlos (1982) 'Laberinto de Pasiones', *5 Dias*, 19 October.
Bergstrom, Janet (1979) 'Alternation, segmentation, hypnosis: interview with Raymond Bellour', *Camera Obscura*, 3/4: 70–103.
Berlanga, Jorge (1984) 'Que hecho yo para merecer esto!', *Diario 16*, 1 August.

Besas, Peter (1985) *Behind the Spanish Lens: Spanish Cinema Under Fascism and Democracy*, Denver: Arden Press.

—— (1987) 'Spanish Culture Ministry issues bleak report on B.O., Theatres', *Variety* 329: 37.

Boletin Informativo de Control de Taquilla, Datos '87, Madrid: Ministerio de Cultura, Instituto de Cinematografia y las Artes Visuales, 2a epoca, año 3, 13, No. 15.

Bordwell, David (1985) *Narration and the Fiction Film*, Madison: University of Wisconsin Press.

—— (1986) 'Classic Hollywood cinema: narrational principles and procedures', in Philip Rosen (ed.) *Narrative, Apparatus, Ideology*, New York: Columbia University Press.

Bordwell, David, Staiger, Janet and Thompson, Kristin (1985) *The Classical Hollywood Cinema: Film Style and Mode of Production to 1960*, New York: Columbia University Press.

Crespo, Pedro (1987) ' "La ley del deseo", un desahogo en la carrera de Pedro Almodóvar', *ABC*, February.

De Cordova, Richard (1987) 'A case of mistaken legitimacy: class and generation differences in three family melodramas', in Christine Gledhill (ed.) *Home is Where the Heart Is*, London: BFI.

Dirigido Por, 'Premios', 11 (101): 12.

D'Lugo, Marvin (1986) 'Historical reflexivity: Saura's anti-"Carmen" ', *Wide Angle* 9 (3): 53–61.

Elsaesser, Thomas (1989) *New German Cinema: A History*, London: BFI.

Ferrando, Carlos and Echeverria, J. (1982) 'Laberinto', *Diario 16*, 30 September: 34.

Garcia de Leon, Maria Antonioa and Maldonado, Teresa (1989) *Pedro Almodóvar, la otra España cañi – sociologia y critica cinematográficas*, Ciudad Real: Autores y temas Manchegos.

Guarner, José Luis (1988) 'Spain', in Peter Cowie (ed.) *International Film Guide 1988*, London: Tantivy.

—— (1989) 'Spain', in Peter Cowie (ed.) *International Film Guide 1989*, London: Tantivy.

Gubern, Román (1983) 'Tendencies, genres, and problems of Spanish cinema in the post-Franco period', *Quarterly Review of Film Studies* 8 (2): 15–26.

Higginbotham, Virginia (1988) *Spanish Film under Franco*, Austin: University of Texas Press.

Kinder, Marsha (1979) 'Carlos Saura: The Political Development of Individual Consciousness', *Film Quarterly* 32 (3): 14–26.

La guia de ocio (1989), 'Cine' June: 28–32.

Lara, Antonio (1982) 'La Provocacion como sistema', *Ya*, 21 October.

Lévi-Strauss, Claude (1968) *Structural Anthropology*, London: Allen Lane.

LLinás, Francisco (1987) *4 años de cine Español*, Madrid: Imagfic.

Molina-Foix, Vicente (1977) *New Cinema in Spain*, London: BFI.

Mulvey, Laura (1988) 'Visual pleasure and narrative cinema', in C. Penley (ed.) *Feminism and Film Theory*, London: BFI.

Neale, Stephen (1986) 'Melodrama and tears', *Screen*, 26 (6): 6–24.

Para, Javier (1982) 'Se rueda "Laberinto de Pasiones" ', *Ya*, 6 March.

Peiro, Julian (1983) ' "Entre Tinieblas", film con mucho "tango" ', *El Periodico*, 13 October.

Santos Fontenla, César (1986) '1962–1967', in A. M. Torres (ed.) *Spanish Cinema 1896–1983*, Madrid: Editorial Nacional.

Vidal, Nuria (1988) *The Films of Pedro Almodóvar*, Madrid: Ministerio de Cultura, Instituto de Cine.

3

IMMIGRANT CINEMA: NATIONAL CINEMA

The case of beur film

Christian Bosséno

Much has been written in France about beur cinema. The magazine *Cinématographe*, for example, devoted most of its June 1985 issue to the subject, though it did extend its field of study well beyond beur films in the strict sense to the whole cinematic output of the North African immigrant community in the first half of the 1980s.[1] Discussion of beur cinema as such focused mainly on the durability of a Franco-Arab school of filmmaking and, above all, on its definition.

Seven years on, it may legitimately be asked whether beur cinema has given proof of any durable existence: is it not doomed by its very nature to auto-destruct as it produces new works? Is it not an inevitable moment of transition, even a vital 'exorcism', for directors and actors whose aim is to integrate into French society?

WHAT IS A BEUR?

Beur, in *verlan* (the back-slang used by young people in working-class areas, particularly the suburbs of big cities), derives from the word 'Arabe' with the syllables in reverse order. It denotes a second-generation child of North African immigrants who was born in France, or else came to France at a very early age. France is the country where these children went to school and have their roots, feel at home and have put down their markers. In almost all cases, they come from a modest background. They live mostly in low-grade suburban housing estates, but also in the few remaining working-class areas in the centre of Paris and other large cities. Most of those who call themselves beurs come from the Algerian, rather than the Moroccan or Tunisian, immigrant community; and the beur cinema reflects that balance.

The term beur is provocative. It refers, somewhat mischievously, to most French people's ignorance of the history of North Africa, which leads them to refer to all the inhabitants of Morocco, Algeria and Tunisia as Arabs.

This is of course incorrect: almost all Moroccans and a majority of Algerians are of Berber origin and were arabized through the Arabic language and Islam, with the result that they now form part of the Arab world.

The beurs are newcomers to the French population, with whom almost all of them are integrating. Through music, books, radio and the cinema, they have created an original new form of cultural expression. To most beurs (some of whom are irritated by the neologism itself), there is no such thing as a problem of integration: they are simply French of Muslim origin. While the roots and culture of their parents are different from those of black Africans, Bretons or Occitans, for example, they are otherwise just young French people who face the same problems as others. The theme of racism, which lay at the heart of the earliest films made by North African (and indeed black) immigrants, is now virtually absent from their works. That does not of course mean that it is not something they suffer from in their daily lives; but it is perhaps precisely because they aspire to forming an integral part of France's younger generation that they prefer not to deal with the subject of racism in their films, where comedy is never far below the surface.

Not surprisingly, then, the Lussas Festival of Regional Cinema broke new ground a few years ago when, in addition to its usual menu of Breton, Occitan, Basque, Chtimi (northern French) and Alsatian movies, it offered filmgoers a chance to discover beur cinema, the product of a new French 'region', the working-class suburban environment.

A RESTRICTED CORPUS OF WORKS

It is fashionable to talk of beur cinema, but its contours are blurred. The few articles that have been devoted to the subject have not helped to clarify it.

Some people opt for an all-embracing definition which classes as beur all films made in France by North African immigrants: they lump together films denouncing the evils of emigration, like Ali Ghalem's *Mektoub* (1964), *L'Autre France (The Other France*, 1974), or Nacer Ktari's *Les Ambassadeurs (The Ambassadors*, 1975), which were made by first-generation *émigrés* and date from before the emergence of the beur phenomenon in the 1980s. Others describe as beur films a number of movies which feature immigrants and beurs but were directed by filmmakers of completely French origin, such as Francis Girod's *Le Grand Frère (The Big Brother*, 1982), Serge Le Péron's *Laisse béton (Just Give Up*, 1983), Gérard Lauzier's *Petit Con (Young Idiot*, 1983), Serge Meynard's *L'Oeil au beur(re) noir (Black Eye*, 1987, a pun on 'beur' and 'beurre' (butter)), Gérard Blain's *Pierre et Djamila* (1986) and Jacques Krier's television film, *L'Ombre des bateaux sur la ville (The Shadow of Ships on the City*). Paradoxically enough, the latter films have more in common with the genuine beur cinema than the militant movies produced by the first generation of immigrants.

Similarly, there are considerable similarities of approach between the beur cinema and recent movies made by Algerian directors who have emigrated to or stayed for a time in France, such as Mahmoud Zemoui's *Prends dix mille balles et casse-toi (Take 10,000F. and Beat It)*, or *Un Amour à Paris (A Love Affair in Paris, 1988)*, by Merzak Allouache, an Algerian director who shares with his beur colleagues the privilege of being young.

Having made these introductory remarks, I shall now attempt to define beur cinema and point to its characteristics: *a beur film is one which was made by a young person of North African origin who was born or who spent his or her youth in France, and which features beur characters.*

When this definition is used, the corpus of beur films turns out to be tiny (if non-commercial movies are excluded): a handful of shorts, including Rachid Bouchareb's *Peut-être la mer (Maybe the Sea)*, Aïssa Djabar's *La Vago* and Farid Lahoussa's *La Poupée (The Doll)*, and a total of seven full-length films: Abdelkrim Bahloul's *Le Thé à la menthe (Mint Tea, 1984)*, Mehdi Charef's *Le Thé au harem d'Archimède (Tea in the Harem of Archimedes 1986)*, *Camomille* and *Miss Mona* (1987), Cheikh Djamai's *La Nuit du doute (The Night of Doubts)* and Rachid Bouchareb's *Bâton rouge* (1985) and *Cheb* (1988), a film which includes a new theme in the beur cinema, that of the return to the home country. All these films were released commercially in France.

But there is another side to beur cinema, which should not be overlooked: alternative beur films made on shoestring budgets which cannot be released on normal distribution circuits. They are shown by local organizations and groups, and form part of a cinema of social intervention. They include super–8 films made by the Mohammed Collective in Vitry-sur-Seine: *Le Garage (The Garage)*, *Ils ont tué Kader (They've Killed Kader)*, *Zone immigrée (Immigrant Zone)* and fictionalized documentaries by Farida Belghoul: *Le Départ du père (The Father's Leaving)* and *C'est Madame la France que je préfère (I Prefer Madame France)*. These films are distributed by Images Spectacles Musiques du Monde and Inter Services Migrants.

At least a score of shorts were made, mainly in Lyon and Paris, before beur films catering for the general public began to emerge from the ghetto of alternative distribution. The common denominators of such films are very distinctive. They involve both genres and themes. On the other hand, they in no way constitute a veritable cinematic 'school', and it would be quite wrong to read a common form of film writing into them. Each director is stylistically distinct from the rest.

CHRISTIAN BOSSÉNO

THE CHOICE OF COMEDY AND A DETERMINATION TO DEDRAMATIZE

All beur films include some elements of comedy, with varying degrees of drama, in order to depict everyday life in the suburbs. In this, they differ from the films of *émigré* directors like Ali Ghalem, who linger on the racism and dramatic and sordid aspects of life. Some beur films even portray the bleak landscape of housing estates in an almost affectionate, and sometimes even 'arty' (in the case of Charef), manner.

Unlike the first films made by North African *émigrés*, or those by certain French directors, such as Yves Boisset's *Dupont Lajoie* (1974), Guy Barbero's *France, mère patrie (France, the Motherland,* 1976) and Roger Hanin's *Train d'enfer (Hell Train,* 1984), which set out to denounce racist attacks, sometimes in spectacular fashion, beur films avoid venturing on to that ground: racism is completely ignored in *Le Thé à la menthe*, and usually alluded to only fleetingly: for instance, in Charef's *Camomille*, an immigrant – a Turk? – in a Salvation Army soup kitchen is elbowed out of the way by another dropout, who shouts 'French first!' In *Le Thé au harem d'Archimède*, Charef is careful to connote racism not as anti-North African but as an outlet for resentment against young people. The masked middle-aged louts who burst into the basement do not shout 'Filthy Arabs!' as they go to work with their batons, but, significantly, 'Stupid young bastards!'

On the contrary, the key themes in these films are friendship, love and the need to escape. In this respect, beur films may sometimes seem mawkish and similar in tone to the 'sweetness and light' school of French comedies, as Françoise Audé pointed out in the very pertinent paper she gave at the Popular European Cinema Conference in Warwick in September 1989. The very real popularity of beur cinema, then, is partly due to the fact that it ignores the themes treated by an earlier school of immigrant cinema, and more particularly racism. But it seems to me unfair to go so far as to accuse it of glossing over reality, or, as I once heard it described in a discussion, of being a 'harki' cinema.[2]

In this respect, it is highly instructive to compare two films, Blain's *Pierre et Djamila* and Cheikh Djamai's *La Nuit du doute*. In the first movie, which is an aesthetically remarkable work, the director shows the implacable series of events that result in the teenage girl Djamila, who has broken with tradition by going out with a French boyfriend, being sacrificed by her brother in the name of that tradition. In *La Nuit du doute*, on the other hand, Djamai illustrates a more closely knit form of tribal complicity, which is probably much more widespread than the exaggerated religious bigotry and sense of 'honour' that lead to the tragedy illustrated by Blain.

A POPULIST VEIN ANCHORED IN DOCUMENTARY

It would be no exaggeration to argue that beur films have revived a tradition of French populist cinema which has often been lost sight of. One of their greatest merits is that they succeed in doing what very few French movies do (with one or two remarkable exceptions, such as Le Péron's *Laisse béton*): they set their stories in a real country, and one that is in crisis. They provide filmgoers with an approach which television, with its long experience of documentary news magazines and 'visual journalism', has succeeded in preserving in a whole series of dramatized documentaries combining quasi-documentary sequences with scripted scenes. One such television film is Krier's *L'Ombre des bateaux sur la ville*, which not only tells the tragedy of a young unemployed man who, in desperation, arms himself and takes refuge on the bridge that leads from the city to the new deserted former shipyards, but also paints the portrait of a wilful 'beurette' (young beur woman).

An example of this approach can be found in the quasi-reportage sequence with which *Le Thé à la menthe* opens. It shows us the Barbès district (in the 18th *arrondissement* of Paris), named after the Boulevard Barbès, which runs along its south side. One of the most celebrated immigrant quarters in France, and currently in the process of renovation, it still contains many old and insalubrious buildings packed with North African and black African immigrants, colourful street markets, shops that are reminiscent of markets in Africa, sex shops and so on. The elevated metro line that runs along the middle of Boulevard Barbès and the colourfully dressed people that throng sidestreets like Rue de la Goutte d'Or are often depicted in beur and other films as characteristic of an area that is at once a racial melting-pot and a gangsters' stamping ground (Barbès is next to Pigalle). Barbès is also regularly used as a setting for French gangster films which feature dusky or black-skinned drug dealers (the 18th *arrondissement* initially had the largest community of immigrants, but they are now found in equally high density in certain soulless housing estates on the outskirts of Paris).

The chief interest of beur films is that by giving substance to a new component of French society and renewing the image of the immigrant in the French cinema they have galvanized the jaded imaginations of those responsible for mainstream productions: more and more movies – those of Jean-Jacques Beineix and Leos Carax, for example – have rediscovered the suburbs. Beur cinema thus marks a salutary return to realism and to real concerns.

In a sense, too, beur cinema taps a realistic, tender source of inspiration that distinguished, for example, the highly innovative filmmaking of a director like Jean Eustache. It is a cinema that is youthful and full of zest, and it is not afraid to force new attitudes and themes on to the French

51

cinema. It is this originality which, despite the very small number of beur films that have been made, assures their importance.

A CINEMA OF INTEGRATION

The central characters of beur films are not 'Arabs' on one side and 'the rest' on the other, since that kind of dividing-line is never regarded as essential by second-generation filmmakers. Young beurs are French like anyone else, even if they do not all have French nationality. In this sense, the small part played by religion in beur films is significant. Most beurs are not practising Muslims. Religion is their parents' affair. In *Le Thé au harem d'Archimède*, for example, there is a sequence full of tender irony in which the teenage beur who does not even speak Arabic shows no interest in religion, while the French tot being looked after by the family mimics the ritual of Muslim prayer. If their parents were not around to keep Muslim traditions alive (after a fashion), many beurs would forget their roots.

Their world is the same as that of their French friends: a concrete jungle of faceless rectangular blocks of flats, threadbare lawns and sand-boxes littered with dog faeces, a universe of basements and staircases. A highly motivated, bearded organizer works his guts out in the 'youth club', with only a bare room and meagre resources at his disposal. But many young people prefer to go to the café because of its more convivial atmosphere and pin-ball machines. Other attractions include the supermarket and its temptations (shoplifting), the bowling alley, the local cinema and petty drug peddling. Most kids leave school at 16; the luckier ones get to Nanterre or Créteil University.

It matters little what colour their skin is or whether they are beurs, blacks, Portuguese, Italians, Turks or (white) French, rockers, punks or rastas: they all suffer the same raw deal to an equal degree. They form spontaneously generated groups of pals, sometimes comprising only two or three close friends. In *Bâton Rouge*, a French lad, Mozart (Jacques Penot), and two beurs, Abdenour (Pierre-Loup Rajot) and Karim (Hammou Graia), dream together of America and, more specifically, of Bâton Rouge, because of a phrase in a Mick Jagger song. In *Le Thé au Harem d'Archimède*, there are just two friends, Madjid the beur and Pat the Frenchman.

The suburban microcosm for people such as these boils down to odd jobs, little fiddles, minor delinquency, academic failure and the job centre. Their aim is to achieve genuine social integration, and this expresses itself chiefly in their hope of getting a regular job. The thematics of beur cinema are naturally drawn from the world I have just described, which has little connection with the militantly Manichaean universe of 'emigration' cinema.

Significantly, when in *Bâton Rouge* Abdenour tries to pick up an American

Plate 4 Kader Boukharef (left) and Rémy Martin (right) in *Le Thé au harem d'Archimède.* By courtesy of the British Film Institute, London.

woman who is visiting the tomb of Napoleon under the Dôme des Invalides he says (in English): 'Abdenour, Napoleon, same country!' For second-generation beurs like him, their country is of course France, even if Algeria is still present 'somewhere' in their subconscious. In *Bâton Rouge* again, when the director Bouchareb shows us an international conference hall, it is no coincidence that he happens to include in the shot the seats reserved for the Algerian delegation, which are indicated by a national flag. This is a nod in the direction of the country where one of the young protagonists' family comes from.

The return to the homeland, even if it may originally be an act of militancy, is almost always experienced as a trauma and ends in failure. This is the theme of Bouchareb's new film *Cheb* (*cheb* means 'young'). It is also the subject of *Les Enfants du Retour (The Children of the Return to the Homeland)*, a poignant documentary made by Rémi Lainé in 1989 and produced by the television channel TF1. (It is the pathetic portrait of a young woman who went back to Algeria with her parents under a government-subsidized scheme, and found that the only way she could escape a serious nervous breakdown was to return to France and find her bearings again.)

The result of proper integration is social and professional success. Take, for example, the final sequence of *Bâton Rouge*, which rather gives the impression of having been tacked on to the rest of the film. After being brutally deported from the United States and arriving back in France, Abdenour and Karim set up a fast-food business with other friends. The director then points out that this upbeat ending was inspired by an actual fast-food collective, California Burg, which had been started up in the Paris suburb of Argenteuil.

The central characters of beur cinema lay down their roots in France.

THE ABSENCE OF WOMEN?

It might be supposed at first sight that beur cinema was a male genre. Here again, though, this 'oversight' may be interpreted as arising from an observation of social realities. Young beurettes, even when they are students, remain tied to the running of the immigrant household. They know they are more vulnerable to the pressure of tradition and realize that the only way they can become emancipated is by going to school and acquiring an education. They are therefore less likely to become involved in the activities of the groups of young beurs that are central to the themes of this cinema. That observation does not, however, apply to the more underground films, which are not theatrically released, such as those by Farida Belghoul or Cheikh Djamai's *La Nuit du doute*, whose central characters are young women.

There are a number of beur women directors, though none has so far succeeded in breaking into the commercial cinema. But they are bound to do so eventually. Some of them have applied for the *avances sur recettes* film subsidy system. Women such as Malika (who is Gérard Depardieu's regular costumier) and Djamila Sahraouï (continuity supervisor and television producer) are beginning to hold down important jobs in television and film.

It is, however, true that in beur films directed by men, beurettes tend to be given less prominent roles. There are no beurette central characters, for example, whereas it is well known that they are the most determined and toughest militants, as well as being the strongest in their belief in the virtues of integration – in other words, their liberation. The character of the North African mother, on the other hand, is always prominent and positive.

In *Le Thé au harem d'Archimède*, the family is dominated by Malika, the mother (Saïda Bekkouch), while the father plays no role at all. He is ill and sits like a zombie in front of his television set, which is always on. Josette (Laure Duthilleul) lives on the same housing estate. She is a single mother – who has been abandoned by her partner – and gives Malika her child to look after during the day. Josette finds herself out of a job after a strike, has a breakdown and is dissuaded from committing suicide only

Plate 5 Beur humiliation in the French school system: *Le Thé au harem d'Archimède*. By courtesy of the British Film Institute, London.

by the comforting, warm presence of Malika, and by her son Madjid. It is Malika again who is called in to try and separate a couple who are having a row.

A CINEMA OF TRANSITION

Because beur cinema describes a stage in the integration of children from a new immigrant community into French society, it necessarily constitutes a stage in its directors' artistic development.

Although in their first film(s) beur directors tend to concentrate on the singularity of their status as French of North African origin, all they seek to do subsequently is to melt into the mass of young people and jobless who live in the suburbs and explain their problems as regards self-expression, social status, work, leisure, housing and so on.

The filmmakers' initial need to give expression to their singularity is quickly superseded by concerns other than the problem of North African immigration. Charef focuses on other people on the fringes of society – homosexuals, the unloved and immigrants (but not necessarily North Africans) in a society in which being marginal is not easy.

And it is here, too, that it becomes clear that beur cinema is one of transition. Charef's work vividly illustrates how a young filmmaker can find himself out of step with his North African origins. His films, which tend to bittersweet realism but contain wonderful excursions into poetry

55

and dream, are about the fringes of society. *Camomille* and *Miss Mona* are movies about dropouts, Barbès, working-class Paris, the suburbs. With hindsight it is easy to see that Charef's closely autobiographical first film, *Le Thé au harem d'Archimède*, fulfilled the function of a much-needed personal exorcism.

A POPULAR AND INFLUENTIAL CINEMA

Beur cinema is a popular cinema. That again is where it differs from the militant cinema of an earlier generation: it relies on well-crafted screenplays which have gained the confidence of producers and distributors, thus opening the way to commercial release.

All beur films have been well received by the general public and some have done very well at the box-office. *Le Thé au harem d'Archimède*, for example, got attendances of 100,000 in the greater Paris area alone and a good reception from the critics (it was selected for the 'Un Certain Regard' section of the Cannes Festival and won the Prix Jean Vigo), despite not featuring any stars (the choice of Rémy Martin to play the young Frenchman was judicious, though – he has turned out to be one of the young hopes of the French cinema).

Beur films aim to be naturalistic but not to carry any message. They do not set out to make spectators ask questions, and in this they adopt the same approach as the commercial cinema. They are constructed along traditional screenplay lines and need to go down well with the general public. They must carry audiences along and make them laugh, as well as adopting a serious and dramatic tone when necessary. They mix genres and rely on tenderness and emotion for their appeal.

It would seem from this brief survey of beur cinema that despite its small corpus of works it displays enough characteristics to be classified as a cinematic genre of its own, and that its influence on the French cinema is quite out of proportion with the number of films that qualify as beur.

It marked an invigorating new point of departure, and was simultaneous with the emergence, in the French cinema as a whole, of more believable themes and new faces. Marginality, after falling out of favour somewhat, has once again become a central concern of the French cinema. Suburban milieux are beginning to take on a more tangible form on the screen. 'Token' Arabs such as Mohammed Zinet and El Kebir have been replaced by new, more complex and more versatile faces. Beur actors of ever greater calibre are playing an increasing role in the French cinema.

Of the fifteen students who won prizes at the 1986 end-of-year examinations at the Paris Conservatoire d'Art Dramatique, no fewer than four were beurs. The success of an actress like Souab Amidou, who is equally at home playing a beurette (such as the unscrupulous dropout in *Petit Con* or the passionate lover in *Le Grand Frère*) or a Portuguese woman on the way to success in *La Valise en carton (The Cardboard Suitcase*, 198?), has demonstrated the ability of beur actors to occupy the place they deserve, and not just to play exotic or Arab-looking characters. Other new faces include Hammou Graïa, Betty Berr, Louné Tazairt, Smaïn and Abdel Kechiche.

Symptomatic of this new trend is the career of Karim Allaoui. A few years ago he was given the leading role in a major television series based on several detective stories by Dominique Ponchardier, whose central character, the Gorille, is an archetypal Frenchman (and lover of cassoulet)! That a beur was chosen to play the part is a sign of the times. But then the man who played the Gorille in Bernard Borderie's 1958 film version, *Le Gorille vous salue bien (The Gorille Sends his Regards*), was none other than Lino Ventura, an Italian-born Frenchman.

The contribution made by immigrant filmmakers such as beurs in France has given a shot in the arm to the European film industry, so it seemed important to illustrate that process with this particular example. There can be little doubt that second-generation blacks in Britain, Indonesians in the Netherlands and Turks in Germany are making stimulating contributions to filmmaking in those three countries. A remarkable Arabo-Belgian school of cinema has also sprung up in Belgium, the most remarkable manifestation of which is Mahmoud Ben Manhoua's *Traversées*.

Translated from the French by Peter Graham.

NOTES

1 See also *CinémAction* 56, 'Cinémas métis – de Hollywood aux films beurs', July 1990.
2 Harkis were Muslim Algerians who fought on the French side, that is to say against the guerrillas of the Front National de Libération (FLN), during the Algerian War. They were mobilized in auxiliary companies, or *harkas*. Some of them did so for the money, but many out of loyalty to traditional leaders who had allied themselves with the French (for example, Bachaga Benaïssa Saïd Boualem, Vice-President of the French National Assembly during the Algerian War).

Many harkis met a tragic fate after Algerian independence in 1962, as they were regarded as traitors and deserters by the new regime. Thousands were arrested and summarily executed. Those who managed to escape followed the French troops home and settled in metropolitan France. Now officially described as French of Muslim origin, they and their children form a community of about 400,000.

Long despised by the Algerian immigrant community in France, and neglected by successive French governments, they have in many cases failed to integrate well. Recently, however, the situation changed. Algerian immigrants seem to have decided to let bygones be bygones and to 'forgive' the harkis. Today it is no longer an insult (at least officially) to be described as the son of a harki. And after rioting by second-generation harkis during the summer of 1991, the French government took steps to improve the situation of the harki community.

4

IMAGES OF 'PROVENCE'

Ethnotypes and stereotypes of the south in French cinema

François de la Bretèque

In France there is a *'question méridionale'*, a southern issue, which structures language, ideology, the production of texts, in a word 'representations'. The 'Midi', the term in current use to describe the south of France, is a term that has meaning only in relation to a north; it is purely demarcational, and external to the identity of the populations concerned. 'Midi' and *méridional* have been vigorously rejected on occasion by the supporters of regionalism, who see them as pretexts to avoid putting a name to the cultural – and perhaps ethnic? – identity of the land, the country in question. Calling it the Midi in fact means not having to say 'Occitania', 'Catalonia', 'Corsica' (Lafont 1971; Pelen 1985).

France has other 'minority' areas but, with a few exceptions – Jean Epstein's Breton films, the militant cinema post-1968 – the Midi is the only one to have had the privilege of inspiring a substantial and popular film output. Why this singular distinction?

First of all there is the fact that, primarily on account of the climate, studios and production units were located near the Mediterranean in the second decade of the century, and then again in the 1930s (Peyrusse 1986: 73–6; Prédal 1980).

But above all production in this locality is undoubtedly a response to the taste for 'internal', domestic exoticism, long nurtured and popularized by regionally inspired literature, which was itself a dynamic genre in the nineteenth and early twentieth centuries, both in French and in the *langue d'oc*, the old Provençal tongue of southern France. Various modes of expression, which I shall be mentioning, took up and developed this exploitation of the regional picturesque. The cinema was naturally one of them.

Nevertheless, we still need to know why the great French public preferred the picturesque which was peculiar to the *méridional* provinces above all the others. The answer has to be couched in historical and ideological terms. For here a dominant culture (French) has supplanted another more

NO.	TRACK	TITLE / DATE	TIME

SICHERHEITSHINWEISE Setzen Sie die CD-R nicht direkter Sonnen- oder anderer UVA/UVB-Strahlung aus. • Vermeiden Sie extreme Temperaturen sowie Feuchtigkeit, Staub und Erschütterungen. • Bewahren Sie die CD-R möglichst in der Kunststoffbox auf. • Vermeiden Sie Schmutzflecken, Fingerabdrücken und andere Verunreinigungen auf der CD-R. • Bekleben Sie die CD-R nicht mit Schutzfolien oder anderen Aufklebern. Tragen Sie keine Überzugsflüssigkeiten auf. • Beseitigen Sie Staubpartikel mit einem trockenen, weichen und fusselfreiem Tuch. Reinigen Sie die CD-R nicht mit Lösungs- oder Reinigungsmittel, verwenden Sie ausschließlich einige Tropfen Ethylalkohol. • Beschriften Sie die CD-R mit einem wasserfesten, lösungsmittelfreien und nicht schmierenden Filzstift. Kugelschreiber, sowie andere Schreibgeräte mit einer harten Spitze können die Beschichtung der CD-R zerstören.

SAFETY INSTRUCTIONS Do not expose the CD-R to direct sunshine or other UVA/UVB radiation. • Avoid extreme temperatures, moisture, dust and vibrations. • As far as possible, keep the CD-R in the plastic box. • Ensure that the CD-R is kept clean of dirt stains, fingerprints and other impurities. • Do not adhere protective foils or other stickers to the CD-R. Do not apply any other coating liquids. • Remove dust particles with a dry, soft, lint-free cloth. Do not use any solvents or detergents to clean the CD-R, use only a few drops of ethyl alcohol. • Only use a water-resistant, solvent free, non-smearing felt-tip pen to write on the label side of the CD-R. Ball-point pens or other writing utensils with a hard tip can destroy the coating of the CD-R.

or less residual culture (Occitanian, Catalan, Corsican), which now only expresses itself apologetically or as seen by the other.

Films offer the means to express this way of seeing very powerfully. And this is why, in French film production, films with southern characters form a special category. At one time they could even be considered as having constituted a genre or rather a 'series', to borrow Claudette Peyrusse's phrase for the 1930s (Peyrusse 1986).

In expanding her thesis, I intend to look at the gamut of images of the Midi and its inhabitants current in French films, even when the Midi is not the principal subject. I will treat them like a galaxy of discursive signs – signs that circulate within the social body generally, outside the cinema as well, and that come to be embodied in a particular character or film. They can be considered as 'identifying markers', i.e. the 'differentiating traits in the eyes of their authors, tending to typify in symbolic fashion the identity of the country in question' (Pelen 1985: 349).

These traits are brought together in types, ethnotypes and stereotypes. These terms are not exactly synonymous. 'Ethnotype' describes in the strict sense the physical type attributed to a 'race' – such as 'the negro' – and has to be used discreetly, with a great many inverted commas, touching as it does on such a delicate subject. The term, it must be understood, in no way describes a reality. It has to be taken as a discursive description. (Hence 'the Arab' in the National Front discourse of today.) 'Type', in this sense, describes a set of distinctive traits that enable you immediately to place the origins of a fictional character. Hence there is a 'Gascon' type in the seventeenth century (in drama in particular), a 'Provençal' type in the nineteenth (in novels, illustrations, etc.). The 'stereotype' covers the previous terms as soon as one of the distinctive traits becomes fixed by the imagination: for example, the boastfulness of Tartarin, the Alphonse Daudet character, becomes stereotypic for the southern character. But the stereotype is not solely confined to people; it can also apply to things and situations (the song of the cicadas, the siesta in the shade and so on).

We can start by noting that the Midi referred to comes down to Provence. This restriction results from a long ideological process, due particularly to Daudet and the 'Félibres'.[1] The cinema is heir to this confusion (Peyrusse 1986: 64). Nevertheless, we have to distinguish between two Midis, corresponding to two opposing inspirations: the comic-maritime vein, which predominates, and the tragic-rural vein that runs counter to it (de la Bretèque 1982). This has been very well formulated by Jean Giono:

There are two Provences. The Provence of Jean Aicard, of Pagnol, Daudet, Mistral; and then there is that other Provence, the one written about by Daudet, again, but also by Stendhal and

Shakespeare. It is not the Provence where you conjure up blue skies, sunshine and flowers, but the Provence of human dimensions: it is not Provence as Mistral understood it.

(Quoted in Mény 1978: 50)

This dichotomy will cut across many films since it is at the heart of the representation of the Midi.

THE FIGURES IN THE VILLAGE MICROCOSM: ETHNOTYPES AND STEREOTYPES

Before the advent of cinema the people living in our Midi had cultural products through which they could project an image of themselves: identity is what people say they are. I shall first look at two of these – the 'Pastorale' and the Christmas crib – followed by the regional literature, the postcard and other representative traditions.

The *méridional* cinema is fed by a whole tradition of live entertainment, to the extent of occasionally drawing on it for its actors (Peyrusse 1986: 44). There was the Marseille operetta, local music-hall, travelling players, etc. There was also the Pastorale, a Nativity play at Christmas and often a pretext for presenting local celebrities. The first in the genre, *La Pastorale Maurel*, dates from 1844 and was published in Marseille. Pastorales have been written and acted all over the Midi and the tradition is still very much alive. The Pastorale has three essential characteristics: the transposing of Judaea to rural Provence, the presence of conventional and traditional characters, and Provençal/French bilingualism, symbolically transcribing the actual linguistic situation, at least up until the First World War, with the angels and the important people speaking French, and the little people, the minor characters, *langue d'oc*. By and large, the cinema was to eradicate the last of these three traits, without dropping it completely – think about who is speaking with what accent in these films.

I believe that this family resemblance has not been given its full due. Films depicting the *méridional* microcosm are wholly imbued with the consensual and unanimist atmosphere of Christmas. Conflicts – and you must have them for there to be a plot – are usually only there as 'McGuffins', an excuse for a grand final reconciliation. And more often than not even in films in the 'tragic vein', this is carried out around a baby's cradle or a wedding, for example the end of *Regain (Rebirth*, 1937) and, particularly, *Angèle* (1934), when the father is reconciled with his daughter who has given birth to an illegitimate child that a good chap, a real Joseph, agrees to take on along with the mother – there's even a donkey to complete the picture (de la Bretèque 1991).

The figures from the Pastorale crop up again in the Nativity of the crib. Less ancient than is often thought, even though they may go back to St

LE VALET DE FERME

Plate 6 Traditional woodcut representation of the southern French farmhand. By courtesy of François de la Bretèque.

Francis of Assisi, their conventions had been established by the early nineteenth century: the first Marseille *santons*[2] date from 1803 (Benoît 1949; Ripert 1956; Bouyala d'Arnaud 1979). Pastorale and crib become popular just when the world they depict is disappearing. In them there is the 'beauty of the dead' that Michel de Certeau (1974) spoke of – a beauty of the dead that the cinema was to prolong, taking it out to new audiences, for whom it would become doubly exotic, temporally as well as spatially.

The village universe presented in these works is stable, fossilized even. It embodies the fantasy of a return to an *ancien régime*, ordered by its guilds. Everyone has his or her place and must stay there. There are three distinguishing features.

(1) *Traditional costume:* here it is worth remembering that the Marquis de Baroncelli (elder brother of filmmaker Jacques de Baroncelli) was responsible for imperceptibly codifying the Arlesian costume. That only happened at the beginning of our century. The silent cinema, in its turn, was to be voracious in its passion for 'traditional' costume: André Antoine's *L'Arlésienne* (1909), the various versions of *Mireille* (Ernest Servaés, 1922, René Gaveau, 1933), and all the 'Camargue' films.

(2) *Occupation:* each had his or her place in the production chain and

could not deviate from it or chaos would ensue. If the baker does not bake the bread, the village catches fire: Henri Verneuil's *Le Boulanger de Valorgues* (*The Baker of Valorgues*, 1952). If he lets his oven go out, the whole community is in a state of anarchy: Pagnol's *La Femme du boulanger* (*The Baker's Wife*, 1938). When the baker's son is born in Verneuil's film his whole career is mapped out: he will be the baker in his turn.

(3) *Character:* this is a stereotype, enabling dramatic and psychological types to be stock-cast in fiction. Each village will have its idiot, its tart, its sanctimonious shrew, its cuckold . . . who will be just that. This characteristic is of course not confined to the Midi. French 'peasant' literature had long since codified these categories, as is borne out by the success of *Clochemerle* (novel by Jacques Chevallier 1934, then a film directed by Pierre Chenal, 1947), and of Jacques Tati's *Jour de fête* (1947). Here we are cutting across another set of issues, that of the representation of country folk and country life (de la Bretèque 1990; Lagrave 1980).

The *méridional* slant comes out in the details, not only of clothing and language but also of the *mise-en-scène*. In the crib each of the characters offers up to the baby Jesus the tools of his or her trade and the fruits of his or her labour. The equivalent of this offertory *mise-en-scène* can be found in the rhetoric of presenting implements and products to the lens, be it that of the postcard photographer or the cine-camera. For this film genre has always had some slight pretension to ethnography.

The museums of folk art and tradition – one of the first of these was in fact the Museon Arlaten founded by Frédéric Mistral in 1896, roughly coinciding with the birth of the cinema – have also familiarized us with this scenario. The postcards show the implement held to the fore while the person behind it is either in repose or miming the movements of his or her trade. The beauty of the implement is mirrored by that of the movement. This 'nobility' of the peasantry is a literary and pictoral cliché, providing support for the academic representations. For example, to quote Mistral himself:

> Tout un pople de ràfi, mesadié, journadié, rastelarello, anavan e venièn dins li tèrro dau mas, quau emé lou rastèu o bèn la fourco sus l'espalo, en travaiavan de-long emé de geste noble coumo dins li pinturo de Léopold Robert.
>
> (A whole host of hands hired by the month or by the day, of women hay-rakers, came and went on the farm land, their rake or fork on their shoulder, and were forever toiling, noble in their movements, as in the works of Léopold Robert.)
>
> (Mistral 1906, 1979: 26)

Léopold Robert is a French painter of the Romantic period who specialized in landscapes of the Roman countryside: here the ennobling reference is twofold. The silent cinema was to rediscover the paths of this academism, at times tempered by the 'naturalist' vein, as with Antoine. There is the grape-picking scene in Louis Feuillade's *Vendémiaire* (1918), the basket-makers in *Mireille*. The taste for it persisted into the talkies. In the Pagnol films the camera does not shrink from pausing to dwell on protagonists behind their implements: the knife-grinders of *Regain* and of *Angèle*, with their 'strop' on wheels; the tool of the trade is sanctified to such a degree that it accompanies its owner into final exile, as when the blacksmith Gaubert, too old to stay on in the village, takes his anvil with him to the town and hides it under his bed before passing it on to Panturle (*Regain*).

The indication that these characters are *santons* is sometimes found in the dialogue: the actual word is used in Giono's *Crésus* (1960) and in Gilles Grangier's *La Cuisine au beurre (Cooking with Butter*, 1963). There is even a film which precisely recreates the Nativity crib, the famous *La Nuit merveill-euse (The Night of Marvels*, 1940) directed by Jean-Paul Paulin, which tells the story of refugees regrouping in a Provençal village after the Débâcle, and concludes with a birth in a stable.

Thus one finds, from film to film, the water-carriers (Pagnol's *Manon des sources*, 1951), reawakening the sculptural convention of the Greek loutroph-oros, statuettes by Tanagra; the peasant with the mule or the ass (Claude Berri's *Jean de Florette*, 1986); the lavender-gatherers (Pagnol's *Manon des sources* again; Jean Renoir's *Toni*, 1934); the miller (*Le Boulanger de Valorgues*); the baker himself, a privileged character in *méridional* films and worth a whole study to himself.

Crowd scenes of people working pose a more delicate problem for the photographer, who must be able to arrange a number of protagonists so that they can still be seen while giving the impression of continuing to work at their occupations. That provides a set-piece beloved alike by opera (Gounod's *Mireille*), advertising agencies and the cinema. You get the olives being harvested, the mulberry leaves being picked, gathering up the cocoons, sorting out the fruit, and, of course, the vineyards and the *vendanges*. Here again these representations are nourished by a pseudo-ethnography: the work being done in front of the camera is not real work, but it has to show all the signs of it (sweat, fatigue and so on), even if those don't always carry conviction – I'm thinking of Angèle haymaking (*Angèle*), a scene worthy of the Marquise de Sévigné.[3]

TYPES, ETHNOTYPES AND ARCHETYPES

The southern characters in films reactivate a number of archetypes or stereotypes, with their origins in folklore or literature. Here we find, brought together, traits of physical characterization, literary types and accessories serving as means of identification, such as dress. Let us run through the main ones:

(1) The plump *méridional*, the voluble, fidgety southerner embodied by Tartarin and the Marius of the 'Marseille jokes', very fashionable in the 1930s – Pagnol knew what he was doing when he chose this name for such a character (Ramon 1925). Raimu, Charpin and several others (currently Armand Meffre) specialized in this type. Their play-acting is often taken for the real thing: expansive gestures, muttering, grimacing, wild gesticulating, etc. Are not these behavioural parameters more likely to be the result of a stage tradition and a viewing habit? In this case the 'reality effect' has been so strong that everyone can swear to having met one of these characters in the street, even to having one in the family.

(2) At the other end of the scale the laconic peasant, stubborn and uncommunicative, as embodied for example by Henri Poupon (who was not originally from the Midi) in *Angèle*, and Gabriel Gabrio in *Regain*, corresponds to the opposite stereotype, that of the austere and isolated rural Provence. That is the counter-myth.

(3) Rather like him, the patriarch, master of the farm and the farmhands, had been immortalized by Mistral in the Mestre Ramon of *Mireille*, based on his own father, 'un grand vièi superbe, digne dins sis prepaus, ferme dins soun gouver, amistadous au paure mounde, rude père èu soulet' (a superb grand old man, of dignified demeanour, with an iron will, kind to the poor, hard only on himself) (Mistral 1906, 1979: 27). These patriarchal figures pleased a Louis Feuillade, a Georges Rouquier (*Farrebique*, 1944). I am not the first to stress the predilection of the southern cinema for paternal figures (Peyrusse 1986: 130). The Midi of the cinema would thus be a vehicle for the archaic values of French society, hinting at nostalgia for strong rule. Its function is that of an escapist fantasy where there is freedom to construct an alternative social Utopia.

(4) Another stock figure in this constellation is the young virgin, with Mireille as the archetype that other heroines set out to copy. This fictional figure, it should be stressed, is also a sociological model that the Félibrige sought to impose through the *festo vierginenco*[4] which still lives on today in certain parts. Conformism, moral repression, exert their full weight on Pagnol's heroines, which doubtless accounts for that 'vacuous' nature of theirs which invariably strikes the spectator.

(5) The farmhand, an indispensable character in any 'rural' film, and a single man devoted to his master's family, assumes in our latitudes a particular colour: that of the innocent, in Provence the *ravi*[5] (another character from the crib). This function can also be devolved to the shepherd. He has been the hero of whole books, for example the *Varlet*

de mas by Baptiste Bonnet (1894) or the *Jean des figues* by Paul Arène (1868). In the cinema it is the Toine of *Naïs* (1945), and the Saturnin of *Angèle*, who describes himself as *le fada*.[6] Both, played by Fernandel (see Plate 7), have the traditional attitude of adoration before the 'miracle child'.

(6) There is often an outsider, who can be entrusted with the narrative function of the disruptive force. He can take the form of a cowherd in the Camargue sub-series (Duret 1984) or of a gypsy, the *boumian* of the crib. In Marcel Camus's *Le Chant du monde (The Song of the World*, 1965, from a script written by Giono in 1941) you have the character Mandru and his tribe, the 'cattle drovers' (Giono 1980). The 'gypsy' enchantress and fortune-teller does not necessarily have this negative hue. Sarah, the gypsy girl of Feuillade's *Vendémiaire* (1918), bears the name of the patron saint of the gypsies, the companion of the three Saint Maries. She is further sanctified by her widowhood, her husband having died for France at the Front.

(7) The bad guy belongs to the maritime and urban Midi, and wears a striped jersey and a scarf knotted round his neck. He is not necessarily from the Midi but the connotation is very much Marseille: Andrex in *Angèle* and in Carlo Rim's *Simplet* (1942).

(8) The witch, more scarey than wicked, haunts the ruins of deserted villages and the desolate *garrigue* (heathland). She is truly the revival of an archetype from folklore, having much in common with Tavan of *Mireille* and Mamèche of *Regain*, or Baptistine of *Manon des sources* (Pagnol, 1951; Berri, 1986). Baptistine appears as the wife of an Italian charcoal-burner, out of a concern for realism that pays homage to the characters depicted in Renoir's *Toni*.

(9) Let us conclude with a completely mythical figure, the wild lass, barefoot and with flowing locks, who lives in the *garrigue* with her goats – like Manon, the child of Pagnol's fantasy, or Hortense in *L'Eau vive* (directed by François Villiers in 1957, based on a script by Giono). Wholly improbable, these apparitions resurrect the fairy figures – dryads or water nymphs – with which the Félibres had allegorically strewn the paths of their imaginary geography.

PLACE AND SOCIAL PRACTICE AS IDENTIFYING MARKERS

Like the *santons* brought together by the marvel of the Nativity, the figures we have been looking at are gathered for collective events, usually of a festive nature – something which makes for the cohesion and affirmation of the identity of the group. These events unfold in an enclosed space, which can be seen as a metonymy for the 'territory' and for the Occitan

Plate 7 The southern French farmhand in his most famous screen incarnation: Fernandel in *Angèle*. By courtesy of the British Film Institute, London.

area as a whole, closed in on itself, bound up in its own internal conflicts, bottled up in its self-celebration.

The village square, with its plane trees and its fountain marking its boundaries and its centre respectively, is this dramatic setting *par excellence* (de la Bretèque 1990). This square, even when filmed on location, is the result of a synthesis of a number of places (*Jean de Florette*, 1986). It is an emblematic square, one already codified by the painting and the postcard. Even the sound details originate from representational codes: 'the Luberon as backdrop, the sun in a solid blue sky and the song of the cicadas to complete the décor' – thus a regional daily described the location of the Berri film. The fountain, the central element of the square, is ever present. It is the source of the very life of the community. With it the circle of the square assumes a distinctly paradisial connotation (Royer and Martel 1978). If not seen, it can be heard; its 'gurgling' accompanies the conversation of the grinder (*Regain*); it enlivens the night of *Comédie*, a 'tourist' film by Jacques Doillon (1988).

The dramatic conflicts crystallize in the centre of the square and do so in representational terms. It is where the 'grocers' confront the 'bakers' (*Le Boulanger de Valorgues*); in the absence of a square it is a canal that unites and divides the two halves of the village, the partisans of the 'Petit Marseille' and those of 'La Sole normande' (*La Cuisine au beurre*). It is in the square that conflicts are also resolved, by the epiphany of the truth (*Manon des sources*). The square is also the place where the idleness of the *méridional* – just taking it easy – is displayed. This is symbolized by the game of boules, a quasi-compulsory passage in any representation of the Midi from Pagnol's *Fanny* (1932) onwards.

The café terrace is the other emblematic place. If you believe the cinema, the essential occupations of the people of the Midi include drinking pastis and playing cards on these shady terraces, under the plane trees or in an arbour. If, in addition, the café has beaded curtains and you can hear the song of the cicadas and the colourful accent of the protagonists, the reconstruction seems perfect.

The square is also the site for the market which brings the village microsociety into contact with the outside world. The popularity of the stereotype of the markets of Provence has been well illustrated by the Gilbert Bécaud song 'Les marchés de Provence'. It was in fact the 1950s and the 1960s, with mass tourism, that saw this cliché coming to reign supreme, as evidenced by the *Gendarme* series starring Louis de Funès.[7] But there had been forerunners of this in the 1930s, such as the Marseille market in Marcel Carné's *Hotel du Nord* (1938), truly a model of the genre!

Let us now look at the activities that take place other than in the public square, but which are still vehicles for collective identity. First, the ceremony of the meal.

Culinary customs are well known as providing an opportunity for

Plate 8 An emblematic space: the café terrace in Berri's *Manon des sources* (centre left; Yves Montand). By courtesy of the British Film Institute, London.

affirming regional peculiarities. These demarcational practices loom disproportionately large in daily conversation. One film – *La Cuisine au beurre* – has even gone so far as to make cooking its very subject. It revolves around the flimsy pretext of a conflict between cooking with oil, espoused by every Provençal, and cooking with butter, which, in the film, has temporarily supplanted it. During a protracted (and revealing) spell of absence by its owner, who has extended his stay as a prisoner in Germany, the restaurant 'À la vraie bouillabaisse' has been transformed into 'La Sole normande'.

The two protagonists are played by Fernandel and Bourvil, both of them strongly coded as regional actors. Two civilizations collide on one of those invisible lines dear to the ethnologists, the very same that divides France as a country and that was currently being highlighted by mass tourism. Eventually, after a highly Gilbertian development (which, to be frank, is quite hard to swallow), the lost harmony is restored. The two adversaries are reconciled under the authority of their joint wife. The Franco-French war will not take place. It's better to be cuckolded (like Fernandel) and learn to live with it. This illusory resolution is the best indication of how practices that give the stamp of cultural identity cannot but regress into folklore. The protagonists will carry on making bouillabaisse, but for the tourists. Many films in our corpus spring from a sharp conflict inspired by food. Mention has already been made of the symbolic importance of bread, and bread is what the conflicts take shape around (*Le Boulanger de Valorgues, La Femme du boulanger*).

In other cases, the dispute hinges on the desire to keep a fetish, an identifying symbol: the village idiot in *Simplet*, a film shot when France was literally divided in two. At the end of the confrontations the reconciliation is sealed by a grand communal meal. 'Southern sociability' serves as a convenient screen backdrop for a reconciliatory and mollifying speech. The village settles its conflicts *en famille*, paternally reintegrating its prodigals. Do we need to press the point? This fine tolerance is, alas, merely begging the question. We recall the prefatory lines from *Toni* – 'the generous Midi, land where the races mix easily and harmoniously' – lines that are in fact belied by the rest of the film.

The Midi on the screen is in fact, with one unusual exception (i.e. *Toni*), characterized by an outward appearance of great homogeneity. The most obvious of these unifying factors is accent, the famous Midi accent, which is actually a maritime Provençal accent, reworked in the school of the theatre and imposed fictionally as the accent for the whole of the south (*Farrebique* being the most notable exception). With accent ruling supreme, the cinema steered clear of representing the actual languages of the south (Provençal, Occitanian, Corsican). 'Regional' French rules; dialects are only there as stereotypic reminders. The languages of other minorities are rarely represented except in *Toni* (Italian) and Agnès Varda's *Sans toit ni loi* (*Vagabonde*, 1985)[8] which opened the door to Arabic. Some, like Peyrusse, consider that it was the accent, and therefore the talkies, that really began the career of the *méridional*, the southerner, in the cinema. Certainly this was the element on which Pagnol built his success. But, however important a part this has played in French cinema, I think it is not the only distinctive sign of the representation of the Midi. It must be combined with other signs, some of which, purely visual, were already present in silent cinema.

The popular success of films with southern characters poses the classic problem of all minority representation. For the 'foreign' public they smack of the exotic – home-grown to be sure, but exotic none the less. For the people concerned they screen representations that some, with irritation, may dispute but in which many recognize themselves. This acceptance should come as no surprise; since Albert Memmi it has been an acknowledged mechanism. This (Jewish Tunisian) writer has shown how colonizers 'create' the colonized, by manufacturing an image of them (obviously one that suits their own purposes) which they then propose to the colonized. The latter, completing a process which ends in the loss of their own cultural identity, finish up by accepting, then by claiming as 'true', this image that has been fabricated for them (Memmi 1957). Would it be thought improper to speak of a colonial relationship as regards the provinces of the south of France? In economic and political terms, undoubtedly (though that is still a matter for dispute). But it is the concept of 'internal colonialism', one of long standing, that best accounts for the tensions in the cultural field that cannot be explained otherwise (Lafont 1954, 1967, 1971).

The cinema, more than other media, has undoubtedly highlighted certain popularizing elements of the stereotype. It has created some others. But above all it has drawn on the stock of representations circulating within the whole of the social discourse, through education, literature, the press. It is not, therefore, the only guilty party (if guilty party there be). Like the regionalist literature, it has played 'the role of emblematic referent guaranteeing and validating a representation that had already been formulated' (Pelen 1985: 355).

As films are fashioned and consumed at a national level it is at this level that the stereotypes we have studied are first refashioned. But the local elites have played their part. One cannot help but be struck by the need manifested in the films to place themselves under the aegis of these cultural guarantees. The silent cinema almost always harked back to some legitimizing literary source – that of Mistral for Servaès and Baroncelli; the same deference runs through the work of Pagnol towards Daudet (rather than to Giono, incidentally); and more recently, by a sort of cyclical repetition, through that of Berri and Yves Robert towards Pagnol.

The models (or clichés) I have cited hardened up long ago. Today they seem susceptible only of pastiche, parody or respectful remake, and archaeological restoration. The vein, however, is not as exhausted as one might think, and is renewing itself elsewhere, in advertising, for example, awaiting better days. The popular stereotype, however fast it may be set, remains dynamic, capable of (indefinitely?) giving rise to fresh fiction and discourse.

Translated from the French by Brenda Ferris, with Robert Short.

NOTES

1 Members of the Félibrige, the society of poets and prose writers formed in 1854 with the object of preserving the Provençal language.
2 Small painted clay figures that decorate the Christmas cribs in Provence.
3 The Marquise de Sévigné's letters provided a vivid but precious account of society during the reign of Louis XIV.
4 Festival of young virgins celebrated in the Camargue and around Arles and institutionalized by Mistral and the Marquis de Baroncelli at the beginning of the century.
5 A Provençal term for a state of blessedness, someone who is 'out of this world'.

6 Simple-minded (literally 'spellbound').

7 *Le Gendarme de Saint-Tropez* (1964); *Le Gendarme à New York* (1965); *Le Gendarme se marie (The Gendarme Gets Married*, 1968); *Le Gendarme en ballade (The Gendarme Takes a Trip*, 1970); *Le Gendarme et les extra-terrestres (The Gendarme and the Extra-Terrestrials*, 1979); *Le Gendarme et les Gendarmettes (The Gendarme and the Gendarmettes*, 1982).

8 Literally 'Without roof or law', a pun on the French expression *sans foi ni loi*, without faith or law.

REFERENCES

Benoît, Fernand (1949) *La Provence et le Comtat Venaissin*, Paris: NRF/Gallimard.

Bouyala d'Arnaud, Alphonse (1979) *Santons et traditions de Noël en Provence*, Marseille: Tacussel.

de la Bretèque, François (1982) 'Images du Midi dans le cinéma français', *Amiras* 4.

—— (1990) 'Le forum villageois dans le cinéma méditerranéen', *Champs/contrechamps, Le Cinéma rural en Europe*, Paris: BPI/Centre Pompidou.

—— (1991) '*Angèle*, un inventaire de représentations', *Lenga e pais d'oc* 20.

de Certeau, Michel (1974) 'L'opération historique' in Jacques Le Goff and Pierre Nora, *Faire de l'histoire*, Paris: Gallimard, 'Bibliothèque des histoires', vol. I.

Duret, Evelyne (1984) *Camargue, terre de cinéma*, Arles: Parc naturel de Camargue, brochure de l'exposition.

Giono, Jean (1980) *Oeuvres cinématographiques 1939–1959*, ed. Jacques Mény, Paris: Gallimard.

Lafont, Robert (1954) *Mistral ou l'illusion*, Paris: Plon.

—— (1967) *La Révolution régionaliste*.

—— (1971) *Le Sud et le Nord*, Toulouse: Privat.

Lagrave, Rose-Marie (1980) *Le Village romanesque*, Arles: Actes Sud.

Mény, Jacques (1978, 1990) *Jean Giono et le cinéma*, Paris: Ramsay.

Memmi, Albert (1957) *Portrait du colonisé*, Paris.

Mistral, Frédéric (1906, re-edited 1979) *Memori e raconte*, Marseilles: C.P.M.

Pelen, Jean-Noël (1985) *La Production d'identité*, Actes du symposium de l'U.A. 041052 du CNRS, Montpellier: Université Paul Valéry.

Peyrusse, Claudette (1986) *Le Cinéma méridional*, Toulouse: Eché.

Prédal, René (1980) *80 ans de cinéma, Nice et le 7ème art*, Editions Serre.

Ramon, Emile (1925) *Histoires marseillaises*, Paris: Les éditions de France.

Ripert, Pierre (1956) *Les Origines de la crèche provençale et des santons populaires*, Marseille: Tacusel.

Royer, Jean-Yves and Martel, Pierre (1978) 'La femme à la fontaine', *Les Alpes de lumière* 65.

5

AUTHOR, ACTOR, SHOWMAN
Reinhold Schünzel and *Hallo Caesar!*

Thomas Elsaesser

There are plenty of fine moments, but as comedy it falters, for lack of structure and a central dramatic idea. Schünzel who plays Caesar ... is on a slippery slope. What he is famous for, his wicked flippancy, his cynicism, his tongue-in-cheek silliness is in danger of turning into a mannerism.

(Lichtbildbühne 108, 1927)

Maybe it is true that ... the material would have been more suitable for a three-reeler than a full-length feature. Szakall, who is a very successful variety artist, has many a fine sketch to his credit. If he gives up writing film scripts, it won't be a great loss. Nobody needs to be good at everything. And Schünzel ought to be reminded that if he didn't just trust his acting skills but took more care over his story material, his successes would be even greater.

(Kinematograph, 8 May 1927)

POPULAR CINEMA?

Reading the reviews, it is fairly obvious that critics at the time did not quite know what to make of *Hallo Caesar!* (Reinhold Schünzel, Germany 1927).[1] They saw a ragbag of more or less successful routines, gags and visual jokes, poorly motivated by a flimsy plot; they faulted the sentimental interludes which detract from the underlying comic premise; and they thought the acting exaggerated. Yet they implicitly made the actor-director's own past performances the measure of their present dissatisfactions, thus confirming that in the mid–1920s, Reinhold Schünzel was considered by the critics a major filmmaker and a comic genius.

With our knowledge of classic German (or Weimar) cinema still largely drawn from Lotte Eisner's *The Haunted Screen* (1969) and Siegfried Kracauer's *From Caligari to Hitler* (1974), this comes as quite a surprise. Here is a popular comedian-director-producer, in the tradition of Charles Chaplin, Buster Keaton, Harold Lloyd, unknown internationally and barely

Plate 9 The star-auteur-showman as dandy: Reinhold Schünzel in the 1920s. By courtesy of the British Film Institute, London.

remembered by German film historians. *Hallo Caesar!* in particular is something of an archaeological discovery: a small chink of light in the solid wall of received opinion about the German cinema as dark mirror of the nation's soul and its authoritarian traits, and thus conceivably giving us a glimpse of the many layers which in actual fact made up Weimar film culture.

Figures such as Schünzel raise important questions about European and national traditions of comedy and their media intertext, about the transitional period between early and classical cinema and the changes from performative to narrative modes, about national film style and the international film industry, and finally, about the discourses that constitute a popular star or performer as a brand-name. A closer study of Schünzel thus would help to reintegrate the German cinema of the 1910s and 1920s into the international production context, and to redress the traditional emphasis on Expressionist vs. realist filmmaking as the dominant dualism of the period.

No national cinema has suffered more from the neglect of the popular in favour of the art cinema and auteur cinema. This is probably due to three factors: first, the scarcity of material that has survived.[2] Second, the overwhelming bias of the German intellectual elite either for the art film, or for American popular cinema, notably slapstick comedy. Third, the general belief that the German cinema has never been capable of good comedy with the exception of Lubitsch who went to Hollywood.

REINHOLD SCHÜNZEL: A TYPICALLY GERMAN FILM CAREER?

Born in Hamburg in 1888, Schünzel started acting as early as 1912 in a *Volkstheater* and appearing in comedy sketches for a travelling troupe. By 1916 he had begun working in films, but first profiled himself as an actor in fantastic genres in the so-called *Sittenfilme* (sex education films) of the post-war period, where he played diabolical figures – seducers, homosexual extortionists and swindlers whose smooth exterior disguised sadistic villainy and fiendish lusts. Of these essentially melodramatic roles probably the best-known is in Richard Oswald's *Anders als die Anderen (Different from Others*, Germany 1918/19), where he blackmails Conrad Veidt over a homosexual affair; he is equally impressive as the double-dealing Duc de Choiseuil in Ernst Lubitsch's *Madame Dubarry* (Germany 1919) and the cold-blooded seducer in his own *Das Mädchen aus der Ackerstrasse (The Girl from Acker Street*, Germany 1920). From the mid–1920s onwards, Schünzel developed an alternative persona, essentially comic, the Berlin street-wise good-for-nothing, turning a notorious 'local' character into a nationally recognized type. Often he played members of the lower orders (servants, waiters, out-of-work artisans) acting as go-between to facilitate fantasies about social mobility and careerism in a society where class was about to be superseded by appearance and raffish style. In this, he was very much a composite identification figure for his primary target audience, the upwardly mobile white-collar workers.

Schünzel carefully nurtured a number of show-business myths centred on being a man of the people. Stories put out by his studio's press office were about him being 'mistaken' for Reinhold Schünzel in provincial towns or working-class districts. Schünzel's favourite plot material in his comedies involved impersonations, mistaken identities, role reversal, con tricks and deceptions (which hints at a deeper connection between his sinister and his comic roles).

Internationally, Schünzel did not become famous until the sound era, when he directed some of the best-known sophisticated comedies of the 1930s, such as *Viktor und Viktoria* (Germany 1933), *Die englische Heirat (The English Marriage*, Germany 1934), *Amphitryon* (Germany 1935). Eight of his films were also made in French-language versions, usually co-directed with Roger Le Bon or Henri Chomette.[3] He also acted in international hits like G. W. Pabst's *Die 3-Groschenoper (The Threepenny Opera*, Germany 1931), or in the German-language version of *Le Bal (The Ball*, Wilhelm Thiele, France 1931). Although Schünzel was Jewish on his mother's side, his films were such big box-office that Goebbels was anxious to keep him on after the Nazi takeover in 1933, and he continued to make popular comedies well into the mid–1930s. When he eventually left for Hollywood in 1937, after censorship difficulties over *Land der Liebe (Land of Love*, Germany 1937), he arrived to a very hostile reception from the German *émigré* community. Under contract to MGM, directing four films for them between 1938 and 1941, he somehow managed to antagonize Louis B. Meyer, who apparently made sure that Schünzel would be out of work as a director. The rest of his career is made up of bit parts in anti-Nazi films, such as Fritz Lang's *Hangmen also Die!* (USA 1942), *The Hitler Gang* (John Farrow, USA 1944), and Alfred Hitchcock's *Notorious* (USA 1946), where he plays the guest of honour at Claude Rains's rather strained dinner party. Schünzel's filmography includes directing credits for forty-five films between 1918 and 1941, and he acted in altogether 140 films between 1916 and 1953.

AUTHOR, ACTOR, SHOWMAN

Celebrating Schünzel as a rediscovery, it is tempting to think of him in terms of an auteur (writing, directing, producing, acting all in one) but this is misleading: he comes from a tradition (in fact, rather similar to the milieu which gave Lubitsch his start) where the performer is perforce a *metteur-en-scène*, if only of his own persona. Contemporary reviews, however, did make a distinction between Schünzel the director and Schünzel the actor. As a director, he was first regarded as a realist with a feel for detail, for seedy settings and underworld types (*Das Mädchen aus der Ackerstrasse* is often quoted as the first realist feature film), while his comedies won praise for understatement. As an actor, by contrast, he was accused of mannerisms and hamming: a dualism the critics resolved by ritually admonishing Schünzel the director to restrain Schünzel the actor.[4]

The Schünzel persona relies heavily on the transvestism of operetta, with its preference for role reversals, and the definition of erotic desire around exchange and substitution. Often, social status and sexual status are conjugated against each other (the impostor who pretends to be the rich uncle from America, or the village simpleton who is suddenly sexually desirable when he becomes heir to a fortune). Furthermore, Schünzel uniquely combines in his roles sentimentality, ruthlessness and cynicism: opportunist but irreverent, the boy next door with a heart of gold but also the street lout without a conscience. Finally and perhaps most characteristically, the Schünzel persona is marked by sexual ambivalence: a homosexual or bisexual subtext is the most obvious common denominator between his diabolical seducer of the late 1910s and early 1920s and his comic persona from the mid–1920s onwards.

Hallo Caesar! was shot during June/July 1926, produced by Schünzel's own firm, with himself as co-writer, director, producer and leading actor. The executive producer was Fritz Grossmann, whom Schünzel seemed to have relied on regularly during that period. The year 1926 was a good one, and Schünzel was at the height of his career. After the enormous success of the Emil Jannings film *Alles um Geld (Everything Turns around Money*, Germany 1923) Schünzel was also taken seriously as a director, and during the next six years he was active in more than thirty films as director or in a leading role. With seven films, the 1925–6 season was one of the best. Those directed by Georg Jacoby: *Der Hahn im Korb (Cock of the Roost)*, Germany 1925; *Der Stolz der Kompanie (Pride of the Regiment)*, Germany 1926; *Der dumme August des Zirkus Romanelli (The Clown from Circus Romanelli)*, Germany 1926 as well as Paul Ludwig Stein's *Fünfuhrtee in der Ackerstrasse (Five o'Clock Tea in Acker Street*, Germany 1926) and Willi Wolf's *Der Juxbaron (The Baron of Fun*, Germany 1926) crystallized and defined Schünzel's spectrum as a comic, which in *Hallo Caesar!* became condensed into a multi-faceted and none the less identifiable type. A poem by the title 'All Star Cast' clearly implies that Schünzel was, with Conrad Veidt, a figure in the front row (of the cinema's publicity machinery).[5] But as one of the trade papers pointed out, this was also a function of his astonishing rate of output: 'Schünzel works without a break, and that is the publicity which serves him best' (*Filmwoche* 9, 1924).

Similarly, judging by the ads placed by UFA studios in the 1926 trade papers, Schünzel had also become a bankable director. In the context of the famous Parufamet Agreement,[6] several Schünzel productions were specifically announced for the 1927 season, and in the UFA Annual Preview (*Lichbildbühne* 151, 1927) much is made of the anticipated December 1927 première of *Üb'immer Treu und Redlichkeit (Be Loyal and Honest*, Germany 1927) and for April 1928, next to 'a Porten-Film' appears 'a Schünzel-Film' (presumably *Gustav Mond . . . Du gehst so stille, Gustav Moon . . . You Move so Silently*, Germany 1927–8).

Such PR work suggests a few questions: was Schünzel at that time valuable to UFA as a star-director or as star-actor? The comparison with Henny Porten points to the latter, but the fact that both 'Schünzel-films' were actually directed by him does not exclude the former, especially since in the same 1927–8 season two more Schünzel films were released through Ufa: *Herkules Maier* (Germany 1927) and *Adam und Eva* (Germany 1928), both with Schünzel in the lead, produced and supervised (as *künstlericher Oberleiter*, artistic supervisor) by him, but with directorial credits going to Alexander Esway and Rudolf Bieberach.

This raises a further issue: were the Schünzel films of the mid–1920s intended for export or for the domestic market? The press releases continue to sell Schünzel to a broad public in Germany, especially provincial audiences: 'In between his important productions he is always concerned to make more modest films, which are above all destined to ensure that a certain public – that of the small cinemas – does not forget him' (*Filmwoche* 9, 1924). The Schünzel anecdotes published in the *Filmkurier* of January 1928 have one single point: to show that, whether among the revolutionaries on the barricades in 1919, among the Berliner street-wise adolescents, or among the working men and Viennese cab drivers, Schünzel was a familiar face, though apparently much better known in his roles as criminal, aristocrat or dandy, than as comedian. Schünzel's own biographical sketch on the other hand tries to prove that right from the start, behind the serious (theatrical) roles, the comedian in him was irrepressible:

> [I must have been] deeply benighted, when I honestly believed I would give the world a new Hamlet or Don Carlos. The Swiss knew better: their stifled laughter was an eye-opener, they discovered the comedian in me. It was a relief no longer having to be afraid of the audience laughing at me.
>
> (*Filmwelt* 4, February 1925: 12)

In the same article Schünzel boasts of his services to ordinary films for ordinary people:

> I don't want to appear immodest, but permit me to point out that I am proud to have been the first director in Germany who, in the age of the big-budget films, dared to make a film on location in Berlin, about the fate of a little servant girl.
>
> (ibid.: 15)

Was Schünzel, as a comic talent, a creator of comedian's comedy or merely an actor of comic parts? A comparison with the early Lubitsch is quite telling. In films where Lubitsch not only directed but also played the lead, as in *Meier aus Berlin (Meier from Berlin)*, Germany 1916, his persona 'Meier' was a character already familiar from variety theatre and newspaper cartoons, so that – parallel to developments in the USA – the persona could rely on a certain amount of audience foreknowledge, increasingly the basis for the fixed characters of comedian's comedy like Chaplin's Charlie, 'Stoneface' Keaton, 'Rubberface' Al St John or 'Babyface' Langdon. Lubitsch soon abandoned comedian's comedy and concentrated on directing, perhaps precisely because the 'Meier' type he had helped to bring to the screen proved geographically and ethnically too limiting, cutting out potentially important audiences and becoming – as much popular European comedy seems to have been – inexportable.

Schünzel did not follow the Lubitsch path until the 1930s when he began to acquire an international reputation for directing erotically suave 'sophisticated comedies' (*Viktor und Viktoria, Amphitryon*) following, precisely, the (American) Lubitsch tradition. What the German film industry did not seem able to marshal in the 1920s, compared to the international competition, were slapstick comedians of wide appeal, who could measure up to Max Linder, Ben Turpin, Chaplin and a host of others. This is not to say that there were not many actors who excelled in comic parts, such as Siggi Arno, Victor Janssen, Julius Falkenstein, but none of them managed the breakthrough to being a star whose (brand) name alone conjured up a one-man genre and guaranteed box-office success.[7]

It seems that one needs to see Schünzel as a compromise figure between a comic character actor and a German star comedian able to compete with the popularity of Chaplin or Harold Lloyd. One of the largest ads of the Reinhold Schünzel-Film GmbH in the *Lichtbildbühne*, April 1928, reads in bold letters: 'Reinhold Schünzel promises a full house for every movie-theatre owner.' Underneath four new productions are previewed: *Der Harem des Mister Fox (Mr Fox's Harem*, not completed; *Aus dem Tagebuch eines Junggesellen* (*From a Bachelor's Diary*, Germany 1928); *Don Juan in der Mädchenschule (Don Juan at the Girls' High School*, Germany 1928); and *Michel im Weltkrieg (Michael in the World War*, not completed); each title is advertised with the phrase 'Schünzel as', following the manner of Chaplin as tramp, as gold prospector, as widower. In 'Kino, Kino über alles' the author Hans Harbeck counts Schünzel among the greatest.[8] One can assume that part of this comparison ('Keaton, Chaplin, Schünzel, Pat und Lloyd') is wishful thinking, or all-too-obvious publicity, for these comparisons had already prompted a critic to vent his doubts, when in a review of *Gustav Mond* he notes: 'the fact must just for once be stated that Schünzel is no Chaplin, Harold Lloyd or Buster Keaton' (*Lichtbildbühne* 305, 1927), against which must be set articles in *Das blaue Heft* or the *Acht-Uhr-Abendblatt*, where Schünzel is mentioned as on a par with Lloyd and Keaton.

HALLO CAESAR!

Considering Schünzel's furious rate of productivity (seven films in 1926, three of them as director), *Hallo Caesar!* would appear to have been a routine picture intended for the domestic market: 'Schünzel has his eye with this – by no means cheap – film firmly on an audience ready to laugh at the slightest occasion, without making too high a demand on its entertainment (*Lichtbildbühne* 108, 1927).

The title itself announces the identity of star and character (Schünzel is Caesar), while the plot is made up of some of the most popular situations of the Weimar entertainment industries (mistaken identity as a satire on social aspirations), which can be found in films, popular fiction and, above all, operettas. Schünzel himself made a film based on one such operetta, *Der Juxbaron*. The American angle is also a staple Weimar cliché (here the chase after the contract replaces the chase after the rich American uncle's inheritance). At the same time, the more unconnected episodes (the taxi ride after he arrives in Karlsbad, for instance) are comic numbers taken straight from the Mack Sennett school of American slapstick. Schünzel knew his audience: with *Hallo Caesar!* the director borrowed from the Hollywood genres his viewers were familiar with, while tailoring the characters and situations to recognizable German issues and conditions. A review of *Gustav Mond . . . du gehst so stille* identified very clearly this aspect of Schünzel's films:

> Despite the viewer being familiar from earlier films with this kind of character, he still enchants in much the same way as Harold Lloyd and Buster Keaton do. In particular, when the frame is as cleverly mounted as it is here, and a few sensations in the American manner are added for good measure.
>
> (*Kinematograph*, 25 December 1927)

Schünzel, in other words, does not aim at the American market, but, on the contrary, shows much more clearly than the art films and prestige spectacles of the Weimar cinema could allow themselves to admit, how popular taste and the German (exhibition) market had become Americanized (taken over by US firms) by the mid–1920s.

The consciously populist streak in *Hallo Caesar!* can be gauged by the title itself, with its convergence of actor and named part, also by its odd mode of address, the 'hailing' of the hero, as if an imaginary public were clapping as he was introduced on stage. This brings *Hallo Caesar!* into the vicinity of a narrative mode that is still very performance-oriented, and some of the faint praise that the film received from the reviewers reflects the preference by 1926 for the totally narrativized full-length feature film. But *Hallo Caesar!* clearly is very attached to the 'numbers' principle of early cinema, perhaps an index that the audience it was aimed at had not yet made the feature film its dominant norm and was quite satisfied with an evening of two- and three-reelers, held together by a recognizable star character, here the Schünzel/Caesar persona. There was in fact a very vivid debate about the desirability of reintroducing two-reelers into the programme, especially for provincial theatres.[9]

Indeed, several factors indicate that *Hallo Caesar!* belongs to what Tom Gunning (1986) has called the 'cinema of attractions', as opposed to the 'cinema of narrative integration'. The gesture of 'showing and telling' (as opposed to just 'telling a story') is very apparent, with Schünzel often taking the audience into his confidence with a wink, or making an exhibition of himself. From the very beginning, at the hairdresser's salon, to which he follows the pair of legs that first attract his attention, Caesar obviously revels in putting on the act of the love-struck pavement beau, failing to seduce the lady with his conjuring tricks and mimic talent, but thereby the more strongly seducing the audience, who are, of course, the real addressees. Thus we have a twofold spectator position: a narrative one, concerned with the progress of the love interest, and a performative one, that justifies Caesar's claim to the contract he so desperately desires. The principle is even more apparent in the subsequent scene, when the lady departs and Caesar rushes after her, though not without putting his 'bride' into the barber's chair and asking the hairdresser to give her a cut in the latest fashion. The bride is one of the salon's own shopwindow dummies, and the hairdresser is already half-way through cutting the dummy's hair before he realizes his mistake. For this scene, the camera has stayed behind, temporarily abandoning both Caesar and the object of his attention. The gag, carefully prepared by Caesar, is wholly staged for the benefit of the audience. In fact, the lady of his dreams all but disappears from the film, and we are as surprised as she is – and as Caesar is – when she turns up again on the Karlsbad promenade.

A whole series of scenes, notably those in the Berlin coffee house, are built up as separate 'numbers', with the coffee house an ideal setting for creating performers and audiences, spectators and exhibitionists. It is as if a constantly gathered diegetic audience doubles and 'represents' the actual audience in the cinema – a clear indication that the film is very conscious of its own performative mode (which has nothing 'theatrical' about it), making *Hallo Caesar!* not so much a 'primitive' film, but one that 'knows its audience'. It is this aspect of Schünzel the actor-writer-director-producer which makes any *Cahiers du Cinéma*-type argument about Schünzel as *auteur maudit* problematic, at least for the 1920s. In performance-oriented films like *Hallo Caesar!* he belongs much more to the (by no means unimportant) line of the filmmaker as showman, a line which can be followed from Méliès to Keaton, from Jacques Tati to Jerry Lewis, and from Federico Fellini to Woody Allen – directors, in other words, whose talent and film material have often been enriched by their drawing on non-narrative traditions such as the circus, variety acts, cabaret and stand-up comedy, but in the German context the intertext is operetta which already in 1913 was denounced as 'the worst enemy of German theatrical art' (Oesterheld 1978).

IRONY OR NOSTALGIA?

One could go even further and argue that *Hallo Caesar!* is not only a satire on the film industry and show business, but quite a sly and sophisticated evocation of an earlier cinema, alluding to it partly ironically, partly out of nostalgia, and thus inscribing possibly two kinds of audiences: let me call them for simplicity's sake the cosmopolitan populist ones, and the rural popular ones.

There is no doubt that the film is full of allusions and in-jokes which are difficult to pick up today. The basic idea of the all-important contract to America for a variety artist is easily decodable as an allegory of the German film industry, which especially in the year of the Parufamet Agreement and with Ufa on its knees, was basing all too many hopes on America.

The chase after the American impresario has thus a certain topical flavour, which is even more apparent when one comes across an item in the film industry trade journal *Lichtbildbühne* of 7 July 1926 (the month *Hallo Caesar!* was shot) about Carl Laemmle, studio head of Universal visiting Karlsbad on his annual European holiday. It reads: 'Laemmle is now the center of a number of Berlin film people who have joined him in Karlsbad, to shake hands with him, partly as friends, partly for business reasons.' Schünzel's Caesar could not have put it better, and Laemmle, himself of Czech origins, is of course precisely the sort of 'Herr Lehmann' that the American tycoon disguises himself as. Ironic, for instance, is also the happy ending. Despite all his troubles, Caesar gets the contract and the woman. But in actual fact, the 'right girl' is really the wrong girl, for the daughter of his landlady is, as the film makes abundantly clear, the maternal type and a homebody, rooted to the small town, and destined to wither if transplanted to Berlin, never mind the American vaudeville circuit. The owner of the elegant pair of legs, who turns out to be the daughter of his new boss, would of course be the perfect partner, personally as well as professionally, and she does not seem disinclined, except at the very end, when she generously renounces in favour of the other. Thus, the plot – pretty feeble if judged in terms of drama and suspense – is quite a witty play of substitution and exchange: Caesar chases the wrong 'American' while he already has the right one as his chum; he pursues the right woman (the boss's daughter) but she is the wrong choice; and gets the right girl who really loves him but who may well prove the wrong one for his professional ambitions. This crisscrossing of erotic and economic object choice would not have been out of place in a Lubitsch comedy such as *The Marriage Circle* (USA 1924), *Lady Windermere's Fan* (USA 1925) and *So This is Paris* (USA 1926), and already anticipates the more explicit and vertiginous exchanges in *Viktor und Viktoria* and *Amphitryon*. What appears to be a happy ending in *Hallo Caesar!* is, in true comedy fashion, simply the beginning of tragedy in another register: say, *Sunrise* (F. W. Murnau, USA 1927).

Equally remarkable, and in a sort of counter-current to the 'simple tale simply told' because displaying its own bravura, is the film's technical sophistication, mainly in terms of lighting, which – unusual for the period – is very 'American': with several light sources, for instance, in the evening and night scenes, rim lighting on the characters for some of the dramatic scenes, and an interesting use of depth of field, as in the daytime exteriors of the environs of Karlsbad, where the landscape, the undulating line of the houses, is offset against the line of the horizon. At night, for instance at the fairground, the space is clearly divided into several action planes, often with an extreme foreground, to emphasize depth or to draw attention to the 'architecture of the looks' between the characters. In the interiors, Schünzel has learnt from Griffith. For example in the extended gag with the water jug and the wash-basin in the hall at the bottom of the stairs, one finds the typically asymmetrical and very powerfully dramatic space of early 1920s Griffith, organized to cut out depth and to emphasize the lateral, since the whole point of the gag turns on entrances and exits, off-screen right and off-screen left, doors and corridors.

But even if the reference to Griffith is not a self-conscious quotation but merely the adoption of a convention, there is no doubt that whole parts of *Hallo Caesar!* are very deliberate pastiches on the classics of film history. Especially in the part that seems to do very little to advance the plot – the hotel fire – we find a veritable anthology of screen gems: apart from the Méliès-type *féeries* that go with Caesar's profession as a juggler and magician, there is Lumière's *L'Arroseur arrosé* (France 1895) lovingly recreated right in the middle of what is obviously Edwin S. Porter's *Life of an American Fireman* (USA 1903), alluding to the fact that every film producer at the turn of the century restaged the popular hits of his competitors. The hotel fire itself, with its Marx Brothers routines and Tati-esque mime sequences (the fire chief endlessly and futilely giving Morse hand-signals to his subordinates) could no doubt, in all its different gags and phases, be traced back to precise examples, whether from Max Linder or Fatty Arbuckle and Ben Turpin. The episode, although renewing his courtship of the boss's daughter, has little other dramatic significance except to show off Schünzel-the-actor's mime and impersonation skills (for one kind of audience) and Schünzel-the-director's skills as parodist and pasticheur (for another – or for the same audience who are getting a whole repertoire of old favourites for the price of one ticket).

82

THE AVANT-GARDE, THE POPULAR AND BEYOND

Obviously, there is a danger of making too much of this, and ending up claiming *Hallo Caesar!* as a sort of deconstructive avant-garde masterpiece. Nothing could be further from my intention, and indeed, it would be rendering Schünzel a poor service. The point is rather the opposite: even a quite ordinary, run-of-the-mill production, such as *Hallo Caesar!*, mass-market product made for the general public, can appear multi-layered to the historically curious gaze. It also raises, in the European context, the question of what is popular as opposed to art cinema. Without being definitive or dogmatic, there are features which deserve to be recalled, because they apply not only to *Hallo Caesar!* but to much of Schünzel's other work: stereotypical plots, comic or dramatic set-pieces; cross-generic intertextuality and allusionism; plagiarism and self-plagiarism; spectacle-attraction over narrative integration; the entertainer/showman as opposed to the director/artist; the star persona defined by his/her roles, but also existing outside in the world of showbusiness. Finally, a popular film will be known by the brand-recognition of the star rather than the genre or the director: a Henny Porten film, a Harry Piel film, an Emil Jannings film.[10]

And yet, the question remains of whether in *Hallo Caesar!* there is a perspective from which the different points of entry, such as the cosmopoli-tan-populist and the provincial-popular, converge, making any hard and fast division between avant-garde and mass culture unnecessary. This would clearly be the issue of sexuality and sexual difference, and the significance of the Caesar persona in this light. Schünzel, as already men-tioned, had a screen presence which was very unsettling in terms of gender, an ambivalence which was due not to his sexual proclivity but to his style, not to any specific 'vice' but to the social role of gender. At first glance, *Hallo Caesar!* is no exception. A homoerotic countercurrent to the plot's heterosexual romance could be indicated by, for instance, the unsatisfac-tory, anti-climactic 'formation of the couple', and Caesar's relation to Herr Lehmann (he dances the tango for Herr Lehmann and dons a huge papier-mâché nose, then the two throw confetti at each other and behave like Laurel and Hardy; their childish pranks only cease when, much to Lehmann's annoyance, Caesar resumes the pursuit of his daughter). In addition, the lady's suitor is outrageously foppish and effete, and Caesar's own juggling tricks are anything but innocent (the billiard balls juggled on a walking stick, the bunch of flowers constantly sprouting from his trouser pockets). At the same time, there are mother-in-law jokes, and an obvious delight on the part of Caesar in fragmenting (the pair of legs, the revue-girls' bottoms), regimenting (the three girls in the coffee house) and fetishizing (the shop-window dummy) the female body, all of which, if they do not support the homosexual subtext, none the less seem to mark the film as mildly hysterical with regard to female sexuality and phallic masculinity.

Such a reading does not altogether answer the question about the Schünzel persona, and its double register of appeal. Female dummies and straw boaters, pairs of legs and chorus lines, walking sticks and billiard balls, flower bouquets and missing pearls: it sounds like a list of props either for a Busby Berkeley musical or an avant-garde experimental film like *Ballet mécanique*. Perhaps the point where the avant-garde and the popular merge in the Schünzel persona requires a different definition of his sensibility as a performer. The figure which comes to mind is that of the dandy, a term that despite its complex cultural baggage seems to me to capture best the ambivalence and duality of many of Schünzel's characters, their subversiveness towards social norms, including sexual norms, but also the fact that this subversiveness is ultimately very conformist, since one of the main attributes of the dandy is his style, his narcissism which he wields aggressively, like a weapon. But Schünzel, especially in his comic parts, is perhaps too little the aristocrat and too much the populist really to qualify as a dandy, which is why, despite the anachronism, one might think of him as camp, in the limited sense that he lovingly devotes himself to popular and even bad taste, not necessarily out of an attachment to kitsch objects or sentimental situations *per se*, but out of an enjoyment of the spontaneity and eccentricity inherent in the act of choosing these objects and situations, in the face of educated or high-brow disapproval and distaste. If Schünzel and *Hallo Caesar!* are in some sense camp, it is thus only to the degree that the term valorizes three distinct moments that I have tried to isolate in the film: the performative-exhibitionist stance, the sexual ambiguity of several of the characters, and the evident love of cliché and pastiche in the plot, the gags and the comic turns.

Yet there is a final aspect to which I want, very briefly, to draw attention. Many of the motifs and scenes I have highlighted can also be read as instances of doubling or mirroring, and exploiting the pleasure of seriality. This, too, is a feature where, historically, avant-garde sensibility and the popular made common cause, for right across the spectrum of the arts, seriality and symmetry became something of a key metaphor during the so-called 'second machine age' (the 1920s). We find it as a celebratory metaphor of energy and vitality in revue girls and bio-mechanics, in the New Photography and representations of Fordism, in the passion for 'time and motion studies' and the jazz idiom. In short, it became Europe's code for Americamania. In *Hallo Caesar!* doubling and the series appear not only in the plot, the coffee-house girls and rehearsing Tiller troupe, the odd use of the (male) Kretschmar twins, but also in the structure – the double and triple comedy of errors, which elevated to a moral mirror maze fairly loses its ideological content: upward mobility. Schünzel's most loving attention in *Hallo Caesar!* ultimately belongs to the mechanical, the serial and the compulsion to repeat. This makes him almost our contemporary: he has, to use a cliché, faith in doubles and in fakes because they are some of the passwords to the popular.

NOTES

1 The film tells the story of an unemployed variety artist who follows a famous American impresario from Berlin to Karlsbad in search of work. But Caesar, told that all it takes to be hired on the spot is to startle the tycoon with a surprise performance, mistakes several well-heeled tourists for the American, baffling them with juggling a plate and a billiard ball on his walking stick. In actual fact, the real impresario is a casual acquaintance of Caesar's who calls himself Herr Lehmann. In the end, Caesar gets the contract and, for good measure, a bride as well (synopsis from *Lichtbildbühne* 108, 1927).

2 Events like the Pordenone festival, which had a retrospective of early German films in 1990 ('Before Caligari'), the annual Hamburg meetings organized by Cinegraph (where I first came across Schünzel in 1988), and the changing policy of access among archives mean that many more films from all periods of German film history are becoming available for study.

3 *Le Petit écart* (Rheinhold Schünzel (R.S.) and Henri Chomette, Germany 1931), French version of *Ein kleiner Seitensprung; Ronny* (R. S. and Roger Le Bon, Germany 1931), French version of *Ronny; La Belle aventure* (R. S. and Roger Le Bon, Germany 1932), French version of *Das schöne Abenteuer; Georges et Georgette* (R. S. and Roger Le Bon, Germany 1933), French version of *Viktor und Viktoria; Idylle au Caire* (R. S. and Claude Heymann, Germany 1933), French version of *Saison in Kairo; La Jeune fille d'une nuit* (R. S. and Roger Le Bon, Germany 1934), French version of *Die Töchter Ihrer Exzellenz; Les Dieux s'amusent* (R. S. and Albert Valentin, Germany 1935), French version of *Amphitryon; Donogoo* (R. S. and Henri Chomette, Germany 1936), French version of *Donogoo Tonka*.

4 There is evidence that Schünzel tried to keep the two sides of his life quite separate: most striking is the contrast between his publicity photographs as director/producer, with a monocle in the dandified manner of Fritz Lang, and some of the stills from his films in which he appears more like one of Dr Mabuse's low-life disguises, or where he casts himself as a 'Berliner Pflanze', a proletarian rough diamond.

5   Ich säh's so gerne: Conrad Veidt den blassen,
   In einem Film mit Baby Peggy spielen . . .
   Und Reinhold Schünzel mit den sanften Mienen –
   Ich säh ihn gern als Mary Carr Entsprossnen . . .
   Wo wär' solch Paar wohl schon vordem erschienen?

(Filmland 1, February 1925)

   I'd love to see pale Conrad Veidt
   Star opposite Baby Peggy in a film
   And Reinhold Schünzel with his gentle features
   I'd like to see him as the son of Mary Carr . . .
   Where could a pair like these be seen before?

6 A commercial agreement signed by UFA with Paramount and MGM in 1925 to try and compensate for the reduction in state finance.

7 It is true, Harry Liedtke and Harry Piel made enormously popular films, and their names were synonymous with the parts they played, but they embodied

only one kind of hero, that of the adventurer and daredevil, not that of the comic anti-hero.

8   Und dann Grotesken, die mit froher Wucht
den Geist der Schwere treiben in die Flucht
und an der Hand von Unsinn immer siegen
Die Keaton, Chaplin, Schünzel, Pat und Lloyd
Lachpillen in das Publikum gestreut
bringen das älteste Gebälk zum Biegen.

(Hans Harbeck, 'Kino, Kino über alles', in Herbert Gunther
(ed.) Hier schreibt Berlin, Berlin, 1929)

And then those slapstick movies which pack a happy punch
Driving away the heaviest thoughts
And always win when taking nonsense by the hand
When Keaton, Chaplin, Schünzel, Pat and Lloyd
Scatter their pills of laughter among the crowd
Even the oldest beams begin to split their sides

9 See, for instance, an article in *Lichtbildbühne* 151, 1927: p 20.

10 Actors in the *Publikumsfilm* (as popular films were known in the 1920s) would not come from legitimate theatre and high-brow acting traditions (such as Max Reinhardt's theatre where virtually all actors of the German 'art cinema' began), but from the Volkstheater, the variety theatre. Similarly, narrative material would not have been adaptations from literature, but drawn from theatrical melodrama, farce, vaudeville sketch, operetta, serialized newspaper fiction (*Groschenromane*) and romance fiction (generically known as 'Courts-Mahler', after the most popular woman author, or *Gartenlaube*, after the magazine of that title).

REFERENCES

Eisner, Lotte (1969) *The Haunted Screen: Expressionism in the German Cinema and the Influence of Max Reinhardt*, London: Thames & Hudson.

Gunning, Tom (1986) 'The cinema of attraction: early film, its spectator and the avant-garde', *Wide Angle* 8(314): 63–70; also in Elsaesser, Thomas (ed.) (1990) *Early Cinema: Space, Frame, Narrative*, London: British Film Institute.

Harbeck, Hans (1929) 'Kino, Kino über alles', in Herbert Gunther (ed.) *Hier schreibt Berlin*, Berlin.

Kracauer, Siegfried (1974) *From Caligari to Hitler: a Psychological History of the German Film*, Princeton NJ: Princeton University Press.

Oesterheld, Erich (1978) 'Wie die Deutschen Dramatiker Barbaren wurden', in Anton Kaes (ed.) *Die Kino-Debatte*, Tübingen.

6

'WE WERE BORN TO TURN A FAIRY-TALE INTO REALITY'

Svetlyĭ put' and the Soviet musical of the 1930s and 1940s

Maria Enzensberger

We were born to turn a fairy-tale into reality,
To extend distances and space;
We've been given reason, steel wings for arms,
And a flaming motor for a heart.

('The Aviators' March', a popular Soviet song)

Soviet popular cinema of the 1930s and 1940s has suffered a peculiar fate in its own country: extolled for several decades as a truly socialist realist representation of Soviet life, since the advent of *glasnost'* it has been subjected to severe criticism as an officially sanctioned falsehood about that life (Alexandrova 1989).

The study of this cinema's relationship to contemporary reality and of the audience's response has been undertaken by Maya Turovskaya who raised the question of the relationship between style and meaning in Soviet cinema of that period. She demonstrated the fairy-tale-like structure of the musical comedies of Ivan Pyriev: *Bogataya nevesta (The Rich Bride*, 1938), *Traktoristy (Tractor Drivers*, 1939) and *Svinarka i pastukh (The Swineherd and the Shepherd*, 1941) and their 'folklorization' of the themes drawn from contemporary Soviet village life. Her conclusion was that their 'embellishment' of Soviet reality should be regarded not as a 'distortion of the truth' – for faithfulness to life was never their aim – but as a standard and perfectly legitimate stylistic mode within popular cinema, the mode that elevates its subject matter into the realm of a 'dream' or Utopia, enabling the spectator to 'rise above' reality and regard it in a more sublime and optimistic manner (Turovskaya 1988).

The purpose of this chapter is to extend the work done by Turovskaya through the analysis of another musical comedy from the same period: Grigori Alexandrov's *Svetlyĭ put' (Radiant Path*,[1] 1940), originally entitled *Cinderella* but renamed on Stalin's suggestion. I intend to examine the way

Plate 10 Traktoristy. By courtesy of the British Film Institute, London.

Plate 11 Bogataya nevesta. By courtesy of the British Film Institute, London.

in which this story of a maid turned Stakhanovite weaver, and subsequently celebrated engineer and deputy to the Supreme Soviet, interweaves symbolic and realistic discourses into a powerful myth of the possibility of personal success in an ostensibly collectivistic society. It should be pointed out at once that the Stakhanovite movement provided a marvellous basis for such a reconciliation of 'capitalist' and 'socialist' ethics.[2]

There are several significant ways in which the Soviet musical of that period differs from its classical American counterpart. Whereas the latter tends to transpose its Utopia in time and space into some sort of 'golden age' or 'exotic community' (Dyer 1981: 187–8), in which everyone (or so one is made to believe) spontaneously dances and sings, the Soviet musical enacts its Utopia in the here and now, the present-day Soviet reality in which everyone works and, for that matter, works miracles. One way in which this phenomenon is integrated into the fabric of the film is that dance numbers are frequently replaced with carefully choreographed labour scenes, made to appear equally liberating and cathartic. Work is thereby presented as fun and pleasure, and endowed with the same sexual overtones that dancing would carry in a Hollywood musical. As a consequence, dancing is almost entirely absent from the Soviet musical of that period. Songs, on the other hand, are often devised as natural concomitants of labour and are designed to uplift and glorify it, for example the girl's song in *Bogataya nevesta* or the 'March of the Enthusiasts' in *Svetlÿĭ put'*.

The other significant difference is that the Soviet non-backstage musical which we are discussing here (by which I mean a musical that is not concerned with the staging of a show) invariably privileges the female protagonist. Her sexual attractiveness, as in a fairy-tale, is featured as an inalienable attribute of her high virtue, social awareness and extraordinary diligence, rather than as an asset in its own right. Presented as a model worker, fully integrated into the process of her country's reconstruction, it is this exemplary woman who sets up the standards which the hero must attain; hence it is she who pushes the narrative towards its inevitable resolution. Thus, it is not the female character who strives to win her male partner over by giving him what he wants, but the reverse: the male character strives to rise to the level of his miracle-worker bride by giving her what both she and the country demand from him.

Like a classic Hollywood musical most of its Soviet counterparts have two central characters – the male and the female poles – so that the narrative, instead of following the fate of a single individual in a syntagmatic linear fashion, alternates between its male and female poles, bringing them into a paradigmatic relationship of parallelism and comparison (Altman 1981). But, while the Soviet musical also postulates marriage as a neutralization of binary oppositions and a means of achieving social harmony, the nature of the male/female opposition acquires a dramatically different twist in view of the different status allotted to women. For the woman in a Soviet musical is portrayed outside the sphere of domesticity that is traditionally assigned to her and which includes an exclusive preoccupation with romance or any other conventional 'female' pursuits, such as clothes or physical beauty. In *Svwetlÿĭ put'* the heroine is contrasted with a girl who is preoccupied with her appearance, and the idea for a scene in which the heroine tries on a fur coat on arrival in Moscow was eventually abandoned (TsGALI).

The Hollywood musical convention of supplying its central characters with substitute parents in place of the natural ones also acquires a different meaning in its Soviet counterpart. As a narrative device this phenomenon is characteristic of Soviet film from that period as a whole, for the substitute parents are invariably depicted as collective-farm chairmen or team leaders, foremen, factory managers or secretaries of party organizations; in other words, the representatives of the party and the state who 'replace' the natural parents, not only for the purposes of narrative intricacy, but also symbolically – as 'social' parents to their 'charges'. The latter are thus presented as the children of the Soviet state itself, the citizens conveniently freed from family ties and personal loyalties. (The absent family of the Soviet cinema of the 1930's and 1940's is a subject worthy of separate investigation.) The most extreme case of this is, of course, the betrayal of his father – the peasant who sabotaged the collectivization-of-agriculture campaign – by Pavlik Morozov, the classic story read by all Soviet children, which was to be the subject of Eisenstein's aborted *Bezhin Meadow* (1937).

Thus the rise-to-public-success story does not merely parallel the romance in the Soviet musical: it becomes its inalienable concomitant, the indispensable condition for its successful resolution. Love and happiness, we are repeatedly told, are the rewards meted out to the outstanding, politically conscious workers, be they male or female. Laziness and philistinism, on the other hand, are vices punished by unrequited love. Thus, culturally conditioned sexual differences are played down in these films: their function as symbols of difference is assumed by minor social or occupational distinctions and the relationship of 'competition' between the protagonists. These supremely conscientious individuals are held apart for the duration of the film only by misunderstandings and the plotting of ill-wishers and rivals: hence the notorious *bezkonfliktnost'* (conflictlessness) of the Soviet cinema from that period.

As in a fairy-tale, characters in the Soviet musical are not personally delineated. The 'personal' is entirely submerged by the 'collective': virtue (i.e. the socialist attitude to work-cum-perseverance, represented by the central characters) is bound to triumph over vice (selfishness, philistinism or conservatism, represented by their antagonists). What is celebrated in the end is in effect the never seriously threatened harmony of the Soviet way of life: in *Svinarka i pastukh*, for example, the marriage of a record-breaking Vologda swineherd to an outstanding Daghestan shepherd, whom she met at the All-Union Exhibition of Agriculture, sanctifies, as the official cliché puts it, 'the friendship of the Soviet peoples'.

The representation of women as leaders in the sphere of production rather than consumption is both a realistic and a consciousness-raising device, for in the Soviet Union women have always been expected to work outside the home on a par with men. This representation is constructed in such a way as to allow for cross-sexual identification. The labour process, invariably depicted as 'competition' and 'record breaking', puts the viewer into the position of a sports event or rather a sports film spectator. The woman performing 'male' tasks (riding a motorbike, driving a tractor or working on a shop floor) is dressed in male clothes – trousers, an overall or even a cap – yet she is never defeminized. Her androgynous image, like every case of carnival clothes reversal, serves to neutralize the male/female opposition threatened by the woman's entry into the traditionally male domain of public life. The woman's power and independence are nevertheless circumscribed within the narrative by the invariable presence of 'wiser' male superiors: she is the 'doer', never the most authoritative 'thinker' or 'decision maker'.

One of the most distinctive features of the Soviet musical of that time – and the reason for its wide popularity – is that it concentrates almost exclusively on the lives of the 'humble' and 'poor' and makes them appear as 'powerful' and 'rich', proud rather than resentful of their lot. The Utopian sensibilities which the musical is uniquely equipped to unleash (Richard Dyer's categories of 'energy', 'abundance', 'intensity', 'transparency' and 'community' are fully manifested in those films, Dyer 1981) uplift and sublimate the off-screen reality: people see themselves as they really are – i.e. workers and peasants – and, at the same time, as they would ideally like to be – glorious heroes and heroines, unique, powerful, prosperous and celebrated. It is this interplay of the symbolic and realistic discourses that turns those films into the most graphic 'documents of the emotions of their time' and enables them, in Turovskaya's words, to act 'not so much as the reflection of their time's objective reality, but rather as the reflection of the reality of its image of itself' (Turovskaya 1988: 132).

Svetlyĭ put' departs from the dual-focus structure of the conventional musical discussed on pp. 90–91: it concentrates on the fate of its central heroine, following it through to her eventual triumph. Its genre can thus be best described as the 'rags-to-riches' or the 'ugly duckling' story. Romance, as fairy-tale conventions demand, serves both as a spur to success and as its traditional culmination.

The film's affinity with the Cinderella story is signalled from the very start by the heroine's ash-stained face and the song she sings in front of the mirror:

> The old fairy-tale tells us
> About magic events:
> Once upon a time there were two sisters,
> The third one was Cinderella.
> I am miserable like Cinderella,
> Torn apart all day long,
> Yet I shall probably never encounter
> A wise old fairy.

Songs throughout the film complement and comment on the narrative, recapitulating the heroine's story as it goes along.

The film makes use of a number of traditional fairy-tale motifs, such as crystal (icicles and chandeliers), mirrors that can answer back, a dream castle and a wooden chest. Having dispensed with many details of the Cinderella story, *Svetlyĭ put'* nevertheless retains its underlying themes: the growing-up process, the role of good and bad mothers, sibling rivalry (Bettelheim 1978), the rewarding of diligence and the eventual reversal of fortunes.

The film opens with a shot of the sky: the title – *Svetlyĭ put'* – flows across the screen, turning into an animated flock of cranes; one of them breaks away and continues its flight above a town surrounded by forests and lakes. A female voice sings:

> High up, under the cloud,
> Above the expanses of fields,
> A flock of cranes is heading
> Towards the south.

As the credits end, the crane reappears and the song continues:

> A strict order, bird after bird,
> Yet sometimes one of them
> Becomes timid and fearful
> And breaks up that strict order.
> Flying for the first time, it is afraid
> Of falling behind its comrades
> Of breaking away from its girlfriends,
> Of getting lost in the grey clouds.
> I can't distinguish the way
> Through the storm and mist . . .
> I am afraid I'll fall behind,
> I am afraid I won't reach my destination.

The camera descends on to a small provincial town, zooming towards a wooden house: in close-up, a cockerel sitting on a painted board – 'Small Grand Hotel'. Through the window the camera introduces us to the interior of a guest-house, where a peasant girl, Tanya Morozova, works as maid to a pompous and capricious lady. The major themes of the film are thereby set in motion: 'sky' versus 'earth'; 'dream' versus 'reality'; lower versus middle class; striving and daring versus philistinism; the will to succeed and the fear of failure; the individual and the flock.

The film was originally conceived as a light comedy in which an exceptionally clever girl outwits everyone around her – the opening scenes of Tanya engaged in her chores retain that slapstick comedy flavour – but it was eventually decided that the fate of an ordinary girl-turned-Stakhanovite should be resolved in a more socially delineated manner (TsGALI).

The narrative is set in motion by Tanya's encounter with a young engineer, Lebedev, who arrives at the hotel from Moscow. The arrival of the 'prince' is coupled with the arrival of the 'villain', an ex-kulak from Tanya's village who later proves to be a wrecker. From now on Tanya wants to improve her lot. At this point another important character enters her life, a 'helper' and 'good mother' (in effect a fairy godmother): Pronina, a middle-aged woman, secretary of the local factory party organization, sends her to study at a workers' school. Tanya's initial response is fear and self-doubt. Every major step forward in her life is punctuated by a song refrain:

Oh I am afraid I'll fall behind,
Oh I am afraid I won't become learned (succeed, and so on).

Tanya's every transformation is signalled in the film by a dissolve of her face, showing her new identity.

The fact that Pronina and all the other characters in the film are single (even Tanya's mistress, who has a child, appears to have no husband) and reside in a hotel or dormitory – the girls' factory dormitory is actually a converted monastery – is one of the devices by which the film suppresses the natural family, foregrounding instead the family of a socialist collectivity.

As Tanya and her mistress ('wicked sister'/'bad mother') vie for the attention of the young engineer, the mistress gets jealous and throws Tanya out. This is the first important moment in her growing-up process. The fairy-tale heroine is often thrown or teased out of her home to embark on her journey towards self-realization. The breaking of the mother-daughter tie is usually enacted by means of displacement and projection: it is not the mother but the stepmother – the mother substitute – who causes the daughter's departure. The rivalry between Tanya and her mistress also re-enacts sibling rivalry for the affection of the parents and later on the 'prince' (Bettelheim 1978).

When Tanya finds herself homeless, Pronina takes her in, promising to take her to the textile factory next day. As Tanya sleeps on Pronina's couch, she dreams of a fantastic castle whose entrance is flanked by giant statues of a man and a woman bearing torches. The castle's gate dissolves into a noisy factory shop-floor where Tanya is entrusted with a broom (her first phallic symbol of potency, later replaced with a shuttle) and starts sweeping the floor.

'Dream' and 'reality' are intertwined into a vision of the factory as the 'entrance' into a 'new life'. The image of a modern factory as a symbol of the construction of a 'better future' is pervasive in Soviet cinema of that time: *Kaĭn i Artyom* (*Cain and Artyom*, 1929); *Vozvrashchenie Neĭtana Bekkera* (*The Return of Nathan Becker*, 1932); *Mechta* (*The Dream*, 1943).

Tanya's fate as a maid-turned-industrial-worker is both realistic, for this was the usual route for a peasant girl in those days, and symbolic of the possibility of social betterment in a developing society. The maid who makes good is a recurrent character in Soviet cinema of that period: *Dom na Trubnoĭ* (*The House on Trubnaya*, 1928), *Vesyolye rebyata* (*Jolly Fellows*, 1934), *Mechta*. It is interesting to note that, whereas in *Dom na Trubnoĭ* the turning of a maid into a deputy to the Moscow City Soviet is still presented as no more than a mixed-identity confusion, in line with the more exalted spirit of the 1930s, this same transformation is depicted as a 'real event' in *Svetlyĭ put'*.

Tanya's rise up the social ladder reproduces the traditional fairy-tale plot of the reversal of roles and fortunes between the 'rich' and the 'poor', the 'strong' and the 'weak', the 'powerful' and the 'downtrodden'. This principle of role reversal was the inspiration behind the October Revolution itself, providing, in the words of the 'Internationale', the motto of the state that the revolution brought about: 'We have been naught, we shall be all'. This may explain the symbolic significance attached to the social rise of women in the Soviet arts of that period: the social revolution that had taken place was epitomized in the rise of the traditionally most oppressed and vulnerable part of the population. In Medvedkin's comedy *Chudesnitsa* (*The Miracle Worker*, 1937) the record-breaking milkmaid, who is called 'Tiny' (Malyutka) is outstripped by an even smaller and younger girl. The role-reversal principle is clearly expressed in the common Soviet oxymoron, noted by Turovskaya, which uses the word *znatny*, meaning 'distinguished', but with implications of nobility, and used only in combination with occupations that are clearly not normally associated with the nobility: for example 'noble milkmaid', 'noble weaver'. This privileging of women as tokens of social role reversal may also help to explain why 'wreckers' in Soviet cinema are almost invariably caught by women, and occasionally children: the 'weakest' in the community overpower the 'ghosts' of the past that threaten the new social equilibrium – *Devushka s kharakterom* (*The Girl with Character*, 1939), *Partiĭnyĭ bilet* (*The Party Card*, 1936), *Arinka* (*Arinka*, 1940); *Lenochka i vinograd* (*Lenochka and the Grapes*, 1936).

The wrecker, another recurrent character in Soviet cinema of that time, is also both a realistic and a symbolic figure. Rather like a monster in a horror film, the wrecker is an embodiment of all the country's fears and obsessions. For purges were not merely an invention of Stalin, as some historians would make us believe: the whole country was seized by spy and wrecker mania. The reversal of roles brings in its wake the fear of reprisals.

In *Svetlyĭ put'* Tanya's interception of a wrecker who has set a warehouse on fire helps her to overcome another of her residual fears and prove her resilience in the face of her first setback at work when she is accused of breaking an already faulty loom. The intervening scene of her sitting alone amidst icicles in front of a skating rink full of gliding couples is reminiscent of another Russian fairy-tale, *Frost* (*Morozko*), which tells the story of a girl left in a winter forest by her wicked stepmother. At the same time, it anticipates the later scene of Tanya celebrating her success amidst the crystal chandeliers of the Kremlin.

Thus Tanya's growing-up process is marked by her gradual surmounting of all her anxieties and inhibitions. Not only does she master the skills of weaving but, in no time at all, she feels capable of operating simultaneously not just eight looms, like all the other women, but sixteen. Her zeal, however, comes up against the resistance of the conservative factory manager, Dorokhov. But Pronina and Lebedev rally to her support (Lebedev's name, deriving from *lebed*, swan, is contrasted with that of a sluggish foreman's assistant Kurnakov, deriving from *kuritsa*, chicken. As Tanya's chosen 'prince', Lebedev is contrasted with the comic figure of the contender for Tanya's hand, the hotel receptionist, Taldykin, or 'windbag'. Faced with a problem, Tanya writes to the chairman of the Council of People's Commissars, Comrade Molotov – the conventions of comedy prohibited the appearance or even mention of Stalin in so light a genre – and she gets a reply congratulating her on her undertaking. The overcoming of another hurdle is marked by another dissolve of Tanya's face, transforming her yet again into a new person. Her ascent up the social ladder is signalled by the scene of her removal from the dormitory to a new flat (the attainment of better accommodation is one of the most significant status symbols in Soviet society) and by the song she addresses to her late mother:

> Mother, look, it's me Tanya,
> No longer downtrodden, but business-like and famous.

In the next scene Tanya is already aspiring to operate 150 looms, bringing to mind another heroine of Russian fairy-tales, Vasilisa the Wise (Premudraya), who performed similar miracles. The scene of this demonstration of her remarkable skill is one of the climaxes of the film, and the spectator is invited to identify with Tanya, as she deftly moves along the looms, through the use of camera-work, editing and the off-screen singing of the 'March of the Enthusiasts'. The words, which include a paraphrase of Stalin's pronouncement, 'Labour in our country is the cause of honour, valour and heroism', are sung alternately by Tanya and a choir and once again express Tanya's newly acquired sense of potency:

> Whether you lean over a machine tool
> Or drill a rock,
> A beautiful dream, still indiscernible,
> Calls you to go forward.
> We have no obstacles in the sea or on land,
> We are not afraid of ice or clouds.

The spectator is implicated in the action by the use first of direct address, 'you' (reminiscent of the same device used in the intertitles of Dziga Vertov's films and in Mayakovsky's poetry), and then the first-person plural, 'we'.

No sooner does Tanya accomplish her feat than she finds herself yet again dejected by the news in the paper of the record set by another weaver, Zvantseva (from *zvat'* meaning to challenge), who has mastered 200 looms. With Pronina's encouragement, Tanya announces her decision to work on 240 looms. Another important piece of news arrives at this point: Dorokhov has been removed from his post. In the original version of the film he was to be replaced by Pronina, but it was deemed more appropriate that Lebedev should be appointed as director (TsGALI).

The Stakhanovite movement and the idea of 'socialist' competition are once again a tribute to the spirit of the time (the film was modelled on the achievements of the two famous weavers, Dusya and Marusya Vinogradova) and a theme of profound symbolic significance (the spirit of sibling rivalry is clearly manifested here), for, like bootlegging for an American gangster from an *émigré* community, or boxing for a black or Italian lad, Stakhanovism was the only way for an ordinary Soviet worker to outreach her or his rank. The material and social rewards were head-spinning, as the next scene, in which Tanya learns she has been decorated, illustrates.

The concluding scenes in which Tanya first receives her order in the Kremlin and then, several years later, appears as an honorary guest in the textile pavilion of the All-Union Exhibition of Agriculture develop another theme characteristic of Soviet cinema of that time: the integration of the individual into Soviet society. Tanya's face cross-cut with the star on one of the Kremlin towers, like many similar cross-cuttings and combinations of an individual with symbolic state sites and buildings (mainly the Kremlin, the Exhibition of Agriculture – the apotheosis of Stalinist architecture – and Moscow as a whole; the town of Kostrov in *Svetlyĭ put'* is sometimes made to look remarkably like Moscow), suggests the unity of the individual with the state, creates the image of a society that envelops the individual and fosters her or his prosperity. The message of *Podkidȳsh* (*The Foundling*, 1939) is that even a little child cannot get lost in Soviet society, but will be taken good care of and safely restored to her parents; the private life of Pyotr Vinogradov in the film of the same name (*Chastnava zhizn' Petra Vinogradova*, 1935) unfolds against the background of Moscow public buildings and recreation sites.

The Kremlin sequence in *Svetlyĭ put'* contains a scene, conceivable only in a musical, of Tanya dancing in front of mirrors, each of which reflects an image of her as she used to be, engaging her in a dialogue with her former selves:

> The fairy-tale come true is being created by us,
> And the inventions of old fairy-tales
> Grow pale before the truth of our time.

The next scene, a phantasmagoric flight of Tanya and her double in a car over the expanses of the Soviet Union (the narrative 'stops', giving way to a breathtaking, cathartic spectacle), indicates the passage of several years, during which Tanya becomes an engineer and a deputy to the Supreme Soviet. It is in this capacity that she appears in the concluding scene at the Exhibition of Agriculture.

Amidst the festivities of Soviet prosperity and abundance (created by people like Tanya – 'millions like us') Tanya and Lebedev meet again. He cannot at first recognize her in a scene parodying Eugene Onegin's meeting with that less fortunate Cinderella, Tatyana, in Pushkin's poem and Tchaikovsky's opera. Yet the traditional 'musical' marriage of opposites, in this case, of hands and brain, of the peasantry, the working class and the intelligentsia (the scene ends in front of Mukhina's famous sculpture of the peasant woman and the male worker outside the Exhibition of Agriculture, which thereafter became the emblem of Mosfilm), of energy/enthusiasm and intellect/reason has already been realized by Tanya's own personal accomplishments. It is with her own double, after all, that she 'flies' over the territory of the Soviet Union. All that marriage to a man can add to her existence is the fullness of being which, as every fairy-tale maintains, can only be achieved by 'forming a truly satisfying bond with another', thereby dissipating the death and separation-from-mother anxieties (Bettelheim 1978: 10–11). Hence the image of sexual potency and fertility – the fountains and a relief celebrating animal procreation – that form a backdrop to the romantic reunion between Tanya and Lebedev.

Thus the film re-enacts in realistic images all the stages of the fairy-tale heroine's/hero's progress from 'once upon a time' through the inevitable stages of 'leaving home', the anxieties of 'going into the world' and struggling there in temporary isolation, to the eventual 'finding of her/himself there', which culminates in the traditional ending 'and lived happily ever after' (Bettelheim 1978: 10–11). Thus, far from being a crude piece of propaganda, the film is in fact sufficently rich in human content to be able to arouse the spectator's interest and empathy on both symbolic and realistic levels (the latter referring to the socio-historical world outside the text).

To demonstrate the film's extraordinary grip not only on its contemporaries but also on subsequent generations of filmgoers, I want to reproduce the letter that Lyubov Orlova, who played Tanya, received in the mid–1970s from the very people whose life the film was intended to portray:

Dear Lyubov Orlova,

We have just seen *Svetlyĭ put'* on television. There were seventeen of us: weavers, spinners, foremen, engineers, metal workers, the secretary of the Komsomol organization, and the former secretary of the party organization.

Dear Comrade Orlova, this film and you – our People's Actress[3] – are our life.

Our factory is the most revolutionary in Nizhny Novgorod. Together with the Sormovo workers, we were the first to raise the red banner and fight on the barricades in 1905.

Nowadays we have more shock workers – weavers and spinners – than appear in *Svetlyĭ put'*. One of them, Barinova, was among the initiators of the movement with Alexeĭ Stakhanov and Dusya Vinog-radova.

Comrade Orlova, we love you, you are a great actress and a remarkable person (with no conceit). We call our daughters after you – Lyubov is the most common and respected name in our factory.

You probably do not know that whenever one of us is decorated or receives a bonus for outstanding work, even at weddings or when flats are allocated, we first of all ask ourselves how would our dear Cinderella, Lyubov Orlova, behave in this situation. Your name is for us the symbol of the Communist attitude to life. Do forgive me, but I am describing it all as it really is.

Comrade Orlova, if you are too busy to visit our Nizhny Novgorod, nowadays called Gorky, then perhaps you could send us your greetings. We have a museum in our club that is devoted to the glory of the Revolution and of labour. Among the other exhibits we display your photograph as both a Stakhanovite weaver and a world-famous actress who reflects our life, the life of ordinary people.[4]

Please forgive me for this clumsy letter, my education consists of the workers' school, the Great Patriotic War, seven wounds – four of them serious. I have two daughters and three sons and I have been decorated twenty-seven times. I am writing to you at the request of the women weavers and spinners. This morning the secretary of the party organization read out this letter at the factory. Everyone there wanted to sign it and even to write to the government, asking it to send you down here, but I posted the letter to avoid any argument.

I apologize once again. We, 4,000 weavers, spinners, metal workers, foremen, engineers, office workers, Komsomol and party members, wish you, our favourite People's Actress, many long years of life and excellent health. We are proud of the fact that – along with Sobinov, Yermolova and Chaliapin – our Russian art has Lyubov Orlova.

On behalf of the workers of the Red October textile factory,
Nikolai Smirnov

(Aleksandrov 1976: 222–3)

NOTES

1 US title: *Tanya*.
2 Stakhanovism was the movement named after the Ukrainian miner Alexeĭ Stakhanov who in 1935 set a productivity record by devising a more efficient system of labour. Workers throughout the country followed him, introducing the spirit of competition and an incentive payment scheme into Soviet industry. The labour elite, *Stakhanovtsy̌*, enjoyed high official esteem and an exceptionally high standard of living and, for this and other reasons, tended to be unpopular with rank-and-file workers.

3 The highest honorary title awarded to actors and actresses in the Soviet Union.
4 One is reminded of a similar tribute paid to Gracie Fields, who was recorded by a cinema newsreel as the star guest at the gala opening of a new factory, thus indicating the breaking down of the distinction between big screen and real life.

REFERENCES

Aleksandrov, G. V. (1976) *Epokha i kino*, Moscow: Izdatel'stvo politicheskoĭ literaturȳ.

Alexandrova, G. (1989) 'Mozhet, eto kasaetsya ne tol'ko nashei semyi' (Maybe This Concerns Not Only Our Family), *Literaturnaya gazeta* 18, 3 May; G. Alexandrova's letter was answered in *Literaturnaya gazeta*, 16 August 1989.

Altman, Rick (1981) 'The American film musical: paradigmatic structure and mediatory function', in Rick Altman (ed.) *Genre: The Musical*, London: Routledge & Kegan Paul.

Bettelheim, Bruno (1978) *The Uses of Enchantment*, Harmondsworth: Penguin.

Dyer, Richard (1981) 'Entertainment and Utopia', in Rick Altman (ed.) *Genre: The Musical*, London: Routledge & Kegan Paul.

TsGALI (Tsentral'nȳ Gosudarstvennȳ Arkhiv Literaturȳ i Iskusstva) (The Central State Archive of Literature and Art) (n.d.) 2450/2/1295.

Turovskaya, Maya (1988) 'I. A. Pyr'ev i ego muzȳkal'nye komedii. K. probleme zhanra' (I. A. Pyriev and his musical comedies. On the problems of genre), *Kinovedcheskie zapiski* 1.

7

STUDYING POPULAR TASTE
British historical films in the 1930s
Sue Harper

In some recent debates, popular historical film has been interpreted either as a passive tool of dominant ideology, or as the site of a repressed proletarian imagination (Elley 1984; Richards 1984; Fraser 1988). Neither of these positions is satisfactory; one is too doctrinaire and the other too sentimental, and both fail to analyse the complexity of the social role of popular cinema. I should like to stress the range of tasks which popular cultural forms fulfil. They have, I think, a fourfold function.

First, they have to win over, on behalf of the ruling bloc, those groups on its boundaries; this is done by according them a symbolic role in texts. Novels or films may produce an image of society in which dissident or insecure groups are safely incorporated. This hegemonic process must not be confused with that of consensual texts, which secure agreement with a politically centrist position by excluding awkward groups.

Second, pleasure is the business of popular texts, and the successful ones which satisfactorily resolve real problems in the lives of their audiences cannot be dismissed as 'false consciousness'. The problem is that a wide range of textual pleasures may obtain in any one period, and audience preferences can shift with bewildering speed. It is the job of the popular cultural historian to chart a map of pleasure, to discriminate between different types and to show continuities and innovations. I suppose one could provide the ritual caveat that the production of pleasure may further contribute to the oppression of subordinate groups. But such miserabilist schools of analysis have had their day. It is possible to produce a radical interpretation of cultural history while at the same time dreading the onset of a coercive puritan moralism.

Third, popular cultural forms may be said to fulfil a quasi-ritualistic function, by endorsing mythic structures of pollution and purity, and thus clarifying confusions about moral or social boundaries. I am here, of course, drawing on the work of Mary Douglas, whose ideas are extremely fruitful for the analysis of mass culture (Douglas 1966, 1970, 1975). However, insights derived from anthropological concepts must always be carefully historicized. Notions of danger and taboo can change within a short space of time, and fictional texts adjust accordingly. Moreover, artistic languages, while not autonomous, do have a history of their own, which must be taken into account.

Fourth, all popular texts make a profit for someone. Walter Scott, Charles Dickens and Bulwer Lytton, for example, tested the water assiduously and adapted their products accordingly.

The key issue is that of intellectual control. A film represents the labours of a wide range of personnel, but at one time, as we all remember, it was fashionable to praise those heroic director-auteurs who imposed their signature on the intractable studio machine. This method is ramshackle. Auteur criticism tends to be predicated on individual enthusiasm; and this, although it may heighten engagement, rarely results in more than a catalogue of a favourite's wrongs or triumphs. Rather, the most valuable way of analysing popular British film in the 1930s and 1940s, and of assessing the relative roles of studio personnel, is through the delineation of the producers' influence. This does not preclude work on individual directors, since the tensions in some film texts may be accounted for by a vexed relationship between the director and the producer. But the producers are the determinant in the last instance; the means of production belong to them or to the investors they represent. They are responsible for delivering the film to the major investor, the film distributor.

This notion of producer-authorship should not, however, lead us into a crude economic determinism. A base/superstructure model of cultural production can be dangerous if not carefully deployed, since it can fatally relegate artistic style to the role of a decorative excrescence laid on the surface of the 'real' text. Rather, we should develop a definition of production control which takes full cognizance of the importance of style for a film's popularity. Visual texture is not superficial; it is the site where we can see the material signs of clashes between different cultural crosscurrents. The relationship between the verbal language of the script and the visual language of the *mise-en-scène* can differ from one studio to another, and sometimes from one period to another in the same studio. And the cultural competence of a producer has extensive influence on the broad definitions which inform a film.

Persuasion, pleasure, ritual clarification, profit: these are some elements which should be taken into account in the analysis of popular film. Historical or costume films are only different in that in certain periods they have a special role in confirming or adjusting notions of a national culture. Films can, of course, never encapsulate national character; they can only select traits which might be elevated to the level of national, class or gender stereotypes. It goes without saying that films give no access to a real set of events, nor can they represent class or gender interests in a straightforward or predictable way. Ideology – that set of social relations preferred by the dominant class – is perforce manifested in popular film; but it is always displaced, complicated or disguised.

An interesting problem is raised in the 1930s by historical film, which dominated the market and underwent considerable stylistic changes. A significant innovation was inaugurated by Alexander Korda's *The Private Life of Henry VIII* (1933); this was profitable and popular, as was his *Catherine the Great* (1934), *The Scarlet Pimpernel* (1935), *The Return of the Scarlet Pimpernel* (1938) and *The Four Feathers* (1939). Michael Balcon, then at Gaumont-British, also produced a range of popular histories: *Jew Süss* (1934), *The Iron Duke* (1935), *Tudor Rose* (1936), *Rhodes of Africa* (1936) and *King Solomon's Mines* (1937). Herbert Wilcox reached the best-seller listings with *Nell Gwyn* (1934), *Peg of Old Drury* (1935) and, most importantly, *Victoria the Great* (1937) and *Sixty Glorious Years* (1938). The only popular historical films which did not fall into these patterns of production were *Under the Red Robe* (1937) and *Dr. Syn* (1938). Historical film in the 1930s is a particularly rich field, and a complete map would locate American-owned production companies, and define the work of British ones like B.I.P. and Twickenham which, although they are of cultural significance, did not attain best-seller status.

It is notoriously difficult to establish profit margins with any finality in this period. A few are available through historical accident; for example, Korda's profit figures were with the Prudential, from whom he borrowed money (Street 1986). But mostly we must construct a popularity map via unsatisfactory means. Key journals such as *Film Weekly* and *Picturegoer* provided surveys and lists of favourites, and *Kinematograph Weekly* produced, from 1937, an annual survey of box-office takings. Some information can be gleaned from studio publicity, autobiographies and 'books of the film', which sometimes give figures. Mass-Observation, letter pages, and the books of J. P. Mayer can be useful (Mayer 1946, 1948). But there is a general absence of hard facts in the field. All that can be said with absolute certainty is that *The Private Life of Henry VIII* and *Victoria the Great* were real block-busters, and that, in between, all the historical films mentioned above appeared in the trade paper listings.[1]

How are we to interpret these listings? It might seem agreeably simple to argue that (for example) *Victoria the Great* was successful because it reinforced the notion of a cohesive and respectable monarchy when the Abdication had produced a crisis of confidence. In that case, how do we account for the simultaneous popularity of *King Solomon's Mines* and *Under the Red Robe*? As I shall show, the former dealt with the male pleasures of empire, and the latter with the lurid charms of the *ancien régime*. A further contradiction is produced by the simultaneous popularity of *The Scarlet Pimpernel* and *The Iron Duke*, which contain radically different political perspectives and aesthetic treatments of a roughly similar area.

In the light of this, we must beware of imposing a false homogeneity

Plate 12 Charles Laughton in *The Private Life of Henry VIII*. By courtesy of the British Film Institute, London.

Plate 13 Leslie Howard (right) in *The Scarlet Pimpernel*. By courtesy of the British Film Institute, London.

upon audience taste. An appropriate metaphor for both cinematic culture and taste might be that of the patchwork quilt. The whole is composed out of different political colours and different cultural/historical orientations. There may be a dominant colour in any one period; but the quilt is held together by fragments of earlier modes of perception. There are also 'fossils' in both artistic production and audience response. Excellent 1930s examples would be the Tod Slaughter historical melodramas such as *Maria Marten* (1935) or *Sweeney Todd* (1936). These certainly provided the audience with a sense of cultural security, since they were deeply embedded in the epistemological and kinesic habits of Victorian melodrama. But too much so; in order to be popular, a film from the developing genre of costume drama needed to display an awareness of recent innovations. Tod Slaughter's efforts were too fossilized to carry any status, and consequently they had no wide audience appeal.

In analysing 1930s audience taste, it is important to make discriminations; perhaps not between upper-, middle-, and lower-class responses, but between high-brow, middle-brow and low-brow ones. The latter were important criteria for the period, and did not have an automatic fit with the class system. For example, it was perfectly feasible for a respondent of working-class origins to have middle-brow tastes, and thereby improve his or her status. It was equally possible for a middle-class cinema-goer to have low-brow enthusiams, although he or she might thereby be suspected of intellectual slumming.

There are clear demarcations in 1930s attitudes to popular historical film. Quasi-official, high-brow bodies like the British Film Institute and the Historical Association were panicky about the effect of venal costume dramas on the innocent populace, and they made strenuous attempts to inhibit the production of inaccurate films, even orchestrating a debate in the House of Lords in 1936. I have described these efforts in detail elsewhere (Harper 1987b, 1990). Middle-brow opinion, probably following this high-brow lead, displayed the utmost distaste for popular historical films; to writers like Graham Greene and John Betjeman, a taste for inaccurate spectacle was coterminous with national decline. But what of low-brow opinion, which, with some exceptions, was the one which brought in mass audience figures?

Of course, with low-brow or popular views, there is a problem of evidence. Mass-Observation reporters could operate as powerful gatekeepers to mass opinion, and they were often unable to decode respondents' irony. Some researchers like J. P. Mayer were hampered by a distaste for popular history, which doubtless skewed their findings. The newspapers could operate as powerful filters through which letter-writers had to pass before they could express their views. Some popular papers like the *Daily Mirror* mounted campaigns against the notion that academic accuracy was appropriate for popular historical film. Other low-brow cinema journals like *Film Weekly* and *Picturegoer* took the opposite view after the mid–1930s. But low-brow opinion (as expressed in letter pages, Mass-Observation and a range of surveys) robustly resisted the blandishments of official bodies and respectable opinion. Almost without exception, these sources indicate that mass audiences patronized those historical films which they thought would provide them with three things: visual pleasure, a greater understanding of their heritage, and the opportunity to expand their empathy with characters from the past. Visual pleasure, in terms of costume and sets, is by far the most frequently mentioned.[2]

The relationship between audience response and successful film production is a dialectical one; a canny producer will have his or her finger on the pulse of public taste and will act accordingly, but at the same time the audience will be in a constant state of readjustment to market changes. Arguably, any film is successful because it evokes and expresses a coherent parish of belief; this process is adumbrated when the cultural competence of the target audience perfectly fits the requirements of the text. Let us now examine the respective parishes of the major producers of popular historical films, in order to assess the definitions of pleasure and social structure that were being offered to their audiences.

I have suggested earlier that Korda's profitable historical films were *The Private Life of Henry VIII, Catherine the Great, The Scarlet Pimpernel, The Return of the Scarlet Pimpernel* and *The Four Feathers*. These films had certain themes in common, which were absent from other historical films of the period. Korda had an unusual reverence for popular history, and also a high opinion of the audience, who 'want their entertainment to be both progressive and cultured'.[3] For him, the final arbiter was not 'some elegant Petronius, but the man in the street, in whom the lowest common multiple was also the highest common factor' (Korda 1937). Korda's intellectual liberalism has rarely been noted; but it is my contention that all the above films have an implicit radicalism in their combination of class with sexual matters. Without exception, they all concerned themselves with the delineation of an aristocratic code. With *The Private Life of Henry VIII* and *Catherine the Great,* royalty were shown as messy and undisciplined in the untrammelled pursuit of their desires; they needed the dignity and control of aristocratic style, which was, by implication, something which all classes could aspire to. Without it, the king became feminized, engaging in uncontrolled orgies of food; and the empress became masculine, and 'the most shameless rake who ever wore a petticoat'. With the *Pimpernel* films, Korda refined this position. Sir Percy Blakeney's manner was a careful mixture of Dandy and Corinthian, feminine and masculine, and his power came from his ability to negotiate his way stylishly through a range of dialects. *The Four Feathers* similarly endorsed the aristocratic code through controlled disguise. Attention to the various scripts of this film shows that Korda wished to highlight the issue of personal bravery and chivalric honour, rather than forcing an overtly political reading of events. All Korda's 1930s histories inculcated the audience with the desirability of class confidence; the learning of the appropriate code was possible for all, and aristocratic virtues could be generally assimilated. Korda also placed a high premium on female autonomy, and he produced a sumptuous visual texture with little attention to realism.

Korda's historical films concentrated on periods when a crisis in hegemony may be deemed to have occurred, and he solved that crisis in the texts by creating a thematic or symbolic union between the aristocracy and the working class. For him, the enemy was the bourgeoisie. This was presented throughout as narrow, puritanical, acquisitive and repressed. It is of great interest to note that, in Michael Balcon's historical films, that group was the hero, and those qualities were praiseworthy. Balcon's organization of his historical films at Gaumont-British in the 1930s was a prototype of his later work at Ealing; he selected compliant, insecure or inexperienced directors whom he could coerce into his own world-view. Films such as *Jew Süss* were combative in their way; they present the past as a site of oppression, whence rescue could only be effected by actively encouraging middle-class values. Hence *Tudor Rose* administered a corrective to *The Private Life of Henry VIII*'s interpretation of the Tudor age. Roistering was dangerous, and could only be neutralized by purity of control and scrupulous discipline. In the later *Rhodes of Africa* and *King Solomon's Mines*, the entrepreneurial spirit was shifted to an empire context. But the notion of empire in both films was structured so as to ensure a very wide catchment area.

Balcon's histories (which, we must remember, did appear in popular listings) were little concerned with local colour or dense visual texture. Moreover, their narratives consistently disfavoured the female point of view. Women could only be listeners or the bearers of tradition. One small example is telling. The symbolic field of the novel of *King Solomon's Mines* is 'Sheba's Breasts': 'On the top of each was a vast round hillock covered with snow, exactly corresponding to the nipple on the female breast.' The males' task is to ascend this 'nipple', and descend down to untold wealth. In the film, the female principle was displaced. The landscape had no sexual resonances, but instead the female qualities of the witch Gagool represented grotesque forces. Balcon's copy of the script suggests that shots of a severed, mummified head be used when she appears. One does not need to be a trained psychotherapist to interpret this aright.

Balcon's historical films, then, were held together by coherent structures; realism, entrepreneurialism, masculinity. The enemy was excess, either of an aristocratic, proletarian or female type. History was a means of promulgating middle-class respectability. Balcon's trajectory was consistent throughout. This provides a contrast with Wilcox, the last of the major producers of popular historical film. His output fell into two distinct halves.

Plate 14 Anna Neagle in *Victoria the Great*. By courtesy of the British Film Institute, London.

Nell Gwyn and *Peg of Old Drury* were both salacious films, which presented the Restoration and the Augustan ages respectively as periods when key liaisons could develop between royalty and the popular residuum. *Nell* encouraged the audience to think that efficient systems of power could also be florid and permissive. By implication, the forgiveness extended to the King's peccadilloes could also be extended to one's own. But the later *Victoria the Great* and *Sixty Glorious Years* took a sterner view of pleasure, and they presented the monarchy as a static icon. The pace of both films was leaden, and the use of intertitles gave them a dated air. The enemy was political radicalism, whether intellectual or working-class; the films' propagandism was close to the surface, which was doubtless augmented by the official support they received at the planning and pre-production level.

Wilcox seems to have been an intellectually craven individual, and a trimmer who lacked flair. His Victoria films provide acute difficulties for those wishing to canonize the popular and make it the hero in the battle against the forces of darkness. As artistic enterprises the Victoria films are uneven and awkward, and their politics are unremittingly right-wing. None the less, a significant part of the audience of 1937 and 1938 clearly needed the naked, undisguised certainties offered by Wilcox. But another part of that audience (or probably another aspect of the same one) could also be gratified by *Under the Red Robe* and *Dr. Syn*. The former was profitable because it reproduced the Korda view of history, and deployed many Korda personnel; the latter was the first of the Gainsborough costume melodramas which were to become so popular in the 1940s, and, like them, *Dr. Syn* defended popular lawlessness in a stylish way.

So far, I have cut the cake of popular taste in a vertical manner. According to this method, different producers represent variously sized slices of the cake. Korda deployed the aristocratic topos in a particularly suggestive way; Balcon reinstated bourgeois respectability; Wilcox opportunistically played both sides against the middle, in that he attempted to balance out bourgeois and aristocratic components so as to privilege a particular definition of the proletariat. This model suggests that audiences were able to predict the product from the reputation of the studio, and choose accordingly. It perhaps also implies that the audience was rigorously segmented according to class, and that those who liked a Balcon film were consciously in revolt against Korda's politics and style. This model also grants major prominence to the Victoria films.

But the cake can be cut in another way. Lateral and horizontal slices may display a linear progression in taste, which can then be related to social change. It is possible to interpret patterns of popularity such that class themes can be seen to have a definable ebb and flow. If we chart historical films of the 1930s according to their release dates and appearance in best-seller lists, it becomes apparent that there are three distinct phases.

The first phase lasted from 1933 to mid–1935, and comprised *The Private Life of Henry VIII, Catherine the Great, The Scarlet Pimpernel* and *Nell Gwyn*. These were all politically liberal, sexually permissive and visually sumptuous, and in their various ways they foregrounded female desire and constructed the bourgeoisie as the enemy.

The second phase lasted from mid-1935 to mid-1937, and comprised *Jew Süss, Tudor Rose, Rhodes of Africa, Victoria the Great* and *King Solomon's Mines*. These films all constructed history as the site of painful struggle; all were politically conservative, and all warned against excess, whether aristocratic, proletarian or female. The monarchy appeared as the bourgeois principle writ large. *Peg of Old Drury*, which appeared in this phase, was really a continuation from phase one.

The third phase lasted from mid-1937 until late 1939, and comprised *Under the Red Robe, Dr. Syn, The Return of the Scarlet Pimpernel* and *The Four Feathers*. It represented a partial return to the principles of phase one. All phase three films, which were from a variety of production backgrounds, gave a privileged role to visual pleasure. They all provided a place for female identification, while eschewing realism and espousing a quasi-aristocratic code. *Sixty Glorious Years*, which appeared in this phase, was really a throwback to phase two.

This has interesting implications. It is possible to argue that phase two films developed as a reaction against phase one, and that they also represented a nervous response to high unemployment, social unrest and the Abdication crisis. Audience taste reacted accordingly, and deployed such films as *Victoria* as a means of neutralizing anxiety. But it is crucial to notice how temporary the change is. If we look further ahead to the war and the immediate post-war period, we can see that mass audiences had an abiding taste for spectacular and inaccurate histories, which celebrated female pleasure and the aristrocratic/proletarian alliance. Two major successes of those years were Korda's *Lady Hamilton* (1941), and Gainsborough bodice-rippers such as *The Man in Grey* (1943) and *The Wicked Lady* (1945) (Harper 1987a, 1988).

In the light of the above, we should interpret films like *Victoria the Great* as a temporary blip in a longer trajectory. The successes of Balcon and the later Wilcox should not lead us into thinking that British audiences had finally come to their senses and had concurred with official views of history. Rather, we should conclude that such films were attempting to function consensually, but in the last analysis could not. Mass audiences displayed an abiding preference for historical films in which marginal groups were ambiguously poised on the purity/danger axis. The popularity of such films is a sure index that audiences could pick their way through the complex demands of the texts, and could turn those texts to their own pleasurable account. Popular historical films required considerable audience creativity, and that is the key to understanding mass taste, which is never simply the prisoner of common sense.

NOTES

1 *Kinematograph Weekly*, 29 March 1934, 14 January 1937, 13 January 1938, 12 January 1939, 11 January 1940. See *Film Weekly*, 5 April 1935, 2 May 1936, 8 May 1937, 24 June 1939. See also *Picturegoer*, 15 June 1935 and 8 August 1936. These all contain surveys, figures or awards.
2 *Daily Mirror*, 25 October 1935, 27 November 1935, 10 May 1937; *Daily Dispatch*, 12 February 1934, 7 January 1935; *News Chronicle*, 10 February 1934; *Everyman*, 16 February 1934; *Evening News*, 28 March 1934; *Daily Express*, 23 August 1935; *The Scotsman*, 12 February 1935; *Yorkshire Post*, 15 October 1935; *Daily Mail*, 25 March 1935. See the letter pages in *Film Weekly* and *Picturegoer* from 1934 to 1939. See also Jeffrey Richards and Dorothy Sheridan, *Mass-Observation at the Movies*, London, Routledge, 1987, and M-O Box 4, File F, at the University of Sussex.
3 *Film Weekly*, 7 November 1936. For other similar pronouncements by Korda on popular taste, see *Picturegoer*, 10 August 1935, and *Film Weekly*, 28 September 1934, 17 August 1934, 12 July 1935 and 23 November 1935. See also the *Morning Post*, 18 June 1936, and the *Daily Telegraph*, 13 January 1937.

REFERENCES

Douglas, Mary (1966) *Purity and Danger,* London: Routledge.
—— (1970) *Natural Symbols*, London: Barrie & Rockcliff.
—— (1975) *Implicit Meanings*, London: Routledge.
Elley, Derek (1984) *The Epic Film: Myth and History*, London: Routledge.
Fraser, George MacDonald (1988) *The Hollywood History of the World*, London: Michael Joseph.
Harper, Sue (1987a) 'Historical pleasures: Gainsborough costume melodrama 1942–47', in Christine Gledhill, (ed.) *Home Is Where the Heart Is*, London: British Film Institute.
—— (1987b) 'Historiography and film: the Historical Association and the British Film Institute 1934–46', *Historical Journal of Film, Radio and TV* 7(3).
—— (1988) 'The representation of women in British feature films 1939–45', in P. Taylor (ed.) *Britain and the Cinema in the Second World War*, London: Macmillan.
—— (1990) 'A note on Basil Dean, Sir Robert Vansittart, and British historical films of the 1930's', *Historical Journal of Film, Radio and TV* 10(1).
Korda, Alexander (1937) 'British films today and tomorrow', in C. Davy (ed.) *Footnotes to the Film*, London: Lovat Dickson.
Mayer, J. P. (1946) *Sociology of Film*, London: Faber.
—— (1948) *British Cinemas and Their Audiences*, London: Denis Dobson.
Richards, Jeffrey (1984) *The Age of the Dream Palace: Cinema and Society in Britain 1930–39*, London: Routledge.
Richards, Jeffrey and Sheridan, Dorothy (1987) *Mass-Observation at the Movies*, London: Routledge.
Street, Sarah (1986) 'Alexander Korda, Prudential Assurance, and British film finance in the 1930's', *Historical Journal of film, Radio and TV* 6(2).

8

WAS THE CINEMA FAIRGROUND ENTERTAINMENT?

The birth and role of popular cinema in the Polish territories up to 1908

Małgorzata Hendrykowska

The history of the very first beginnings of popular cinema in Poland has not yet been definitively written, and for many reasons deserves to be reassessed today. The traditional view is that the years 1900 to 1908 were a period of 'fairground cinema', an expression which originally referred to the way films were shown but eventually became an aesthetic term and was used above all in a pejorative sense. According to that view, then, pre-1908 Polish cinema was fairground entertainment, its spectators were fairground people with corresponding needs and tastes, and the world portrayed in the films did not extend beyond that of the fairground.

Is that an accurate view? Is it in fact true to say that at the turn of the century the popular entertainment known as 'animated photographs' was the same thing as fairground entertainment? Is it right to apply a single term 'fairground cinema' to describe the way the earliest cinema functioned in countries with diametrically opposite economic and social conditions and in societies with widely differing levels of knowledge and education? And can the way films were shown and where they were shown really be used as an interpretative key to the understanding of 'animated photographs' up to 1908?

Those who argue that pre-1908 cinema was fairground entertainment tend to analyse it as though it were monolithic. In their quest for features to confirm their argument, they generally mix up several different facets of the one problem. A distinction should, however, be made between: (1) the birth of the cinema as an institution and the first attempts at distribution resulting from that phenomenon; (2) appreciation of the films' aesthetic values; (3) the position of the cinema in social consciousness.

I am not trying to argue that there are strict dividing lines between these questions. On the contrary, they interact and affect each other, and a description of each one would require a different approach. Above all, they need to be discussed in a wider context.

It is by analysing the function of film in social life in its broadest sense, while also taking into account the cultural context and, more particularly, cinema's links with popular and 'high-brow' culture, that it should be possible to provide an exhaustive answer to the question of whether film was fairground entertainment.

It is precisely that context which is crucial to understanding many of the reactions and preferences of spectators in various countries and in different cultural environments. While there remain fundamental similarities, the cinema's position and role were different in France and in the United States, and different again in the Polish territories that had been annexed and divided up between the three neighbouring powers, Prussia, Austria and Russia.

In offering my own view of the way the cinema functioned up to 1908, I propose to use examples drawn from the Polish territories, which are not widely known beyond them, and to demonstrate through them that it is inaccurate and misleading to describe film as 'fairground entertainment'. It implies a contradiction between film and 'real culture', and puts the former on the same level as the most primitive and crudest forms of entertainment; it also results in a paradox whereby the term 'fairground', used in connection with the way films were distributed, is automatically transposed into the area of aesthetic value judgements. I also hope to illustrate, by refuting the fairground nature of film in that sense, the role played by this popular form of entertainment in Polish society at the turn of the century. Some of the questions discussed here are typical only of the Polish territories, but many undoubtedly apply to the cinemas of other countries, and in particular those of central and eastern Europe. I hope that what I have to say, in the unavoidably limited space available, will at least partly correct the schematic and uniform picture that most people have of pre-1908 cinema and go some way towards answering the question of why it was so popular.

In the course of describing how the cinema functioned within the fabric of Polish society at the turn of the century, I shall necessarily touch upon the question of where films were most commonly shown in public between 1900 and 1908, namely in the controversial fairgrounds that later so distorted the image of the cinema. To answer the question of how films came to be shown in circuses and fairground stalls, one has to go back to about the middle of the nineteenth century.

There can be no doubt that most films, especially in small towns, were shown for the first time in a fairground context. But the nineteenth-century fair was not at all the kind of event that might be imagined nowadays. In addition to its fundamental purpose, which was commercial and social, it had many other functions which might today be described as educational. Nor was the phenomenon confined to the fairground itself. Hundreds of showmen, offering the most unexpected kind of wares, visited the Polish towns and cities in the three partitioned zones. Adam Chodyński (1972), a historian specializing in nineteenth-century regional matters, has drawn up an inventory of the public shows put on in Kalisz between 1821 and 1854. He describes some extraordinary things. One Jan Heffner exhibited, for money, his exceptionally obese son-in-law, Jan Dalke. Josef Schütz of Potsdam called forth spirits, while a woman called Lothe Daburger clenched a red-hot iron between her teeth and swallowed boiling tar. But alongside such exhibitions, and during the same period, we find Konrad Springmann showing models and pictures of ore mines, Barbara Kosak operating a camera obscura, and Wolfgang Philadelphia demonstrating an acoustic ball and other scientific apparatuses. Carlo Aureggi explained the uses of various pieces of meteorological equipment and Karol Elzner gave a lecture on the Copernican system using paintings and drawings.

From the mid-nineteenth century on, every kind of chemical, physical and optical invention that could have had an application was demonstrated at fairs. Over ten years before *tableaux mouvants*, the public was shown a kind of primitive telephone. If it had been within their power, the showmen would probably have demonstrated Röntgen rays or the internal combustion engine. The cinema, then, was shown at fairs not as some primitive form of entertainment like a magic mirror booth, but as one of the many inventions that fascinated the public.

The end of the nineteenth century and the beginning of the twentieth was a period of extraordinary inventiveness. There were major and lasting inventions such as the electric light bulb, the car, the telephone and the aeroplane, and other more modest ones devised by inexperienced engineers in, say, Wągrowiec and Drohobycz. Almost every illustrated Polish periodical worthy of the name had a regular column that listed the latest discoveries and innovations. It was widely thought that people's daily lives could be improved by technical inventions. From time to time such columns contained truly weird reports. In a section called 'The most recent discoveries at home and abroad' in the Warsaw weekly *Wędrowiec*, we find, under the letter W, 'electric ventilator', 'pen-wiper' and 'the raising of sunken vessels'. The section also featured 'apparatus for throwing away flowers' and 'envelope-moistening instrument'. Another column, in the weekly *Biesiada Literacka*, reflected the public's fascination with electricity, which was catered for by such 'practical' contraptions as an 'electric rat trapdoor', an 'electric horsewhip', an 'electric cradle for the maid', an 'electric cane for self-defence' and 'electric paper', whose application was not described. Also featured were an 'electric paper-knife' and a drawing of a 'machine to alter a misshapen nose'.

This utter confusion, which may seem funny to us today, should be interpreted as evidence not of scientific ignorance on the part of those responsible for such columns, but rather of the state of emotional ferment that had overtaken people's minds at that time. Those dozens of suddenly discovered objects, whose relative importance to each other has since been greatly modified, and which as far as we know had no use at all but were regarded at the time as convenient and useful, were the expression of a deep conviction that science would find an answer to everything. The nose-correcting machine and the electric paper-knife looked forward to an era of universal bliss, where the right kind of machine would even spare people the chore of throwing flowers away. It was only in 1914 that that idyllic image of technology was shattered.

But at the turn of the century the latest inventions did more than catch the public imagination and rally the interest of scientists and intellectuals: they quickly and spectacularly swept the board in little comedy theatres and circus rings. The owners of various entertainment companies seized upon every new technical discovery in an emotionally naïve manner and for their own purposes, showing in this way the connection between their productions and the most recent inventions of science and technology. Interestingly, at the turn of the century, acrobats in the Ciniselli circus started tightrope walking on telegraph wire instead of the traditionally used rope. Other such examples come to mind too. Warsaw theatres became interested in electricity only in 1887, whereas circuses had been using it since 1883. In 1886, in the Mach Brothers' panopticon (exhibition room for novelties), spectators were fascinated by the 'theatrophone', a contraption which broadcast music through fifty microphones and thirty telephones. Newfangled machines like the velocipede, penny-farthing and bicycle amazed circus audiences before they were to be seen on the streets of Warsaw. The cinema invaded every place of popular entertainment just as soon as it became possible.

Does that mean that the cinema was fairground entertainment? Before attempting to answer that question, let me point to another interesting example. The first demonstration on Polish soil of the Lumière brothers' Cinématographe took place on 14 November 1896, on the stage of Cracow's august municipal theatre. Are we to regard this event as an atypical and extraordinary phenomenon in the history of Cracow's traditional theatre?

To see things in perspective, let us examine the kind of shows that were put on in Cracow towards the end of the nineteenth century. Theatregoers enjoyed not only Molière and Shakespeare, but Chinese acrobats and gymnastic exhibitions by thirty bedouins. A little later, the same theatre featured a woman tamer of wild animals, Oriental magic shows and optical and astronomic experiments (Michalik 1988). All these attractions either were shown on their own or formed part of the supporting programme of plays. Now it would clearly be absurd to regard Molière, Schiller or Beaumarchais plays staged at the Cracow theatre as fairground entertainment just because they were accompanied by conjurors or animal shows. Cracow's estimable classical theatre lost nothing of its dignity as a result; nor did the presentations of animated photographs seem drastically out of place on the stage of the municipal theatre. It was simply that the two approaches to the aims and duties of theatre – to procure a memorable experience and to provide entertainment – far from being mutually exclusive, coexisted and complemented each other. In short, cinema's supposed affinities with fairground culture were in fact rather loose and superficial.

The cinema was above all a discovery, and it functioned as such not only during the earliest months but also for the first few years of its existence. The place where film demonstrations were organized is of secondary and even marginal importance compared with the essential issue: the vision of the world that fairs and the cinema offered spectators.

The most common subjects treated in films during the first few years of the twentieth century would seem to have been news items and documentaries (visits by VIPs, pictures of disasters and reports from various parts of the globe) or reconstructions that looked like documentary material. Then come films which re-enact well-known historical, political or social events (for example the Dreyfus affair,[1] the Captain of Köpenick affair,[2] and Marie Antoinette, 'a historical event in ten tableaux'). Next most common are pictures connected with a well-known literary original (such as the adventures of Don Quixote, Gulliver and others). All these types of film occur more commonly than those that might be classified as 'invented stories' or 'funny adventures', with which fairground cinema is usually identified. This classification of subjects emerges from a study of regularly published film programmes and from other occasional shows organized in the Polish territories. The programmes and main attractions of certain authentic fairs of the time can today be listed almost as precisely as the subjects of film shows.

Between 1903 and 1907, for example, in the centre of Poznań, which then had 130,000 inhabitants, fairground attractions included a lion woman, a bearded lady, the athlete Nordini who dived into a barrel full of water and got out of it by breaking its iron hoops, a footless Indian who predicted the future, and, exhibited in a cage, a child brought up by wild animals. At the same time Leon Mettler's cinema in Poznań showed *The Coronation in Delhi*, *Trip through Paris along the Seine*, *Panorama of Danish Islands*, *The Cherry-blossom Festival in Japan* and *Haymaking in Scotland*.

When the cinema programmes and main fairground attractions of the time are compared, it is easy to measure the gulf that existed between the nascent cinema and fairground entertainment. Fairs and film shows both offered spectators certain wares, but those wares were of a very different kind. The fairground always set out to astound its customers with weird phenomena that were at once incomprehensible, unbelievable, strange and terrifying. The cinema, from its very beginnings, tended to offer spectators experiences that were common to all. It satisfied their cognitive needs by showing women workers coming out of a factory, a baby being fed, the Russo-Japanese War, blacksmith in a smithy, Paris

116

Plate 15 1906: the Plac Wolnosci in Poznań, site by 1907 of three permanent cinemas. By courtesy of Małgorzata Hendrykowska.

Plate 16 1903: the first cinema in Poznań in Leon Mettler's restaurant. By courtesy of Małgorzata Hendrykowska.

squares, and waves breaking against a cliff. Unlike the offerings of the fairground, everything the cinema showed was 'true', immediate and comprehensible. Those were the characteristics which caused the cinema, through its integrative function, to extend far beyond the walls of the first picture palaces. Could a fairground entertainment ever have gripped the hearts, minds and imaginations of the masses to the same degree as the cinema? What was responsible for the cinema's unique popularity and success? Was it solely the result of the public's need to be entertained?

The simplest and most commonly proposed answer to those questions is that city populations increased sharply, creating mass audiences and, consequently, a need for cheap and easily accessible entertainment. That answer is also valid outside the Polish territories, and explains the popularity not only of US amusement arcades, which attracted polyglot crowds of immigrants from all over the world, but also of the film marquees erected in the suburbs of Saint Petersburg. The reasons for the popularity of the cinema go much deeper, however, and do not only have to do with the need for cheap and universal entertainment, which could so easily be gratified by the fairground. We need to set the cinema against its cultural context in the broadest sense.

Apart from the already mentioned presentation of the Lumière brothers' invention, the earliest film showings in the Polish territories usually used Edison equipment. That was the case in Warsaw (June 1896), in Lvov (September 1896), in Poznań (November 1896) and in Przemyśl (1896). The film projector soon became one of the most widespread new inventions in the Polish territories. The first Polish film showings took place in a very different cultural context from that of, say, France or Britain. The fairground showmen who set up their projectors and primitive screens in marquees, booths or amusement parks showed those first films to a Polish public that lived on the periphery of the Russian, Prussian and Austrian empires. There would be no point here in going into the political, social, economic and psychological complications endured by a nation that had been deprived of its statehood in 1795 and carved up between its three invaders, Russia, Prussia and Austria.[3] It is, however, worth mentioning a number of specific phenomena arising from that situation which throw interesting light on the way the earliest films were received by Polish society.

The three great powers regarded their Polish territories as unimportant border areas in which there was no point in carrying out any further public investment, and they expected Polish society to adopt the role of a conquered nation. As a result of Russia's deliberate policy towards its part of the annexed territories, where two-thirds of the Polish people lived, 69.9 per cent of the population were illiterate in 1897. In Warsaw alone, 41 per cent of men and 51 per cent of women were illiterate; the equivalent figures for Łódź were 55 per cent and 66 per cent. In the territory annexed by Russia, there were only three cities apart from Warsaw which had mains water in 1904. In fifty-eight towns there was no hospital, and in fifty-three no hotel. At the beginning of the twentieth century, only fourteen cities had gasworks. Whereas there was one post office for every 13 sq km and one telegraph office for every 37 sq km in the territory belonging to Prussia, one post office had to serve an area of 189.5 sq km in the Russian sector. It was only in 1907 that Warsaw was illuminated by 400 electric lamps; in 1906 the first few electrically lit train carriages made their way across the Russian-annexed territories; and the first electric trams started operating in Warsaw in March 1908 (Pazdur 1963).

It was in that world that the cinema made its first appearance. In 1896, by the time Warsaw got its first glimpse of an automobile, which was described by the newspapers as 'a small Benz-system closed carriage' with a maximum speed of 20 km per hour, spectators at the Ciniselli Circus had already watched, on a screen set up under the big top, a parade of automobiles through the streets of Paris. Before the first electric tram appeared in the streets of Warsaw, cinema audiences had already seen *A Journey through the Streets of London and Leeds*, *The Lights of Venice* and *A Trip down Broadway in New York*. It would be difficult to overestimate the cognitive role played by the cinema in the Polish territories at that time. While the illustrated press, which was so successful elsewhere in the world, proved to be a relatively inaccessible source of news to the Poles because of their high illiteracy rate, the cinema, the cheapest and most popular form of entertainment, became the medium through which they learnt about the world. Between 1904 and 1906, dozens of films were shown in all the main cities. They included not only films about discoveries, but ones which could be said to have had an educational function, such as *The First Automobile Journey*, *The Pilotable Air Vehicle*, *Visit to an American Locomotive-building Factory*, *The International Balloon Race*, *The Japanese Fan Factory*, *How Our Newspaper is Made* and *The Whole Production Process in the Jam Industry*. Such films brought spectators in Poznan, Warsaw, Vilnius and Lvov into closer intellectual contact with the outside world than ever before.

Polish spectators found films appealing for other reasons, which also apply to most of their counterparts elsewhere. The cinema was one of those wonderful inventions that anyone could watch and understand. It was highly democratic: films shown to the King of Romania, the Tsar of all the Russias and Kaiser Wilhelm II could be seen a few weeks later by the inhabitants of Toruń or Drohobycz. Yet it was not that aspect of the cinema that attracted spectators from various milieux.

The increasing amount of information that reached members of the public through either the illustrated press, postcards or reproductions (depending on their intellectual possibilities) did not satisfy their curiosity. On the contrary, it simply whetted their appetite for more information. Photographs and drawings could excite interest only in bits of things. Even

119

the most accurate illustrated report or most realistic and detailed drawing eventually proved incomplete and inadequate: they always reproduced only a single moment, movement or situation; there was always only one atmosphere and one point of view. The published illustration was never 'true' in every respect – it always required retouching. Irrespective of the circumstances, Tsar Nicholas's or Kaiser Wilhelm's face always bore the same forbidding and formal expression. Photographs and press illustrations, then, always seemed to be at one remove, whereas the motion pictures shown in the cramped and stuffy conditions of the earliest cinemas had an infinitely greater suggestive appeal: spectators were given the illusion that they were taking part in the events they were watching. Most people felt that the cinema showed the truth. It was utterly genuine. They could see how Tsar Nicholas moved and detect a moment's weariness or impatience on his face. They could also enjoy the comical side of the royal couple boarding a gondola in Venice and the 'true' appearance of the 'savages' who were building the railways. No written description or illustration could be a substitute for such pictures. No one who has read the writings of the film director Bolesław Matuszewski (who was also a pioneering film theorist), and more particularly his booklet entitled *A New Source of History* (1898), could possibly doubt that his contemporaries were convinced of the total credibility of film and believed that it was only on the cinema screen that the truth could be perceived. 'What the cinema shows', he writes, 'is indisputable and absolutely true.' He goes on: 'It may be said that animated photography has a quality of authenticity, accuracy and precision that is peculiar to it alone. It is the truthful, infallible eye-witness *par excellence*' (Matuszewski 1898).

It was precisely that deep need for truth and authenticity which in 1898 led the Jews of Żytomierz to ask a travelling photographer, the French cameraman Francis Doublier, for genuine documentary footage of the Dreyfus affair. Their request prompted Doublier to commit an unusual piece of deception: he stuck together pieces of film in his possession, thus apparently creating the first montage film in the history of the cinema. He needed only to put together shots of the sea with some land on the horizon, high walls and a marching army, for his spectators to believe they were seeing a genuine Captain Dreyfus, the walls of his prison and the place he was deported to – the 'real' Ile du Diable. Doublier showed his 'documentary photos' for several months, and his crude trick would probably never have come to light but for the chance presence, in a cinema in one of the cities near the border of the country, of a keen follower of new inventions. The man in question knew that the cinema had not yet come into existence when Dreyfus was tried in 1894 (Bottomore 1984).

During the first ten years of the cinema's existence, spectators were apparently much more interested in experiencing the phenomenon of authenticity than in watching 'invented stories'. This is reflected in advertisements and posters, where the authenticity of the photography is explained and even guaranteed to the spectator. When I look at advertisements which offer a 100 per cent guarantee of 'the authenticity of the pictures' I realize there is something more involved here than a mere question of authenticity. The cinema in the first decade of its existence satisfied to a great extent audiences' cognitive requirements. Nowadays almost every schoolchild is familiar with the skyscrapers of New York, the canals of Venice and the squares of Paris. But audiences at that time consisted mostly of people who had never set foot outside the local café: they were seeing such pictures for the first time. The cinema, which was the most popular entertainment of all, was very often their only link with Europe and the rest of the world.

It is hard for us, who have been made blasé by television and are used to travelling easily and quickly from one place to another, to imagine how curious people at that time were about the world and, consequently, how much they dreamt about it. Here is another characteristic example of the kind of attitude that was prevalent at the time: in the early 1890s, the Kalisz municipal theatre, which was a highly respectable institution and certainly had nothing in common with a fairground, put on a highly successful production based on Jules Verne's *Around the World in Eighty Days*. Performers in the show included monkeys, giraffes, an elephant, a snake, 'Redskins' and Brahmins; also depicted were the explosion of a ship and – something the inhabitants of Kalisz dreamt of – a railway. Was this a case of the fairground moving into the theatre? Or a distant echo of the theatre of André Antoine?[4] Neither, in my opinion. The presence of the elephant, the snake and the railway on the municipal stage may have had another explanation: this was a case of a provincial theatre pandering to the most secret fantasies of its spectators: fantasies about travel, dangerous natives, wild animals and the railway. The cinema was in a perfect position to satisfy that curiosity about the world a second time.

The earliest films exerted an enormous influence. Itinerant film exhibitors from Łódź, such as Antoni and Władysław Krzemiński, covered tens of thousands of kilometres a year between 1901 and 1908 with their projector. Using numerous means of transport, from train, horse-drawn carriage, raft and steamboat to horses and camels, they took their films out to central Asia. In 1907 alone, the cities they visited included Grodno, Tula, Vologda, Archangel, Chelyabinsk, Symbirsk and even Tashkent. Meanwhile, they had founded the first permanent cinemas in Polish provincial towns. They showed *The Indians in Canada*, *The Streets of Tokyo* and *Foxhunting in England* (Hendrykowska 1989). At the same time, Leon Mettler's first permanent cinema in Poznań featured *The Transport of Private Despatches via Lake Baikal*, *The Building of the Railway in Manchuria*, *The Felling and Transport of Timber in California*, *The Kirghiz Horse Trials*, *Pictures from North Borneo*, *Bullfighting in Madrid* and *The Construction of the Railway by Savages*.

Lake Baikal and Canada, Tokyo and California, Indians and the Kirghiz
– the world had grown smaller and at the same time very much larger.
Audiences at those earliest showings certainly did not realize to what
degree their eyesight, so to speak, was being improved, with the result
that they experienced an increasingly close spiritual bond with the outside
world. To a more or less conscious degree, they felt and sought not so
much aesthetic sensations as experiences lacking in their daily lives, that
is to say a substitute for the social relationships and contacts available in
their tenements and drinking places. They were not an educated public
that spent its time travelling between Paris and Saint Petersburg but, on
the contrary, one that was deprived of the opportunity of wider contacts
and not very demanding when it came to reading matter – a family or
social get-together was their main source of news more often than the
newspaper. The showing at more or less the same time in Brazil, Saint
Petersburg, New York and the Polish territories of *Fox-hunting in England*
or *La Sortie des usines Lumière* brought people and continents together to a
hitherto unparalleled degree.

This feeling of spiritual union with the rest of the world was fostered
not only by documentary reports, but by dozens of 'directed' films about
current events that were very much in the news in Europe and elsewhere.
*Massacre in Macedonia, The Murder of the Serbian Royal Couple, The Captain
Dreyfus Affair, The Death of Pope Leo XIII, The Captain of Köpenick Affair, The
Murder of Grand Duke Serge* and *The Maximilien Lebaudy Affair* were just some
of the titles of reconstructed newsreels made at the time. When Georges
Méliès carefully re-enacted the coronation of Edward VII, when he built
a large aquarium and placed behind it a cardboard model representing
the sunk cruiser *Maine*, when he used papier mâché to evoke the explosion
of the Mont Pelé volcano or reconstructed the Pax balloon disaster, he
was in each case catering to a more or less conscious degree to the deepest
needs of human nature: the need to know more about the world and the
need to share the experience of true and exciting events.

The concept of cinema as fairground entertainment assumes the passivity
of spectators who, after entering the tent for a brief look at, say, a bearded
woman, happened to see the film programme. But the cinema soon created
its own public of regular filmgoers precisely because, from the very beginning, there was an active reciprocal link: people went to the cinema because
it depicted their own problems.

Up to 1908, at a time when most films shown in the Polish territories
tended to be of an informative nature, the cinema was capable of living
up to the expectations of various social groups. It was the film medium
and the cinema which, by featuring such subjects as the Russo-Japanese
War, the fake Captain of Köpenick or the train disaster near Berlin,
encouraged broad sections of society to get involved in some of the more
disturbing problems of the contemporary world. It was the travelling

cinema that broke the vicious circle of *petit-bourgeois* interests, while at the same time bringing together people in big cities who lived separate lives and did not know each other. The popularity of the cinema in this very early period – and I refer to the situation obtaining in the Polish territories – was due to the fact that it was above all a source of news and knowledge, a form of identification with culture, a medium through which people could find their place in the world, not a passive, unthinking and easily assimilated form of entertainment. That situation changed with the passage of time; but that is not of concern to us here.

The habit of going to films, and in cities to permanent cinemas, was the factor that gave people a sense of belonging to a community and a new society which tempered the feelings of bewilderment and loneliness common among the city-dwelling masses at the turn of the century. For the thousands of people pouring from the countryside into the cities, who were cut off from their earlier contacts and cooped up in narrow streets and rented tenements, the cinema and the pictures it offered were the only thing they had to hang on to in a society in which they had placed such great hopes. The cinema, with its 'pictures from various parts of the world', its popularized versions of well-known fables and its reconstructions of current events that people talked about in streets, cafés and shops, meant that for the hundreds of illiterate peasants who flocked into the cities each year the new and incomprehensible world of urban society became for the first time, if only partly, tamed and systematized.

It would be wrong to deny that the cinema had an entertainment value or awakened certain sensations of an aesthetic nature. But those qualities were essentially different from the feelings generated by fairground entertainment. The cinema was the only field of aesthetic emotions in which the scale, nature and rhythm of the topics touched upon tallied with people's lives at the time: it echoed the multitude of news items that the spectator would have seen in newspapers or the illustrated press. A cinema of that kind, with its rich and well-balanced subject matter, was the only artistic form capable of capturing the all-pervasive, complex hurly-burly experienced by people living in the middle of a large city. That kind of cinema, then, not only provided a singular form of assistance for people wishing to dominate a new psychological and social situation, but also became an aesthetic necessity.

At the same time – and as if against both the progress of civilization and the development of industry, physics, chemistry, biology and printing – traditional models remained the rule as far as the arts in general were concerned. It is true that innovations were being made by the avant-garde in certain artistic fields such as painting; but the canons and norms that had been established decades earlier were still widely respected as regards music, architecture, fashion and indeed mores. The cinema, one of the most democratic inventions of the nineteenth century, was not hindered

123

by such considerations when it offered spectators a 'true', authentic, up-to-date and shared imaginative involvement in all the essential issues of the times.

So was the cinema fairground entertainment? I fear that the epithet 'fairground' cannot be entirely and definitively erased from the history of the cinema. It was not anyway my intention to attempt to erase it with the zeal of the novice, but simply to accord it its proper place. That a fairground element was one aspect of the cinema's existence at the time is undeniable. In the Polish territories, that element resided chiefly in a specific type and system of film distribution. But there was no absolute rule, and what I have attempted to show is the cultural complexity of the phenomenon and the fortuitousness of the cinema's links with the circus or the showman's booth. What needs to be firmly challenged, however, is the use of 'fairground' as an aesthetic category, or the idea that the cinema and fairground entertainment can be equated. I admit that it is tempting to approach the issue from a historical point of view and see a direct line leading from the invention of the cinema to 'genuine' film art via fairground entertainment. Yet the importance of the cinema in the first decade of this century and the role played by moving pictures in the minds of the first filmgoers were infinitely more significant than I had originally suspected. The many volumes of memoirs, reports and statistical data corroborate that view, though to a degree that would certainly not satisfy modern cultural researchers. But we should allow our imagination to have as much say as historical facts, always supposing that we are able to liberate it from a certain oversimplified and comfortable way of thinking. It is after all up to our imagination to suggest what people were actually seeking, after squeezing into the small cinemas of the early years, once the novelty of the invention had ceased to work its charm and all that was left was a bright screen and flickering 'animated photographs'.

Translated from the French by Peter Graham.

NOTES

1 Alfred Dreyfus, a French General Staff officer of Jewish origin, was wrongly arrested in 1894, accused of spying, sentenced and exiled to Ile du Diable. He was exonerated in 1906. The Dreyfus affair divided public opinion, caused considerable political turmoil and featured in many press reports, illustrated articles, serials and filmed fantasies. (See Stephen Bottomore, 'Dreyfus and documentary', *Sight and Sound* 4, 1984).

2 On 16 October 1906, ex-convict Friedrich Wilhem Voigt dressed up in a stolen captain's uniform and placed under his orders a group of soldiers he had met by chance. Nominally 'commander' of the group, he arrived at the town hall of Köpenick near Berlin, ordered the arrest of the mayor and chief treasurer, and withdrew 4,000 marks from the offices of the municipal treasury. The affair was seen in Europe as an example of the kind of blind obedience generated by

124

military uniforms. A German filmed reconstruction of the incident, *The Affair*, was shown in early December 1906 in the Polish territory annexed by Prussia.

3 By agreement between its three neighbours, Prussia, Russia and Austria, Poland was partitioned three times during the second half of the eighteenth century. It was in 1795, after the Kościuszko rebellion had been put down in 1794, that the third and final partition took place. It effectively liquidated the Polish state for a period of more than 100 years. Austria annexed Cracow and an area of about 47,000 sq km; Prussia took over several cities including Poznań and an area of about 55,000 sq km; and Russia annexed Warsaw, among other cities, and an area of about 120,000 sq km.

4 André Antoine (1858–1943), a French actor-producer, and the leading figure of the naturalistic school of drama.

5 The first permanent cinemas in the Polish territories were opened between 1903 and 1907 in cities (Warsaw in 1903, Poznań in 1903, Cracow in 1906) and between 1909 and 1911 in smaller towns.

REFERENCES

Bottomore, Stephen (1984) 'Dreyfus and documentary', *Sight and Sound* 4.

Chodyński, Adam (1972) 'Widowiska publiczne w Kaliszu', in Stanisław Kaszyński (ed.) *Teatralia kaliskie, Materiały do dziejów sceny kaliskiej* (1800–1970), Łódź: Wydawnictwa Łódzki.

Hendrykowska, Małgorzata (1989) 'Filmowe peregrynacje braci Krzemińskich (1898–1907), *Kino* 11.

Matuszewski, Bolesław (1898) *Une Nouvelle Source de l'histoire*, Paris: Imprimerie Noirette.

Michalik, Jan (1988) 'Odwaga czy konieczność. Teatr Miejski w Krakowie – kinem', *Kino* 2.

Pazdur, Jan (1963) 'Rozwój kultury materialnej', in Stanisław Arnold and Tadeusz Manteuffel (eds) *Historia Polski*, vol. 2, Warsaw: PWN.

Wyka, Kazimierz (1960) 'Kultura polska w drugiej połowie XIX wieku', in Stanisław Arnold and Tadeusz Manteuffel (eds) *Historia Polski*, vol. 3, Warsaw: PWN.

9

THE FINN-BETWEEN

Uuno Turhapuro, Finland's Greatest Star

Veijo Hietala, Ari Honka-Hallila, Hanna Kangasniemi, Martti Lahti, Kimmo Laine and Jukka Sihvonen

The popularity of the phenomenon called 'Uuno Turhapuro' is unique in Finland. The statistics speak for themselves: six out of the seven most successful Finnish films of the last six years (1984–90) were Uuno films. The largest audience for a single Finnish film in the 1970s and 1980s was for *Uuno Turhapuro armeijan leivissä* (*Uuno Goes Military*, 1984, 750,000 spectators), only narrowly beaten by two foreign films, *One Flew Over the Cuckoo's Nest* and *Papillon*.[1] The subsequent television presentations of most Uuno films have attracted further audiences of millions.

Since 1973 Pertti 'Spede' Pasanen has written and produced fourteen films with Uuno Turhapuro as protagonist and two films with cameo appearances by Uuno in one or two scenes. Every autumn for eighteen years (with the exception of 1974 and 1989) Finnish cinema audiences have enjoyed a new Uuno film. In thirty years Finnish culture has not produced another fictional hero who is known by everyone and who attracts so many kinds of film audiences regardless of the crises elsewhere in national film production.

Like any other nation, Finland is an inherently ambivalent one. Uuno is a good example of the various ways in which this ambivalence does and does not become represented within a specific culture. From this perspective the first observation is that despite its culturally widely acknowledged existence and popularity, Uuno's world, the Uunolandia, is in many ways ambiguous, self-contradictory and incomplete. It exemplifies the spaces of which Homi Bhabha writes: 'What emerges as an effect of such "incomplete signification" is a turning of boundaries and limits into the *in-between* spaces through which the meanings of cultural and political authority are negotiated' (Bhabha 1990: 4).

Our aim in this paper is to examine Uuno's world as an 'in-between space'. We do not think of Uunolandia as maintaining or subverting certain culturally and nationally specific values, but rather take it as an imaginary

126

space in relation to which people in Finland try to make sense of their cultural ambivalence.

BACKGROUND AND RECEPTION

The Uuno character – played by Vesa-Matti Loiri – was created by Spede Pasanen for his television show in the early 1970s. The first appearances consisted of short sitcom sketches with Uuno lying on the couch and having constant arguments with his wife. Spede is a sort of institution in Finnish entertainment: producer, scriptwriter and comedian, loved by the person in the street but sniffed at by critics and the cultural elite. Originally a familiar voice in radio shows in the late 1950s, Spede has since established his status as the prominent figure in and behind the most popular TV shows and film farces:

> The world is littered with comics whose wit, like Swiss wine, cannot be exported. Pasanen's jokes depend a great deal on current affairs, figures, and incidents in Finnish life. So the foreign viewer may be perplexed by the ecstatic response of audiences in Helsinki or provincial cities; even more puzzling, however, is the experience of watching a Pasanen movie alone on video. Then it becomes almost impossible for a non-Finn to laugh.
>
> (Cowie 1990: 120–2)

The triumph of Uuno films has taken place at a time when the rest of the Finnish cinema needed considerable subsidies from the state to survive. Due to the decline in audience attendances, the Finnish Film Foundation, founded in 1969, has systematically supported national film production, for instance by channelling a small percentage of ticket income into it. In spite of this the downhill course culminated in 1974 with only two Finnish feature films – and a break in the Uuno series.

These changes in film production have naturally had an impact on the films themselves: one is more likely to acquire state subsidies for morally uplifting and aesthetic subjects than, say, farces. This is why it has been difficult for Spede to get financial support from the Foundation. Yet this has also provided the Uuno films with a flavour of counter-culture: Uuno represents all those features that the official cultural hegemony stands against. In Uuno's early years, the first half of the 1970s, a time characterized by a strong polarization of party politics, Uuno's (un)popularity transgressed even political oppositions: to put it roughly, the young cultural left called for socially radical realism, whereas the right wanted national subjects to support traditional conservative values. Uuno did not fit into either of these policies.

The film critics' arguments were basically virtually identical on the right and on the left. First, Uuno's grotesque appearance and irresponsible behaviour (laziness, over-eating, boasting) insulted good taste. Second, the films were perceived as repetitive and formulaic with stereotyped characters and recurrent situations, their structure episodic with no signs of the continuity of 'correct' film narration. Third, they were considered implausible and illogical. Even the technical quality of the image, the critics argued, did not meet the requirements of film art: Spede made use of television equipment to cut down costs which, of course, partly guaranteed economic success. All these arguments notwithstanding, the critics mainly took the films as 'realistic', that is, Uno was conceived as an object of identification, thus evidently teaching the masses wrong values and bad models of behaviour; the situation was aggravated by Uno's alleged popularity among youth and relatively uneducated adults.

Over the years Uno's appearance has not changed much; he is still the same country boy who became more urban than the natives within two weeks of moving to Helsinki. After his marriage opened up the possibility of easy and comfortable living, Uno changed his clothes for a loose, sleeveless shirt and the grey work-trousers with braces. Uno's attitude towards his looks is similar: uncombed hair and unshaved face. On the other hand, if needed, Uno can and will take greater care of his appearance: for example, when he wants to conquer the blonde next door he immediately appears with sunglasses, slicked hair and skin-tight shorts. This is the recurrent and most obvious metamorphosis inscribed in Uno's body. But there are also other unusual abilities hidden beneath the shaggy looks. For example, in *Uuno Epsanjassa* (*Uuno in Spain*, 1985) Uno shows that he can move as a king of the discotheque or a champion of the golf course as well as an immortal matador. Meanwhile he has an opportunity to show his expertise in rare butterflies.

All of this should be seen in terms of the character's contradictory image. In spite of his appearance Uno is extremely popular with women in the films. At the same time his marriage seems to stay on course. Uno's education is based on the primary school but this does not prevent him from becoming an officer in the army or a professor at the university.

Vesa-Matti 'Vesku' Loiri's multiplicity is well known throughout Finland. In his Uno figure it reaches a world in which he can, with remarkable ease, play 'through' Uno roles from executive to Don Juan. On this elementary level the Uno films are as impure as the world of Uno itself. As an image, Uno is a recognizable hedonist but he can also be very rational. Moreover, these two sides seem to live happily together in him. Uno is against the ethics of work in the same way as he is against almost everything that dates back to the high values of the Enlightenment. But again, at least in some respects, he is hyperactive, namely when it comes to food and sleep.

All this exemplifies the multifarious structure of Uno's world and the Uno films. One can ask whether this kind of behaviour represents merely pitiful inability and impotence (that is, is Uuno only an *uuno*, a numbskull?) or a passionate and honourable commitment to one single thing (that is, is Uuno, *uno*, the number one?)[2] After all, questions like these may show that Uuno is not only against social control and order; he also creates and follows his own set of controlling and ordering devices. He can adapt new circumstances extremely quickly to his own world view.

CHANGING PHASES, UNCHANGED FACES

Of the fourteen Uunos, eleven can be divided into three successive phases. The first four films familiarize the audience with the character: the fourth, *Häpy Endkö?* (*Happy End?*, 1977), consist of a summary of Uuno's life in Helsinki since he left home in the country as a youth. The second phase contains the next four films up to 1983, and the Uuno cameos in two films (1979 and 1980) directed by Spede himself; this period completed the Uuno world and saga with his rich father-in-law and other people around him. In the three films of the third phase (1984–6) Uuno's world is tested against other, non-domestic discourses, army, tourism, rural life, etc. All these films were directed by Ere Kokkonen, a member of the Spede team since 1966. The most recent Uuno films were directed by Spede, Hannu Seikkula and Pertti Melasniemi.

Although the first Uuno feature, *Uuno Turhapuro* (1973), adheres to the formula of short TV sketches common in Finnish entertainment, it already has a classical narrative structure with 'an undisturbed stage, the disturbance, the struggle, and the elimination of the disturbance' (Bordwell 1985: 157). The film presents Uuno literally in an undisturbed stage, cosily lying on the couch, while the disturbance consists in his extraordinary success as an autodidact violinist. However, money brings nothing but unhappiness, because he has no time to enjoy it. The TV background is evident at this stage: the diegetic space is mostly restricted to the Turhapuros's flat and there are considerably more close-ups and medium close-ups. The film concentrates on Uuno almost entirely, with only one segment without him, and the rhythm of narration is determined by jokes and gags, rather than the plot itself.

The other three films of the first phase contribute to completing Uuno's world before the second phase, beginning with *Rautakauppias Uuno Turhapuro, Presidentin vävy* (*Ironmonger Uuno Turhapuro, the President's Son-in-Law*, 1978). Now Uuno's team, played by the same actors since the fifth film, includes his wife Elisabet, the rich father-in-law Tuura who is a political VIP (later the Minister of Defence, though not finally elected President), the nice mother-in-law, and, in addition, two working-class friends, Hartikainen and Sörsselssön, who 'work' as repair mechanics at a garage. The sixth member is Tuura's secretary, a stereotyped dumb blonde.

The diegetic space of the first and second phases contains few separate locations: Uuno's home, the garage where his friends work, Tuura's office in Helsinki and Tuura's summer-house nearby. The characteristics of the locations may change between films: in almost every film Uuno's home looks different, following quite closely the changes in the ways in which middle-class homes have been furnished in Finland. There are some recurrent narrative motifs, however: Uuno and his friends expecting the (natural) death of Tuura and the huge inheritance which they are due to share, Tuura attempting to make his daugher and Uuno divorce, Uuno's 'philosophical' arguments and long explanations and his immediate flirtatious tricks at the sight of pretty women.

The second phase is characterized by formal features common to many other Spede films. Narration is split into many narrative lines – the main characters each have their own stories – with no necessary connection to each other. In this phase the narration is far from classical as regards time, specified location and causality.

The third phase extends the diegetic space beyond Helsinki. *Uuno Turhapuro armeijan leivissä*, the most successful in the series, is formally identical with its predecessors with split narration and parallel story lines. Under the obvious impact of the military farce genre (popular in Finland in the 1950s), the narration again acquires a logic of time and space. The protagonist declares his ultimate goal as a newcomer recruit: 'Next week I'll be a major.' There is a narrative tension, for although the audience certainly know that he will attain his improbable goal, the question of how he will do so creates suspense. As a major, after once more outwitting his father-in-law, the present Minister of Defence, Uuno again learns the loneliness of success which reaches its climax in the scene where his fellow soldiers respond solely to Uuno the major, not to Uuno the man: in spite of his attempts to speak to his subordinates as a buddy, they respond to him according to his rank as a superior officer.

Since the third phase Spede has produced three more Uuno films. The first and second of these *Uuno Turhapuro, kaksoisagentti* (*Uuno Turhapuro the Double-Agent*, 1987) and *Tupla-Uuno* (*Double Uuno*, 1988), return to the triangle of the second phase – home, garage, Tuura's office – and its familiar plot constructions. The latest film of the series, *Uunon huikeat poikamiesvuodet maaseudulla* (*Uuno's Boisterous Bachelor Years in the Country*, 1990), however, differs from the earlier ones in taking the entire Uuno world back to the protagonist's assumed adolescence. Basically this resembles the collision of discourses typical of the third phase, but taking the familiar Uuno world to narrate about Uuno's own childhood and adolescence creates a network of temporal relations such as has been seen in the art film tradition, for example the films of Alain Resnais. Of course, 'experimentality' in this Uuno film becomes possible because of the assumed knowledge concerning Uuno's world.

Uunon huikeat poikamiesvuodet maaseudulla tells of Uuno's past, of which one has seen and heard different versions already. The film itself does not, however, count on these. Instead, it presents yet another story about how Uuno met his wife-to-be, Elisabet. This confirms the idea about Uunolandia as a self-sufficient universe in which the temporal and spatial continuums of our everyday world are not valid.

BETWEEN CULT AND CULTURE

We can see behind Uuno's appearance an image dependent on contradictions and the logic of turning oppositions upside-down. Through Loiri, Uuno creeps into a wider set of discourses. Loiri's star image is built on the stage: as a serious actor in theatres (and in films); as a jazz musician singing Eino Leino's ballads; as a TV star and comedian; as a public figure. The image lives in discourses which include one of the major poets of the national literary tradition (Leino) as well as Uuno. In examining this set of different discourses, we could first suggest that Loiri's Uuno performance seems to take its basic form in relation to its opposition, to the high-cultural face of his stardom. In this way jazz, theatre and Leino would constitute one pole in a binarism where the other would be Uuno. On the other hand this relationship is not as clear-cut as it seems since Uuno's figure already carries with it the entire field of Loiri as a star. Thus Uuno's world also contains the high-cultural element (albeit in a repressed form), and Loiri's star image also includes impure and contradictory elements of hierarchized popular and elitist discourses.

This is concretized in the ways the commercial world can take advantage of Vesa-Matti Loiri's star image. The full page advertisement for Apple Macintosh in *Helsingin Sanomat*, the largest Finnish newspaper, in December 1990, makes use of both the high-cultural and popular aspects simultaneously present in Loiri's star image: the ad aims at organizing and hierarchizing these aspects. The advertisement claims to shatter the boundary between high and popular culture by representing two ends of Vesa-Matti Loiri's star image, popular Uuno and high-cultural flautist, as parallel and alternative. The verbal frame, however, reveals the supposed nature of this parallelism of roles. Vesa-Matti Loiri's high-cultural side, the serious artist, controls the opposite popular role, 'makes him dance to his music'.

Here the ad utilizes the interplay between surface and depth structuring the star image, the contradiction between the 'represented' and the 'real', which the text in the picture regulates: 'With his Apple Macintosh Portable Computer at hand Vesku Loiri makes Uuno, Tyyne, Kusela, Uncle Nasse, Auvo, Pizza Boy, Vili, Heimo Meskanen [Loiri's well-known comic roles] and others dance to his flute.' Thus the spectator is persuaded to perceive the right-hand Loiri as surface in comparison with the left-hand 'authentic' Loiri. The ad makes use of a strategy that allows the spectator the safe

Macintosh tuo työniloa luovaan kaaokseen.

Apple Macintosh

Plate 17 Vesa-Matti Loiri: Uuno Turhapuro – high culture, low culture. By courtesy of Apple (Finland).

pleasure of otherness. From a high-cultural 'reality' perspective, Uuno's assumed inauthenticity becomes an exotic spectacle which is an exciting environment to visit.

The presence of such heterongeneous elements in both Vesa-Matti Loiri and Uuno may in part account for the latter's popularity, because they contribute to the pleasures of different audiences. There simply is no first, innocent watching experience for Vesa-Matti Loiri's audience, but, rather, the Uunos are processed through successive watchings inside the larger Uuno text created by Finnish culture and constantly present therein.

Spectators face Uuno films with their own Uuno and Vesku texts in their pockets, and, in a sense, relive their previous viewings while, at the same time, negotiating those experiences. Because of their TV background and serialization the Uuno films offer themselves for almost infinite appropriation.

The source of pleasure may consist in the desire to experience, with the high-cultural Vesa-Matti Loiri, the opposite, the culture of the grotesque, as well as the desire to see how the Uuno saga is retold this time. In the latter case the recurrent references in the films to the earlier Uunos yield a certain pleasure, for through them the spectator may recognize her/his own expertise ('I know Uuno'), thus differentiating her/himself from those novices in the Uuno cult who do not catch the allusion. Consequently, the films may feed the spectators with a comforting impression of a community of Uuno devotees sharing a certain cultural capital and expertise in the Uuno world. Thus the traces of popular and high culture inherent in Vesa-Matti Loiri's star image and in Uuno neither undermine nor confirm the boundary between these fields, but, rather, foreground the boundary and make it visible. This strategy may fit better into the self-fulfilling Uuno world, where one does not know – perhaps does not want to – anything about the world beyond. Uuno acts on contradictions, abuses of social norms. He is totally dedicated to the rituals, norms and values that shape bourgeois existence, whether they concern money, family, sexuality or marriage, the measuring units of social value, but simultaneously he pushes them to their boundaries thus making them visible by his extreme action. On the one hand, then, Uuno contributes to maintaining the bourgeois world (after all, he does not know any other) by constantly attempting to adapt himself to it and pursuing its measures of value, economic and sexual power. On the other hand, Uuno's behaviour betrays those values, embodies their reverse.

UUNO STRIKES BACK!

The Uuno logic recurrently intervenes in everyday logic by means of various tactics. According to Finnish Lutheran ethics one has to work, shedding sweat and tears, to get rich and/or survive. Uuno, on the contrary, relies on his wife's income, the future inheritance and, in addition, various more direct manoeuvres, such as lotteries and mixing in his father-in-law's business dealings. Further, the Uuno character seems to shatter the status quo of certain social relations: the country boy who lives in the city has married into a bourgeois family but his best friends come from the working class (at least emphatically coded as such). Recurrently Uuno is presented in a position where he should not 'belong' (university professor, army officer, travel guide, in the business world, in the foreign service, even as a woman), thus seemingly questioning the social, political and even sexual hierarchies.

Uuno also intervenes in various fields of high culture. In *Uuno Turhapuro* he acquires international fame as an autodidact violinist. In *Uuno Turhapuro, kaksoisagentti*, he conducts a symphony orchestra with enormous success. Uuno's performance as the Russian conductor Jetvushenko is so brilliant that the critics are willing to change the title of the composition (which is Sibelius's *Finlandia*) to *Russlandia*. Further, he turns out to be a virtuoso in such 'refined' sports as billiards, golf and tennis. This, of course, tends to question the boundary between vulgarity (inherent in the Uuno character with his 'bad' manners) and the elite culture, as also does Uuno's expertise as a gourmet.

In addition, Uuno appears to transgress class and gender boundaries as effortlessly as the allegedly more universal boundaries between adult and child, human and animal. In Uuno there seem to be no limits or boundaries.

Having lost his memory in *Uuno Turhapuro menettää muistinsa* (*Uuno Turhapuro Loses his Memory*, 1982) Uuno thinks he is a woman. As a result he assumes the cultural signs of the female, such as motherhood and the importance of 'to-be-looked-at-ness': Uuno imagines pregnancy, attempts to breastfeed a little girl, supposedly his child, and makes a fuss about calories and his appearance. In *Uuno Turhapuron Aviokriisi* (*Uuno Turhapuro's Marital Crisis*, 1981) he adapts himself to the animal sphere: his extraordinary sense of smell, which enables him to distinguish between various foods through a shop window even with eyes blindfolded, takes him to a school for dogs – as a pupil.

Uuno's appeal to child audiences may result from the fact that he seems to represent children's logic in adult reality, thus defying the strict adult/child boundary. Even in his appearance the classic signs of a young rascal are easily decoded: torn and dirty clothes, missing teeth and messy hair. Uuno resembles the monster child of the horror genre who is able to destroy the order and logic of the adult world with her/his magical powers. With an innocent look on his face Uuno recurrently sabotages his father-in-law's enterprises, advancing his career and acting adequately in his roles as father, husband and business manager. Uuno's opponents, his wife and father-in-law, resort to multiple strategies (stopping short of exorcism) to control Uuno, but eventually find themselves unwillingly realizing his

Plate 18 'The classic signs of a young rascal': Vesa-Matti Loiri as Uuno. By courtesy of Spede-yhtiöt, Helsinki.

desires. For instance, Uuno's and Elisabet's marriage and the constant attempts to annul it are a sort of infernal carousel, whose speed Uuno increases every time the father-in-law perceives an opportunity to pull his daughter out.

In principle, it might be easy to interpret Uuno's character as questioning these structuring oppositions of culture. However, as already mentioned, Uuno's sojourns at the limits of dichotomies seem to foreground rather than question these boundaries, in accordance with the logic of Uunolandia which ignores the world outside.

Uuno's 'transgressions' adhere strictly to gender difference. Masculinity incessantly seeks its identity at various limits. In the Uuno films femaleness (Elisabet) represents the repressing and containing forces of adult and civilized society – education, sociality, commitment – which males often try to escape in their fantasies. Uuno's wife is the norm of 'normalcy' and responsibility, from which Uuno escapes into the realms of infancy or bestiality. In relation to Elisabet, Uuno realizes the masculine fantasy of the male as active and transgressive and the female as stable and passive. From this perspective Uuno, playing on the borderline between adult and child bodies, may not be a radical transgressor but, simply, a man repeating a masculine fantasy.

In fact, one might trace the birth of the Uuno character back to the popular discourses of the early 1970s in which the Finnish male was increasingly criticized, especially in women's magazines. The Finnish man may behave in a gentlemanly way at the dating stage, according to criticisms, but after the wedding he soon turns into a lazy, untidy beer-drinking couch potato. The first Uno film displays this transformation right at the beginning. Clean, shaved and appropriately dressed, Uno is seen with Elisabet at the altar and the ceremony is concluded. In the next scene, after the ensuing opening credits, we see the 'Uunoized' Uno figure lying on the couch, drinking beer and arguing amiably with his wife who reproaches him for his changed outlook and habits. In addition, 1970s popular discourses described the Finnish male as a lousy, unromantic lover who does not know how to talk to women – if he talks at all – when compared to passionate Latin males, now familiar as a result of the increasing popularity of package holidays in the Mediterranean. Against these discourses the Uno character might be seen as a male counter-attack in which the hidden potential of the Finnish male was revealed, and at the same time perhaps as a regressive male fantasy in defence against the increasing demands for sexual equality and women's rights from the early 1970s onwards.

Uno may be 'a bit untidy' but, when needed, he can conquer any woman he wants; he may try to avoid the deadening routine of daily work, but his resources are inexhaustible when it comes to money making or climbing the social ladder. Actually this hopeless couch potato is an invincible virtuoso in many fields of life, whether sports, cuisine or the arts. In other words, as in Clark Kent, the ordinary-looking reporter, a real superman with all the right connotations hides behind the modest façade of the Finnish male.

While Andy Capp could be seen as a British version of the common man, Uno is apparently – from the producers' perspective, at least – designed to caricature the values of the average Finnish male. He is untidy, carelessly dressed, lazy (in an early film he did not even recognize the word 'work'), and loves food, frequent naps on the couch and beautiful women. All these features are taken to a caricatured extreme in the films. His wife tries to force him to look for a job and constantly intervenes in his attempts to empty the fridge of its contents. But while Andy Capp is happy with his drinking, pubs and soccer, Uno is most enterprising in escaping domestic control and, above all, getting involved in his father-in-law's public career. The plots of the films mainly deal with Uno's success in humiliating his father-in-law in various social, political and economic undertakings, to his own benefit, of course.

THE IMPURE AND THE GROTESQUE

The possibility of comic surprise depends on quick changes in narrative and emotional response. They in turn depend on the contradictions in values and expectations that spectators already have in relation to their everyday experiences. Thus, comedy attempts to surprise spectators in terms of both its narrative strategies and its verisimilitude. What is predictable and appropriate refers to the two levels of verisimilitude: the conventions of the genre and the norms of public opinion (Neale and Krutnik 1989: 83). Characteristic of comedy is its dependence on inappropriateness and incredibility. What appears as such, however, depends on national, cultural, generic and temporal variables. Hence, the many conventions so typical of comedy can be referred to the modes and norms of limited cultural and social behaviour. Broadly, these modes and norms offer possibilities for a transgression of the familiar as well as a familiarization of the transgressive (ibid. 93).

According to Bakhtin's *Rabelais and his World*, the carnival is both a Utopian vision of the world seen from beneath and a transgressively joyous criticism of 'high' culture (Bakhtin 1968: 109; Holquist 1990: 89). Its method is to turn the existing hierarchy upside-down. Peter Stallybrass and Allon White propose in their *The Politics and Poetics of Transgression* that Bakhtin's ideas about the carnival should not be blunted by essentiallistic binarisms like 'Is the carnival subversive or not?' (Stallybrass and White 1986: 14–15). For Bakhtin, the carnivalesque can be related for example to notions of the classic and the classical body in relation to their negations, their others; that is, to everything which the classical excludes in the process of searching for its own identity. Stallybrass and White argue that the notion of the carnival should be used analytically to clarify what kind of symbolic forms temporally and spatially determinable cultures use when speaking to themselves, when thinking of themselves.

Stallybrass and White analyse the development of the cultural imaginary among the (mostly English) middle classes from the seventeenth till the end of the nineteenth century and they divide the high/low opposition into four domains: psychic forms, the human body, geographical space and the social order. The fundamental cultural division is based on everything that the notion of the classical signifies. For example, in the realm of the human body 'the classical body' would refer most concretely to ancient Greek statues. Its opposite, then, would be 'the grotesque body' which includes many of the features excluded from the classical body. This kind of distinction can be found in Bakhtin, but according to Stallybrass and White, he still uses it in ambivalent ways. Another possibility is to see the grotesque as a hybrid form which is not only 'outer' or 'lower' but rather questions and complicates the correctness of the binary model itself. The grotesque, seen from this viewpoint, can include both 'high' and 'low', both 'closed' and 'open', both 'pure' and 'impure'. From this perspective the Apple Macintosh advertisement is exemplary in the way it includes both the classical and the grotesque, though its meaning is still strictly dependent on cultural knowledge concerning Loiri's stardom.

The prototype of the classical body in Finnish culture might be the statue of the famous Finnish long-distance runner, Paavo Nurmi.[3] Instead of embodying muscularity, the statue expresses such traditionally typically 'Finnish' characteristics as endurance and obstinacy (which come together in the Finnish-language word, *sisu*). The statue also embodies the notion of 'the flying Finn' which was originally one of Nurmi's emblems and was later attached to Finnish rally drivers. By contrast Uuno represents the grotesque body, including such features as untidy clothing, clown-like make-up, gaping mouth, distended belly and clumping feet. Moreover, Uuno embodies the basic sign of the grotesque body, namely the importance of food. Whereas the classical body is closed, homogenized, monumental, pensive, centred and symmetrical, the grotesque body is open, multifarious, distracted, deformed and impure. In this sense the Uuno films themselves follow the discursive norms of the grotesque body: open, multiple, cheap, fragmented and disordered. Even film reviews have recourse to references to excrement and waste to characterize them.

Because of this grotesque body, it is not at all easy to propose that there actually exists a kind of unitary and single 'Uuno discourse'. Rather, Uuno as a larger cultural phenomenon seems to act as a space for several discourses, which, furthermore, can be in contradiction with each other. The fundamental collision occurs in the Uuno films between, on the one hand, the abstract Uuno discourse (the sign of which is the image of the grotesque body) which is continuously in a process of becoming, and on the other, the national high culture with its closed, conserved and contained values. The constant becoming of the Uuno discourse in the films themselves is due to the fact that this discourse can build its own figure and form only as negations. Its structure is totally dependent on how it reflects the part of the Finnish culture (and its normative value system) which it mockingly takes as its critical 'mirror'. It may be family or marriage as institutions, a mechanism of social power and order (such as the army) or some cultural phenomenon which is in fashion (such as package tours). Hence, the obscure and unidentified limits of the Uuno discourse are perceived in the way it itself frames and transgresses the much sharper boundaries of the targets of its mockery and criticism.

The limits of what is seen as appropriate and credible are defined in and through language. The conventions of public opinion deal with what is said and, above all, what can be said and where. Levels of appropriateness and credibility correspond to the spatial contexts of language, and the ability to control these contexts means linguistic power over what can and cannot be said, and where. As a linguistically marginal and tribal culture, Finland is subdivided according to these 'verbal spaces': home, school, church, even sauna are framed according to what may not be said in them and in what way that is so. This kind of nationally specific negativity is one of the ways in which Uuno's criticism and transgression operates. In relation to these negations Uuno is represented as a negation of negation: he denies and circles the values and norms of a culture so powerfully founded on various different denials and prohibitions.

Nationality, 'Finnishness', exists in both the images of Uuno and the Uuno films always through and according to this kind of counter-attitude and position within the existing power relations. Uuno's world belongs to the cultural imaginary of the Finnish middle class of the 1970s and 1980s, and Uuno is Finnish only in so far as this imaginary space can be seen as culturally specific. In this imaginary fantasy world there have always been Utopian positions for mythical heroes whose main purpose is both to question and to embody the basic elements of Finnish, white, middle-aged masculinity such as endurance, obstinacy, shyness, inability to show emotions, repressed aggressivity, speechlessness and excessive drinking (which, in the Uuno films, is metaphorized in the mode of excessive eating). These social satires have traditionally been seen in ambiguous ways: on the one hand as objects of identification ('If only I dared do that!') and on the other hand as ideologically distanced reflections ('Isn't that stupid!'). Repression and repulsion on one level appear simultaneously at another level as symptoms of secret desires and hidden fears. In this way the movement of the divergent discursive fields in the Uuno films reaches the space between the spectator and the screen. Presumably the producers manipulate these various movements every time they market a new Uuno film: spectators have already been taught to wait for Uuno, to find out what is new in this familiar world, what is framed, structured – and transgressed – this time in relation to this world.

Thus the Uuno films incisively exemplify the nature of 'the logic of the absurd' which, as Jerry Palmer argues, always 'points to a variety of possible subject positions' (1987: 182). Because of this the Uuno films – as comedies and modifiers of the 'essence of humour' – are both subversive and conservative, both offensive and inoffensive, both serious and ridiculous. But of course there are limits to these possible subject positions, namely the boundaries which signify the supposed inexportability of these films. In this sense nationally popular film comedies, like the Uuno films in Finland, can never be really excessive, or, to put it another way, they can only touch the borders of excess since these limits are, nevertheless, linguistically, culturally and historically determined.

The perversities of rational and/or irrational behaviour can produce laughter only in so far as they do not insult supposed common sense. And this common sense has traditionally been rather clearly defined in tribal societies like Finland. *Uuno Turhapuro armeijan leivissä* is a good case in point: we can read the image of the military system as a miniaturized image of Finnish society at large.

Hence the Uuno films are in a sense conservative: their transgression is still ruled by the imaginary of common sense. Yet, in the process they emphasize the extremes of this Finnish common sense of the 1970s and 1980s, they subvert its various forms, or at least offer possibilities for such a subversion to the spectator. In general, the secret of Uuno's success may be in expert maintenance of the ambivalence of this culturally and historically distinctive symbiosis of conservatism and subversion.

NOTES

1 According to the statistics compiled by the Finnish Film Foundation, audience attendances in Finland in 1990, for example, were about 6 million per year.
2 The name 'Uuno Turhapuro' might be translated as 'Numbskull Emptybrook'. Uuno is a Finnish male forename but in slang it also connotes a fool or dummy.
3 Lived 1897–1973, winner of nine gold and three silver medals in three Olympic Games. According to a Finnish saying, Nurmi 'ran Finland on to the map of the world'.
4 In fact, as Benedict Anderson argues, language played an essential role in the national liberation movements in Europe between 1820 and 1920: 'in almost all of them "national print-languages" were of central ideological and political importance' (1983: 66). One of Anderson's examples is Finland: 'The leaders of the burgeoning Finnish nationalist movement were persons whose profession largely consisted of the handling of languages: writers, teachers, pastors, and lawyers' (ibid.:72).

REFERENCES

Anderson, Benedict (1983) *Imagined Communities; Reflections on the Origin and Spread of Nationalism*, London and New York: Verso.
Bakhtin, Mikhaïl (1968) *Rabelais and his World*, Cambridge, Mass.: MIT Press.
Bhabha, Homi (1990) 'Introduction: narrating the nation', *Nation and Narration*, London: Routledge.
Bordwell, David (1985) *Narration in the Fiction Film*, London and New York: Methuen.
Cowie, Peter (1990) *Finnish Cinema*, Helsinki: Finnish Film Archive and VAPK Publishing.
Holquist, Michael (1990) *Dialogism: Bakhtin and his World*, London: Routledge.
Neale, Stephen and Krutnik, Frank (1989) *Popular Film and Television Comedy*, London and New York: Routledge.
Palmer, Jerry (1987) *The Logic of the Absurd: On Film and Television Comedy*, London: BFI.
Stallybrass, Peter and White, Allon (1986) *The Politics and Poetics of Transgression*, London: Methuen.

10

THE INEXPORTABLE

The case of French cinema and radio in the 1950s

Jean-Pierre Jeancolas

This chapter, which does no more than touch on its subject in the hope of initiating a more comprehensive, European-wide examination, sets out to make a simple point: that during the period from the beginning of sound cinema until the mid-1950s (or rather until television took over as the new dispenser of banal, easily assimilated or demagogic images and consequently robbed cinemas of some of their patrons), there existed in all the major European industries (certainly the French and Italian, probably the West German and Spanish, and possibly others – work remains to be done on this) a category of low-grade films that were destined to be seen only by audiences in their country of origin. In at least one case, that of Italy, it may be that some of those films were aimed solely at filmgoers in specific regions.

I would describe such films as inexportable, because they were too insignificant and/or unintelligible to be appreciated by spectators outside a given popular cultural area, which was at once uncouth, coded and based on recognition.

A rough typology of the genre based on the example of France would look as follows:

(1) Inexportable films are above all based on a form of complicity that is limited both spatially and temporally. That (reassuring) complicity may focus on: (a) a form of entertainment that existed before the film was made: a specific or dialectal type of play, a radio programme, a game or a sport; (b) an actor or actress, or a couple, or a group of singers or musicians. They often had connections with singing (this type of cinema relied above all on sound, whether it took the form of talking or singing), and were popular even before they appeared in films: it was their presence alone which justified the making of a film commercially; (c) an anecdotal interpretation, usually ironic or satirical, of the history of the country concerned.

(2) Inexportable films are not auteur films, and are dealt with by film historians only from an economic or sociological viewpoint. They are in all respects of poor quality and have no artistic ambitions.

They may also be of interest to cultural historians in so far as they are 'multi-media': they often combine film with one or several other categories of popular culture, such as the theatre, song, radio or strip cartoons.

(3) Inexportable films may on occasion be a springboard for an actor's or actress's career. This may sometimes result in a film being subsequently legitimized and thus included in a retrospective season or filmography. But up to now, no work has been done on inexportable films as such.

(4) Inexportable films can be defined in terms of production (they are based on a pattern, on the complicity I referred to in point (1). They can also be defined in terms of consumption. Until the end of the 1970s, the French industry produced a number of films targeted on garrison towns. These 'garrison films' were probably the last examples of the genre: they were aimed at young men doing their military service, particularly in eastern France, who had nowhere to watch television when they went on a night out from their barracks. Around 1978 national servicemen were catered for by such remote descendants of the military vaudeville movies of the 1930s as Philippe Clair's *Comment se faire réformer* (*How to Be Discharged From the Army, 1978*) and *Les Réformés se portent bien* (*The Rejects Are Doing Well*, 1978), Michel Gérard's *Arrête ton char, Bidasse* (*Stop Fooling Around, Bidasse*, 1978), and Claude Bernard-Aubert's *Les Filles du régiment* (*The Girls' Regiment*, 1979). The last manifestation of the genre came as late as 1983 with Michel Caputo's *Les Planqués du regiment* (*The Skivers of the Regiment*).

One last remark: it would seem that French hard-core porn films, which peaked in popularity from 1976 to 1983, and which worked within strict limitations as regards both production and content, by no means constituted an inexportable genre.

In other words, inexportable films belonged to an ill-codified genre that was aimed at relatively uneducated audiences. They left little trace, as critics were not interested in them (some films were even released directly in provincial towns and small cities without getting the kind of first run in Paris that normally helps to launch new releases). Foreign distributors were not interested in them either, though they do seem to have been widely shown in what used to be called the French colonies, chiefly North Africa and Black Africa.

I propose to look in greater detail at one of the types defined above: the popular cinema and its relationship with radio.

In the 1930s, songs from operetta and elsewhere – people heard them in theatres, including travelling theatres of which there were still many in

France, particularly south of the River Loire, more often than on the radio or on gramophone records, which were uncommon in working-class households until the immediate pre-war period – often served as a point of departure for a film, which might borrow no more than a title, a tune, a story or a basic musical backing. But it would only rarely borrow a performer: songs in the 1930s were not automatically associated with a given singer: they were volatile and were governed by ill-defined copyright laws.

In the 1950s, radio became a popular medium *par excellence*. At that time, France was covered by the national radio network and a few peripheral stations such as Radio Luxembourg, then from 1955 on Europe 1 in northern France and Radio Monte Carlo and Radio Andorra in the south (transmitters were set up just across the border from France). Radio game shows and daily serials with very distinctive, immediately identifiable comperes' and actors' voices were immensely popular at that time. There were Raymond Souplex and Jeanne Sourza, Jean-Jacques Vital and his Famille Duraton, Ded Rysel, Yves Deniaud and Pierre Dac, and games which were sometimes recorded by touring companies in country towns or by Radio Circus (the circus was also fed by radio): this was the heyday of France's 'radio days'.

A form of cinema that was meaningless except to regular listeners of such programmes (the complicity was in this case generated by the link with radio) naturally thrived on radio's territory. Low-budget productions, very minor directors and mainly provincial distribution were all typical characteristics of inexportable films. For a more detailed picture one would have to look at the cinema attendances of such films by consulting the records of the Centre National de la Cinématographie, but it would be an inordinately lengthy task.

There were two ways in which the tie-up between radio and cinema might take place. One would be for a character created on the radio (usually identified with an actor, or rather the voice of an actor) to find himself or herself caught up in some fairly rudimentary plot which would use the radio identity as a starting point.

A typical case was that of Piédalu, a traditional caricature of the gauche but wily peasant, immortalized by Ded Rysel. He was the central character of three films by Jean Loubignac, *Piédalu à Paris* (*Piédalu in Paris*, 1951), *Piédalu fait des miracles* (*Piédalu, Miracle Worker*, 1952) and *Piédalu député* (*Piédalu Goes to Parliament*, 1953). The screenplays were based on well-tried formulas worked out in the early 1930s: the country bumpkin who ends up in Paris, the contrast between town and country, and an excuse to show Paris and its music-halls and cabarets. The films would be sprinkled with numbers – they would be called video clips nowadays – that showed musical stars or bands in action: the first *Piédalu*, for example, featured 'the duettists Monique and Josette', and the third, much more exotically,

Sidney Bechet and Claude Luter's band[1]. Another case was Leguignon. The *lampiste* (dogsbody) Leguignon[2] starred in *Le Tribunal (In Court)*, a programme put out by Radio Luxembourg every Sunday. Each programme took the form of a trial, and the man in the dock was always Leguignon, who was played on the radio by Yves Deniaud. The cinema soon got interested in him, and in 1952 Maurice Labro made *Monsieur Leguignon lampiste (Monsieur Leguignon, Dogsbody)*. The credits mention that it was 'based on Picq and Ferrari's radio programme'. Three years later, Labro made *Leguignon guérisseur (Leguignon Healer)*. Deniaud naturally played Leguignon on the screen: his drawling voice and outraged denials were a quintessential part of the character.

And then there was *La Famille Duraton*, a daily serial broadcast just before the evening news on Radio Luxembourg; it was already being put out before the war, and in 1939 Christian Stengel made a film version called *La Famille Duraton* based on a screenplay by Jean-Jacques Vital, the producer of the radio programme (and many others). In 1955 André Berthomieu directed *Les Duraton*, with Vital again responsible for the screenplay. Some of the radio actors appeared in Berthomieu's film, among them Ded Rysel and Jeanne Sourza. Also in the cast was the young Jean Carmet, who remembers spending many years of his early acting career lending his voice to the character of Gaston Duvet, the rather oafish woolgatherer who drops in on the Duratons every day.

In these three cases, the film functions as what would nowadays be called a spin-off of a radio programme. It is sold to spectators who, so to speak, are already part of the family.

The second type of transition from radio to cinema, unlike the first, does not transfer a popular 'hero' (in fact an unheroic hero, a typical product of a restricted imaginary at the confines of populism and Poujadism[3]) from the air to the screen, but gives a programme, usually a game show, the status of an institution, generally a show whose filmed image – a vehicle of truth, along the lines of the innocent principle underlying the early cinema: 'I saw it, so it must be true' – is both a justification and an advertising medium. Below are three examples of radio programme titles being used unchanged in film titles.

One of them was *Sur le banc (On the Bench)*, a daily programme (not a game show) broadcast at lunchtime, which was the day's peak listening time. In 1954 Robert Vernay made a film of the same name, with a screenplay and dialogue by Raymond Souplex. The programme was a dialogue in the best *chansonnier* tradition – that is to say, it made jokes about a not too sensitive topical subject, more with nudges and winks than with genuine audacity – between two tramps, Carmen and La Hurlette, huskily played by Jeanne Sourza and Raymond Souplex. The scenario of the film relied on an old device: a legacy. The two tramps suddenly find they are rich, and go to spend a huge amount of money at a seaside resort in Normandy – Cabourg, to be precise, though no reference is made to Marcel Proust. Also in the film, in the minor part of Sosthène, was Julien Carette, an actor who certainly deserved a better fate but had to earn his bread and butter somehow.

Then there were two popular game shows. Here, the aim was to use motion pictures to lend them credibility, in other words to give flesh and blood to people who were not actors but comperes. The first was *Cent francs par seconde* (*One Hundred Francs a Second*, 1952), which was directed by Jean Boyer and written and coproduced by Jean-Jacques Vital, an old hand at broadcasting who realized, before television came along, that the kind of radio show he produced and sold had everything to gain from being backed up by pictures.

The screenplay tells a story that concentrates solely on the possibility of making an enormous fortune in a very short time, even though people were still using old francs: a particularly clever or lucky contestant in the game *Cent francs par seconde* manages to lose the fabulous winnings he has clocked up so as not to ruin the game's organizer, who happens to be his girlfriend's father. The film featured two well-known figures of 1950s radio, André Gillois and 'Monsieur Champagne', a former deputy headmaster of a lycée who started a new career as a mastermind and judge of contestants' answers.

The other film was Robert Vernay's *Quitte ou double* (*Double or Quits*, 1953), which exploited even more explicitly a radio programme that used to be recorded in the various places toured by Radio Circus. This real circus, which was devised by Louis Merlin, offered grassroots France a mixture of traditional numbers (trapeze artistes, clowns and horses) and live game shows broadcast by Radio Luxembourg. *Quitte ou double* was a quiz, based on an American model, where contestants could double their money every time they came up with the right answer to a question put by a smooth-talking, moustachioed compere in a loud check jacket, Zappy Max, who plays himself in the film. Max falls in love with a young woman contestant from Bourganeuf, a small Limousin market town whose name in itself condenses and symbolizes reassuring provincial life, combining in its reality – the 'reality effect' again – the notions of *bourg* (small town) and *neuf* (new). What is more, the woman wins the jackpot. The icing on the cake is Line Renaud, then a singer at the height of her fame, who appears in the film in the part of 'the singer'.

The reader will have noted that all the films mentioned in this list were released during the first half of the 1950s. By 1956 and 1957, television was beginning to catch on, albeit only in the form of a single black-and-white channel, which also had its own popular programmes. But it was still a luxury: it was expensive and by no means covered the whole of France.

So in 1957 it was only natural to make a film like *C'est arrivé à 36 chandelles* (*It Happened at '36 Chandelles'*, directed by Henri Diamant-Berger, with a screenplay and dialogue by Jean Nohain), which extended the boundaries of a television variety programme compered by the same Jean Nohain and called *Trente-six chandelles*. The plot is a simple love story involving a case of mistaken identity (the central characters lose each other, then are reunited) which takes place in a television studio: the film shows the compere of the programme and his guests on set, as well as what goes on behind the scenes. Nohain, a radio pioneer before the war and a television pioneer after, realized that in the mid-1950s television still needed the cinema if it was to reach wider audiences. That period was shortlived.

From 1970 on, it was of course television which took over the production and broadcasting of inexportable screen artefacts.

Paradoxically, too, it was in the early 1970s that the inexportable cinema came to grips, in France at least, with contemporary history, which it interpreted in a most unusual way, as I mentioned at the beginning of this chapter. For obvious economic reasons (producers had to get their money back from distribution on the domestic market alone), inexportable films had to be widely popular; in other words, they had to generate consensus, if not unanimity. The seam they were working was necessarily a memory or an imaginary of reconciliation. They were therefore films which, to take a specific example, were very careful not to get involved in the familiar and acrimonious controversy that generally flares up among the French as soon as any attempt is made to deal seriously with such issues as the Second World War, the resistance and the collaboration with the Germans.

A single factor (the death of Charles de Gaulle and the consequent watering-down of historical Gaullism into a form of conservatism that also accepted the legacy of Vichy) paved the way in France not only for documentaries as detailed as *Le Chagrin et la pitié* (*The Sorrow and the Pity, 1971*) and *Français si vous saviez* (*French People, If Only You Knew, 1972*), which probed the nation's collective memory by dredging up conflicting eye-witness accounts and documents, but also for engagingly demagogic popular comedies, of which the archetype could well be Robert Lamoureux's *Septième compagnie* trilogy: *Mais où est donc passée la septième compagnie?* (*Whatever Happened to the 7th Company?*, 1973), *On a trouvé la septième compagnie* (*They Found the 7th Company*, 1975) and *La Septième compagnie au clair de lune* (*The 7th Company by Moonlight*, 1977), as well as, to a lesser extent, another film by Lamoureux, *Opération Lady Marlène* (1974) (Jeancolas 1975).

In all these films ordinary French people, whether soldiers called up in 1940 or the citizens without rights of Pétain's France, find themselves caught up in personal adventures which illustrate not only their adaptability and resourcefulness, but also, when it comes down to it, a low-key but gratifying courage. The bad guys in these stories (German soldiers or collaborators) are caricatured but above all marginalized. Decisions (the right decisions) are taken without any problems of conscience or recourse to extreme situations. Such films, as I have already pointed out, offer a unanimous, reconciliatory view of the period. Lamoureux and his many imitators relied on flabby consensus fifteen years before it became the buzz word of French ideology.

The *Septième compagnie* films were a very different kind of inexportable product from the cinema mentioned earlier: they were not low-budget movies slapped together on the fringes of the industry, but Gaumont productions (the Gaumont International division run by Alain Poiré). The first of them was a French-Italian coproduction, the second a Franco-German coproduction, and the third a wholly French production – which suggests that Gaumont's foreign coproducers came out of the deal rather badly. The films' subjects and their allusions to a complex historical situation meant that they only went down well with audiences who were at least rudimentarily informed, and who were both in step with the subjects of the films and keen not to find themselves ridiculed in them. According to Alain Poiré, 'our characters, who were so French, or rather Gallic, brave, skiving, grousing, never completely heroic but never truly cowardly either, reminded my compatriots of a period they knew well' (Poiré 1988). That was certainly true, and still is: the *Septième compagnie* films are regularly screened on television and always get very high ratings.

The analysis could be taken further. The inexportable cinema would then take on an ideological flavour, not only through its referents, its subjects and the way they are treated in it, but also in relation to the time when the films were shot and distributed; indeed, it is precisely this relationship with their first spectators that is their main interest.

It would be fascinating to see if other European film industries, and in particular the Italian and West German industries, produced the same type of low-grade comedies, and if so when (against what background of domestic politics): comedies describing (justifying) the behaviour of compatriots during the same war. A film like Comencini's *Tutti a casa* (*Everybody Go Home!*, Italy 1960) does not of course fall into that category, nor even does the *08/15* series produced in West Germany during the 1950s. Could self-justification be an exclusive characteristic of unimaginative French feature films?

Translated from the French by Peter Graham.

NOTES

1 At that time, the first half of film shows in the provinces was often taken up by shorts consisting of three or four songs unimaginatively recorded with the singer

standing behind a microphone. The aim was simply to 'show' sound, nothing more than that.

2 The real nature of the *lampiste*, a word first used in that sense by the satirical magazine *Le Canard enchaîné*, is itself coded: it denotes the degree zero of the social ladder, the universal scapegoat. That meaning of the word came into common usage before the First World War.

3 A shoddy ideological movement founded in January 1953 by Pierre Poujade, a stationer in Saint-Céré, under the name of Union de Défense des Commerçants et Artisans (UDCA, Union for the Defence of Shopkeepers and Artisans). A corporative and antiparliamentarian movement, the UDCA gained a surprisingly large following in the archaeo-capitalist sectors of production and distribution, winning 12.5 per cent of the votes and fifty-two seats at the January 1956 general election. Poujadism, which was on the far right of the political spectrum, suffered a split over the Algerian question and petered out as a political force after 1958.

REFERENCES

Jeancolas, Jean-Pierre (1975) 'Fonction du témoignage, les années 1939–1945 dans le cinéma français de l'après-guerre', *Positif* 170.

Poiré, Alain (1988) *200 films au soleil*, Paris: Ramsay.

11

THE OTHER FACE OF DEATH

Barbara Steele and *La maschera del demonio*

Carol Jenks

It's not me they're seeing. They're casting some projection of themselves, some aspect that I somehow symbolize. It can't possibly be
me.

(Barbara Steele, quoted in Warren 1991: 68)

Angela Carter (1982: 120) named the three surrealist love goddesses as
being Louise Brooks first and foremost, followed by Dietrich and Barbara
Steele. With regard to Steele, however, not all the following descriptions
emanate from surrealists caught in the grip of *amour fou:*

The very symbol of Woman as vengeful, alien and 'other'.

(Nicholls 1984: 52)

Her sculpted features and wildness of eye quickly typecast her as the
dark goddess who can dole out pleasure and pain in equal measure.

(Hogan 1986: 168)

All at the same time, a fairy with claws like the drawings of Charles
Addams and the Vera of the Count of Villiers.

(Jean-André Fieschi, quoted in Beck 1978: 296)

She glides about with the elegance and eroticism of a black patent-
leather high heel.

(*Cinema*, quoted in Beck 1978: 308)

Her image, more than any other, is the emblem and fetish of the
[horror] genre.

(Hardy 1985: 149)

It is the last statement that demands attention. How can such a claim be
made for a woman who appeared in only eleven horror films between 1960
and 1968, nine of them Italian, which were released haphazardly outside
Italy through exploitation companies in cut, dubbed versions and of which
she herself remarked that they were 'hardly worth creating a cult around'
(quoted in Crawley 1983: 42)? And beyond that, what can explain such

ambiguous ecstasies, such a mixture of fear and desire as a response to an image?

The key term, of course, is fetish, since supposedly only a woman can constitute a fetish object, although in the context of the horror movie Roger Dadoun disputes this when he sees the male vampire figure, Count Dracula himself, as being the maternal phallus incarnate, the visible fetishistic substitute for the absent, non-visible archaic mother[1] (Dadoun 1989: 41). The latter is a mythical being of crucial importance in trying to account for the textual workings of Steele's films, which constitute a distinct and specific subgroup of their own amidst the overall explosion of Italian horror in the first half of the 1960s.

At the time, they were the films on which attention focused, due to her star presence, but the later developments of horror in Italy evolved from quite other strands. The type of narrative where a nominal framework is provided by an investigation into a series of murders but in which any actual coherence or resolution is completely overwhelmed by the excessive violence of the murders themselves as spectacle could hardly be better summed up than by the stark title of Mario Bava's *Sei donne per l'assassino*. (*Blood and Black Lace*,[2] 1964), which anticipated the work of Dario Argento. A complacent, non-gender-specific description of the film, 'the murders are photographed to appear gorgeous and titillating, forcing the audience to feel an accomplice's share of the assassin's pleasure' (Lucas 1985: 30), gives a clue to the drives fuelling the narrative and the answering emotions it expects to evoke in the (male) spectator.

The very different concerns of the films starring Steele suggest how hermetically sealed is the body of work dedicated to and celebratory of her image. The cultural fantasies embodied by the films, and the lure they hold, have perhaps ultimately more to do with the figure of the all-devouring *femme fatale* than with any crucial stage in the development of the horror genre. Their very cultishness, even by horror film standards, places them outside the mainstream, as does the purely practical problem of their extreme difficulty of access. This latter factor, of course, is often an important one in the very existence of a cult, but here it seems to have the added resonance of creating a particularly intense and ardent desire to see a mysterious and inaccessible being whose rare manifestations are thus extremely precious.

The question remains, however, why such an anachronistic figure was enabled to reappear in the form and in the country she did at the beginning of the decade of Cool, the 1960s, whose affectless heroines represented a notion of sexuality as liberation (however false), not as the promise of a sadomasochistic dance of death.

To discuss the provenance of the killer *femme fatale* (and the veiled figure of the archaic mother in the shadows behind her) is entirely outside the scope of this chapter. Her death throes as a European cultural icon took place with the advent of the First World War. Immediately prior to that, she had found the new medium of cinema a fitting place for a final incarnation. It was the Italian cinema's extravagances in the areas of fantasy and spectacle, using the words in their widest sense, that accounted for its early international predominance and influence. In the late 1950s, popular cinema harked back to its roots by reviving the various male and female figures who had inhabited historical epics and peplum fantasies, taking what had once been regarded as the art of the film and turning it into genre material.

However, as the only outright horror film of the Italian silent period was a version of the archetypal dyadic fantasy dependent on the expulsion of woman altogether, namely *Il mostro di Frankenstein (Frankenstein's Monster,* 1920), it is clear that this recreation of scenarios from the early national cinema cannot have led in some simple or direct fashion to the first wave of Italian horror.

A figure not normally considered even remotely in relation to horror and who dominated the terrain of early Italian films could provide the missing link - the diva. Francesca Bertini, Lyda Borelli and others were arguably the first women in world cinema to fulfil the role of star, and that to the utmost. Their grandiloquent, heiratic acting had to take the place of the missing voice, and the emotions it created, of the opera singers from whom they took their title.

The melodramas created to display them, actually called *divismo* films, were usually contemporary in setting and dress but dealt in archaic fantasies, formerly pinned on historical figures: 'The woman as predator, as the dominating figure, the man in subjugation: this is a situation virtually unprecedented outside the Delilahs, Shebas and Cleopatras, outside tales of princes in thrall to courtesans' (Shipman 1985: 17).

It is the invocation of Cleopatra that is particularly interesting here. Lucy Hughes-Hallett, in her study of Cleopatra through all her historical changes as a cultural icon, identifies what she calls the killer-Cleopatra as a romantic archetype of insatiate lust and cruelty, a phallic figure of 'equivocal gender' in 'splendid but transparent drag', a projection of male masochist drives, 'or at least a part of the male psyche' (Hughes-Hallett 1990: 229), who bears no relation whatever to any real woman. The very last manifestation of the killer-Cleopatra, as Hughes-Hallett notes, was in the person of Theda Bara in 1917.

Bara had been consciously created as the American cinema's answer to and incorporation of the Italian diva and she was remembered as the woman who put the vamp in vampire when the divas had become the concern solely of professional film historians. Remembered to the extent that in 1964, *Cinema* magazine could evoke her in relation to Steele, whom it described as going 'on her own high-heeled, porcelain-skinned, vamp-eyed way to stardom as a modern Theda Bara' (quoted in Beck 1978:

151

308). The idea of anybody in 1964 being a modern Theda Bara on screens ruled by Monica Vitti and Julie Christie bespeaks the depth of cultural dislocation and anachronism involved, a revival of fantasies grounded historically elsewhere, re-emerging from out of the past.

The key figure in the return from the repressed of Italian neo-realism of various mythic/historical female figures was Riccardo Freda, whose career as a director began in 1942 and who had kept up the tradition of melodramatic spectacle. In 1953 he had cast his wife, Gianna-Maria Canale, as the Empress Theodora and he revived the archetypal victim, Beatrice Cenci, in 1956, the same year as he made *I vampiri (The Vampires*[3]*)*, a film so entirely isolated generically, with no national tradition to back it up and predating the Anglo-American horror revival, that it can only be accounted for as a final step from melodrama into overt Gothic, for the purpose of enabling a new female figure to be added to the cinematic repertoire.

Freda once declared, 'I am not in the least interested in banal humanity, everyday humanity' (quoted in Lephrohon 1972: 179), and it is possible that he wanted to extend the imaginative field of operations of the literally imperious woman, by turns either actively suffering and imperilled or personifying what has been designated as 'the promise of cinema – the beautiful, cruel woman' (White 1987: 80). This hypothesis is supported by the fact that *I vampiri* was inspired by the female standby of horror film makers, the Bloody Countess, Elizabeth Bathory, and that having cast her as his Theodora, Freda again used Canale in the lead role. Also, the plot, concerning an older woman whose lover brings her young women whom she can drain in order to rejuvenate herself, clearly foreshadows the fascination with a symbolic 'monstrous' mother figure. When rejuvenated she passes herself off in society as her own niece, an enactment of the fantasies of incorporation and loss of identity that are particularly supposed to haunt dyadic relations between women.

It was the film's very isolation, however, that ensured its utter failure both in Italy and on the export market, and it appeared at the time to be an experiment that would lead nowhere. It was the immense success of the Hammer *Dracula* (1958) in Italy that changed the reception climate. When Mario Bava was offered the chance to direct a film of his own choosing as a reward for taking over, uncredited, from Jacques Tourneur on *La Battaglia di Maratona (The Giant of Marathon,*[4] 1959), his request to be allowed to base a scenario on Gogol's *Viy* was granted by the producers, Galatea Film, something very unlikely to have happened pre-*Dracula*. He used the popularity of the British film to argue that Italian audiences were now ready to accept a 'new wave' of horror.

When the finished product, *La maschera del demonio (The Mask of the Devil,*[5] 1960), was discovered by international critics, who turned it into a cult movie, they praised it for its ability to create atmosphere, 'brilliant intuitions of the spectral' (*Time*, quoted in McGee 1984: 139), through visually poetic black and white photography, thus linking it to the classical tradition of the horror genre. But they also commented on its power to shock by the introduction of a new element, overt images of sadism and bodily corruption, which almost overwhelmed narrative drive and coherence. The success of the film ensured that Bava became the only Italian director of the period to work almost exclusively in the horror genre for the rest of his career, apart from the occasional excursion into spoof spaghetti westerns or the exploits of Viking marauders. The allegations, which became habitual, that he sacrificed narrative to image were conventional in the case of someone who had had a long and distinguished career as a cameraman prior to his directorial début.

In *Maschera* the images which arrest his fluidly mobile camera in contemplation are of the face and body of his star, Steele, formerly a small-part actress in British films whose services he had gone to great lengths to acquire and who was transformed into something undreamt of by the J. Arthur Rank Charm School, whose last contract starlet she had been. She came into the studio system immediately prior to its disintegration and as the available 1950s range of female types was going into bankruptcy, but the accident of her looks would have debarred her from the coming 'realism'.

Raymond Durgnat, lamenting that British directors failed to explore the possibilities of certain actors who didn't 'fit', credits Bava, conventional auteurist-style, with having recreated Steele Pygmalion-like. Her British films, he claimed, revealed only 'a weakly pretty face', not the 'spiky, whiplash strength' unleashed by *Maschera*, which rendered her 'mesmeric' (Durgnat 1970: 184). The tell-tale imagery here gives away the nature of the projection involved: the male critic praising the male auteur for having brought an image into being that is determined by their own need to see it and from which the actual woman is entirely absent. Her weakly pretty face – as the face is traditionally the mirror of the soul, the words cunningly suggest a trivial or vacuous personality – becomes a mere *tabula rasa* to be sculpted by the intense play of light and shade.

It follows logically that in her career in Italian horror, Steele was removed from the arena of language, literally reduced to silence by the process of redubbing. She disliked the absence of psychological realism in horror movies, the fact that there were no characters, only situations, and that they were directors', not actors', films. As a compensation, she brought a mimetic style of acting into play, diva-like, becoming a figure in a landscape, an essence, a mimed emotion. Two extraordinary examples are the scenes in Antonio Margheritis's *I lunghi capelli della morte (The Long Hair of Death*, 1964), in which she lets her mother's ashes run through her hand, while her knee-length hair and the long velvet sleeves of her dress are whipped up by the wind, and her protracted death scene in Massimo

153

Pupillo's *Cinque tombe per un medium (Terror Creatures from the Grave,*[6] 1966), a series of jerky, flailing gestures across the length and breadth of a room, as angular and contorted in relation to the actual lines of the body as anything to be found in Expressionist acting.

This concentration on the body of the woman raises further questions: the same writer who found Steele to be 'the emblem and fetish of the horror genre' also thought that her face 'is probably how Norman Bates remembers his mother in *Psycho*' (Hardy 1985: 149). Leaving aside the absurdity of the writing, this is a very overt invocation of the primal mother, archaic, phallic, all-consuming. Instead of Dadoun's male fetish-figure, who stands in for this hidden being, *Maschera* attempts to realize the implications of actually making her present and visible.

The film's textual sadism is marked out from the beginning by an extreme violence towards the audience, an aggressive desire to wound the very site of vision, the eye. The unspoken agreement of the cinematic contract is broken: the spiked mask of Satan is carried forward into the camera to pierce the gaze of the spectator. There are then two further shots of the mask, but these are marked as being from the witch Asa's point-of-view and punctuated by a reverse close-up of her huge-eyed terror.

Asa is thus presented as the owner of a violated gaze, one which she shares with the spectator. This immediately introduces issues of gender and identification, because it is a profoundly held tenet of film distributors that the spectator of a horror movie will almost invariably be male, no matter what empirical evidence can be brought to refute this. It is unquestionably true that many women do avoid horror films, and not only on the grounds of aversion to their overt violence. They are a disreputable, marginal cultural form, second only in that respect to pornography, which in certain manifestations – the work of the French Jean Rollin and the Spanish Jesus Franco – they actually fuse with. Horror has been perceived as functioning for men as melodrama does for women, that is as a cathartic working through of the impossible contradictions between desire and the social dictates appropriate to gender.

If, then, a film whose own hypothetical constructed spectators are male places a woman about to have her eyes put out as the figure to whom they are sutured in the text, there is an obvious point of crisis, an almost literal ravishment. The conventional interpretation would be that it is raising the spectre of castration, which would easily fit a view of horror as concerned with specifically male anxieties.

Another way of looking might reveal a fantasy not necessarily predicated upon the axis of castration, because predating the Oedipal scenario and its ensuing subject positions – a refusion with the primal mother, a merging of identity with her, thus a 'becoming feminine'. However, the resultant loss of gendered subjectivity, the dissolving of the self's boundaries in

Plate 19 The temptation of monstrosity: Barbara Steele as Katia in *La maschera del demonio*.

the return to an imaginary undifferentiated state, albeit one of plenitude, inextricably threads desire with fear.

This means that the figure who embodies the prospect of refusion will be represented negatively, as a threat, as the other face of death. What is so unexpectedly fascinating about the narrative proper of *Maschera*, which starts after the prologue, is that it seemingly leaves direct anxieties about male subjectivity by the wayside, deflecting the threat towards another female figure, Katia. Katia is the descendant and double of Asa, who desires literally to 'fuse' with Katia in order to 'regain her life completely', as the priest, who wishes to prevent such a thing ever happening, expresses it.

A title tells us that we are now two centuries on, fixing Asa all the more as that being who is always in the past, mother. The image-trace of her prehistoric existence is her portrait, which affects Katia strangely. 'There's something alive about it, something different about the eyes, the hands, as if it were hiding something. Sometimes I'm afraid to go near it.' The prince, her father, is obsessed by the history of an earlier descendant of Asa's, the princess Masha, who died as she reached the age of maturity, 21, and who was 'the very image' of Asa. He believes Asa will try to take Katia in turn, who is also just 21 and 'her living image'.

What is being presented here is a version of the construction of female subjectivity as something demonic. Whereas the male subject is constituted

155

Plate 20 Barbara Steele as Asa the witch, Katia's tempting ancestor in *La maschera del demonio*. By courtesy of the British Film Institute, London.

precisely by leaving mother behind, the female must 'become' her own mother through the process of identification, in order to attain access to subjectivity, albeit precisely a subjectivity characterized according to orthodoxy as perpetually incomplete and in the grip of regression. Mary Ann Doane has gone so far as to claim that the loss of subjectivity in the paranoid state, the place where meaning collapses, 'characterized by the foreclosure of the paternal signifier' (Doane 1988: 144), while identified as 'perversion' in the male, and a residue of unresolved feminine identification, is therefore in essence the very condition of the female, who can only endlessly erase herself.

To confine consideration of the problematic nature of such a claim to the text of *Maschera*, why does this version of mother-daughter relations cause such fear in the male that it has to be represented as something monstrous? And how might an actual female spectator respond to the spectacle of such a dyadic relation, particularly when it is placed in the context of witchcraft? If, as has been claimed, the climactic encounter in the classic horror text is always between the heroine and the monster, patriarchy's two freaks mirroring one another (Williams 1984: 87), then what can such a confrontation mean when the figure designated as the monstrous is the heroine's double, her other self, her-self?

Hélène Cixous provides a witty answer to the last question by asking rhetorically, who, surprised and horrified by the fantastic tumult of her drives (for she was made to believe that a well-adjusted woman has a . . . divine composure), hasn't accused herself of being a monster?

(Cixous 1981: 246)

The political/erotic celebration of witches and witchcraft by certain women writers, Cixous among them, in terms of the potentially explosive consequences that the return of patriarchy's ultimate repressed outlaw could have, points a way to read Asa and what she represents differently, to read from what Teresa de Lauretis calls 'an elsewhere of vision' (de Lauretis 1984: 83).

For Asa is literally an explosive force: in the self-propelled blowing open of her tomb she gives birth to herself. She is also a deflecting force, reducing reason and scientific knowledge to ineffectuality. The symbolic father-son pair of doctors, an all-male substitute for the more usual heterosexual couple, never reach their destination. The staple of the horror movie, the broken axle-wheel/projector that halts one narrative and begins another, initiates a complete turning away for them.

They leave the road that keeps them in the world of men and are drawn towards the being whom the prehistoric narrative of the prologue supposedly repressed for ever, as they are lured into the space of the feminine, the internal labyrinth of the castle, in which all hidden passageways lead ultimately to only one destination, Asa's tomb. The castle is the House of Incest that Raymond Durgnat perceived as the key locale of Italian horror, the decaying Gothic halls in which a return to archaic states preceding the Oedipal can be acted out (Durgnat 1968: 28).

One of the chief attributes of witches, the power to 'call', is linked to the even greater power of the primal, parthenogenetic mother, when Asa summons her dead lover back to life, 'Rise, Javutich. Javutich, Rise!' The answering scene, in which he fights his way out of the erupting earth, his hands appearing covered with a web of mucus, is an obvious mimesis of birth. The fact that he is thus symbolically placed as her son as well as her lover and exists only to serve her and carry out all her wishes ensures that he does not fulfil the safeguard role common to witch and female vampire films, the male control from whom the supposed protagonist actually receives her desires and the permission to enact them. (This is entirely consistent with the general disempowering of the male figures in the film, with the exception of the priest, the one untainted by desire.)

It is this dual son/lover position that represents and exposes even more within the film the threat of incest and its alliance with death for the male. When he speaks rapturously to Asa of how they will live again, there is an immediate cut to a close-up of Dr Kruvajan, who, having 'known' Asa, has now become, as she proclaimed he would, 'dead to man'. As incest is entirely constructed by the film as desire for the maternal, the text has to go to the most extraordinary lengths to disavow the symbolically very obvious threat to Katia from her risen father. When she addresses him by that name, he responds, 'I am no longer your father. The spirits of evil have rent that tie between us for ever'. This seems so manipulatively unconvincing that only the narrative as a whole can explain it; his attack on her is prevented and she is immediately abducted to the tomb where Asa is awaiting her. What Katia has to be saved from is being transfixed for ever as a daughter of the mother, not the father.

What is striking about *Maschera* is how completely it inhabits the realm of the uncanny. The text deploys virtually all the signifiers that Freud identifies as hallmarks of that ambiguous area, at once linguistically 'homely' and 'unhomely'. The threat of violence to the eye is central to the text, as is its converse, Asa's burning, penetrating gaze, the stare that petrifies. Uncertainty as to whether a body is animate or inanimate is exemplified both by Asa's half-revived state and by the question of whether her portrait is 'alive' and has altered or not. Moreover, the entire narrative is predicated on the phenomenon of the double, in the form of Asa/Katia's dual being.

The eeriness of the uncanny has to do with that which 'ought to have remained secret and hidden but has come to light' (Freud 1985: 345). Its apogee is the return of the sexualized body of the mother from repression, in the spectre of the female genitals, the point of entry to where the subject was before, the womb, the first home. Even outside the regime of neurosis, the gaping genitals are therefore always seen as uncanny to some extent, always taboo, the signifier of danger of castration and death.

But why should this need exist to render the revealed mother as the other face of death? The petrifying gaze in the list of uncanny attributes recalls something else that Freud mused over – Medusa's head, which man cannot look upon and live. Yet he turns to stone, becomes 'stiff' (Freud 1964: 273). What threatens castration and death also arouses. Of this, Cixous mocks,

> men say that there are two unrepresentable things: death and the feminine sex. That's because they need femininity to be associated with death: it's the jitters that give them a hard-on!
>
> (Cixous 1981: 255).

There is no doubt that Steele was constructed as a Medusa by her devotees: the favoured French adjective for her hair was *vivante*, evoking the snakes. The American poster for *Maschera* consisted of a drawing of her face, from which her hair undulates out in non-naturalistic 'serpentine' ripples, and the publicity slogan first invites the audience to 'Stare into these eyes', and then promises that the film will '*paralyse* you with fright!' (my emphasis). The extreme close-ups of the landscape of her face, the slant of her cheekbones, her eyes, sometimes looking into the camera, her parted mouth and teeth in *Maschera*, turn it into an abstraction. The camera seems to go in so close because it wants to become an X-ray, to reach the skull beneath the skin. In later films her long thick hair was increasingly styled so that it fell over her cheekbones and cut out, as it were, the shape of a living skull from the planes of her face. In the two films she made for Antonio Margheriti, *I lunghi capelli della morte* and *La danza macabra (Castle of Blood*,[7] 1964), she plays a woman who is dead. This is revealed to the male protagonist after he has had sexual relations with her. In *Lunghi capelli* the man is trapped between her materialized image as a ghost which is flawlessly beautiful, dressed in white brocade and her hair threaded with pearls, and her actual mouldering, worm-ridden corpse in its tomb.

It is very clear in such scenarios that if the desire for refusion with the primal mother is a nostalgic longing for 'home' in the uncanny sense, a place the (male) subject has by definition irretrievably left behind, then it can only be represented as a drive journeying forward to the sole other undifferentiated state – death. (The central paradox of the vampire myth depends on this – to have conquered death, the ultimate affront to subjectivity, to have re-entered a state of pure, absolute desire, signified by primal orality, one must actually be dead.) The only adequate explanation for the necrophiliac responses to Steele's image, and the construction of that image itself as it developed, is contained in this syndrome. The following rhapsody could hardly be clearer: 'Beneath the flowing robe of this young woman with so beautiful a countenance there appear, distinctly, the tatters of a skeleton. Is she any the less desirable?' (Jean-Paul Torok quoted in Durgnat 1967: 148). (That such a profoundly masochistic response is summoned up by an image embedded in horror texts is suggestive, for the entire body of such texts is always an invitation to masochistic conversion: from the spectacle of the unpleasing, the frightening, comes pleasure. The taboo nature of the desires involved in this form of spectatorship makes it a limit case and may be a partial explanation of the marginalization of the genre.)

However, suppose the female viewer left the main road of male Oedipal subjectivity and found wandering off into the labyrinthine byways of female desire more interesting? What would she discover about the desire of the woman, who, according to Mary Ann Doane, is permanently endangered by the regressive pull of the maternal and whose subjectivity is literally in the dark? Asa's great triumphant speech over the unconscious Katia is certainly intended as the climactic point of the 'monstrous' in the text, as it gives expression to this pull:

'You did not know that you were born for this moment. . . . But you sensed it, didn't you? That's why my portrait was a constant temptation to you. You felt that your life and your body were mine. You felt like me because you were destined to *become* me. The love that young man had for you could have saved you, do you know that? You might have been happy together, but *I* was stronger.'

Regression, narcissim and lesbianism all merge together here. The priest's description of how Asa's resurrection can only come about through 'possessing and entering the body of another young woman' does not leave the sexuality in doubt and *Maschera* is listed by Bonnie Zimmerman, along with *I vampiri* and *La danza macabra*, as an early example of the lesbian vampire movie in her article on the subject (Zimmerman 1981: 23). From this threat Katia is saved only by the father's mark, the cross, which will protect and reclaim her and prevent her from being arrested for ever as a victim of maternal incorporation, the fate she must be rescued from and wrenched instead into heterosexual subjectivity. Katia felt herself forbidden to respond to Andrei's very obvious feelings by 'a sense of terror, a present-iment of death, of being destroyed by something that's inside me'.

Yet this demonic maternal figure, however constructed by male cultural fantasies as the monstrous, something vengeful and rapacious, still signifies the disruptive possibilities of autonomous female desire and a desire between women. Even Katia felt it: Asa's portrait was after all a 'temp-tation'. And, more specifically, she signifies the desire of the mother herself in all her original power and completeness. When Asa and Katia do finally fuse, enabling Asa, however temporarily, to regain her life completely, a transformation takes place. Asa's 'marks' heal, close up, her face no longer bears visible wounds but becomes whole. The insignia of castration have vanished away.

For the mask that pierced and wounded her was literally put on by men, the figures of the Inquisition. At one point in the text their mask functions as an actual fetish; found in the graveyard, it becomes the part that stands in for the whole, but the whole is the body of Javutich, who tore it off, but whose wounds never heal. However unwittingly, this betrays that castration is a term circulated entirely between men, that 'woman' is absolutely outside its regime but forcibly marked by it through patriarchal institutions as a defence against the knowledge that in her original pleni-tude she constitutes both a lost paradise and a threat to the myth that it is the male who is the 'whole' subject, a myth shored up precisely by fetishism and the construction of sexual difference after the inevitable entry into the Oedipal order, with all the losses that gendered subjectivity entails.

For the horrible – the truly horrible – fact of sexual difference is the repressed knowledge that the mother is the uncastrated, not the site of lack but of too much body. The primal mother, for women, need not at all be the shadow that threatens annihilation but Cixous's mother, 'who makes everything alright, who nourishes, and who stands up against separation; a force that will not be cut off but will knock the wind out of the codes' (Cixous 1981: 252). And as for castration: 'Let others toy with it.

160

What's a desire originating from a lack? A pretty meagre desire' (ibid.: 262).

Asa had so much desire, so much body, that the Inquisition ordered its complete disintegration, that it should be consumed to ashes. When this finally takes place, she consumes the text along with her, bringing it to an end as the screen becomes a wall of flame – this body, which should have remained hidden but insisted on becoming visible, is, in more than one sense, burning up.

NOTES

1 The archaic mother is a transposition of the pre-Oedipal mother to the status of a mythic, archetypal force, but an ambivalent force with the power to consume as well as to nourish. The dyadic relation of the pre-Oedipal, where subject boundaries have not yet been established and are instead literally characterized by fluidity and absorption, in the form of primal orality, is crucial to the vampire myth. For a brilliant discussion of the deployment of these fantasies in horror fiction, see Hodges and Doane (1991).
2 Literally, 'Six women for the killer.'
3 Also known as *The Devil's Commandment* (US), *Lust of the Vampire* (GB).
4 Literally, 'The battle of Marathon'.
5 Also known as *Black Sunday* (US), *Revenge of the Vampire* (GB).
6 Literally, 'Five graves for a medium'.
7 Literally, 'Dance macabre'.

REFERENCES

Beck, Calvin Thomas (1978) *Scream Queens: Heroines of the Horrors*, New York: Collier Books.
Carter, Angela (1982) *Nothing Sacred: Selected Writings*, London: Virago.
Cixous, Hélène (1981) 'The laugh of the Medusa', in Elaine Marks and Isabelle de Courtivron (eds) (1981) *New French Feminisms*, Massachusetts: Harvester.
Crawley, Tony (1983) 'Interview with Barbara Steele', *Halls of Horror* 3(2): 40–4.
Dadoun, Roger (1989) 'Fetishism in the horror film' in James Donald (ed.) *Fantasy and the Cinema*, London: British Film Institute.
de Lauretis, Teresa (1984) *Alice Doesn't: Feminism, Semiotics, Cinema*, London: Macmillan.
Doane, Mary Ann (1988) *The Desire to Desire: The Woman's Film of the 1940's*, London: Macmillan.
Durgnat, Raymond (1967) *Films and Feelings*, London: Faber & Faber.
—— (1968) 'The Long Hair of Death', *Films and Filming* 14(7): 28.
—— (1970) *A Mirror for England*, London: Faber & Faber.
Freud, Sigmund (1964) 'Medusa's head', *Complete Psychological Works*, vol. XVIII, London, Hogarth Press.
—— (1985) 'The uncanny', in Albert Dickson (ed.) *The Pelican Freud Library*, vol. 14, *Art and Literature*, Harmondsworth: Penguin.
Hardy, Phil (ed.) (1985) *The Aurum Film Encyclopedia*, vol. 3, *Horror*, London: Aurum Press.
Hodges, Devon and Doane, Janice L. (1991) 'Undoing feminism in Anne Rice's

Vampire Chronicles', in James Naremore and Patrick Branlinger (eds), Bloomington: Indiana University Press.

Hogan, David J. (1986) *Dark Romance: Sex and Death in the Horror Film*, Jefferson, NC: McFarland & Co.

Hughes-Hallett; Lucy (1990) *Cleopatra; Histories, Dreams and Distortions*, London: Bloomsbury.

Lephrohon, Pierre (1972) *The Italian Cinema*, London: Secker & Warburg.

Lucas, Tim (1985) 'Bava's terrors', *Fangoria* 43: 30–4, 64.

McGee, Mark Thomas (1984) *Fast and Furious; The Story of American International Pictures*, Jefferson, NC: McFarland & Co.

Nicholls, Peter (1984) *Fantastic Cinema; An Illustrated Survey*, London: Ebury Press.

Shipman, David (1985) *Caught in the Act; Sex and Eroticism in the Movies*, London: Elm Tree Books/Hamish Hamilton Ltd.

Warren, Bill (1991) 'Princess of Darkness', *Fangoria*, 102: 15–19, 68.

White, Patricia (1987) 'Madame X of the China Seas', *Screen* 28(4): 80–95.

Williams Linda (1984) 'When the woman looks', in Mary Ann Doane, Patricia Mellencamp and Linda Williams (eds) (1984) *Re-Vision*, Los Angeles: American Film Institute.

Zimmerman, Bonnie (1981) 'Daughters of darkness: lesbian vampires', *Jump Cut* 24/25: 23–4.

12

POPULAR TASTE

The peplum

Michèle Lagny

What I propose to discuss here is the extent to which one may gain an idea of 'popular taste' from a certain cinematic genre, the peplum,[1] which is regarded as 'mass entertainment' both because of the large audiences it draws and because of the contempt in which it is held by most film historians and critics. For it is a fact that although sociological research has been done on this subject it is very hard to ascertain what sort of reception such films get in social milieux which do not habitually express themselves, or at least leave few detectable traces of their opinions, and what 'cultural uses' spectators make of them. I shall start by postulating that it may be possible to gain some idea of that reception by analysing the films' recurring themes and formal mannerisms.

Taken in the broadest sense of 'mythico-historical spectaculars', peplums started as a genre in the very early Italian cinema and were soon adopted by Hollywood. There were two golden ages of the peplum, the first during the silent period, and the second from the late 1940s to early 1960s, at which point the genre fell out of fashion. A measure of its success is the way films of the same type were made again and again over a period of years: mass production of this kind is justified only when attendances generate healthy profits (and it ceases as soon as profits fall off). They were pre-prepared commodities of the 'international cuisine' type: outside Hollywood – that is to say in Cinecittà – and during the post-war period in particular, the considerable budgets of such films (even with minor actors and corner-cutting during shooting) meant that their distribution base needed to be broadened. As a result they were mostly coproductions with backing from various sources.

Qualitatively, the peplum is a minor genre which caters for rather uneducated audiences and does not appeal to 'sophisticated' filmgoers (with the exception of a few wayward enthusiasts); and film critics tend either to dismiss the genre with mild sarcasm or to lambast it for being ideologically unsound.

Any attempt to ascertain the way in which peplums are understood or culturally used is all the more interesting because elements of a learned

163

culture, the classical humanities, feature in them. Moreover, audiences seeing peplums of the second golden age (those dating from the silent period are now more or less forgotten, except by historians of the early cinema) cannot be described as homogeneous either geographically (the same blockbusters were seen more or less simultaneously in Europe and in the United States) or temporally (peplums are enjoying a second lease of life, as they are now being shown again on certain television channels and are available on video). Their success with non-contemporary social groups may have to do with an anthropological conception of a popular ethos rather than a sociological one.

In order to get to grips with the problem as precisely as possible, I shall suggest a 'qualitative snapshot' by establishing an analytical grid based on a single film; then I shall attempt to project that grid on to other films of the same period, so as to check its relevance and draw broader conclusions.

LA BATTAGLIA DI MARATONA

La Battaglia di Maratona (*The Giant of Marathon*, Italy) was shot in 1959 and came out in 1960. It was a Franco-Italian coproduction involving four companies, Titanus and Galatea in Rome, and Lux Film and La Lyre in Paris. There were two directors, the French-born but Hollywood-bred Jacques Tourneur, and the Italian Mario Bava, who had already worked as a director of photography on successful peplums by Pietro Francisci. The actors, like the technicians, were a mixture of nationalities: American (Steve Reeves in the starring role), French (Mylène Demongeot) and Italian (Sergio Fantoni as a traitor). The film was a commercial success: according to the film historian Gian-Piero Brunetta, it made over 500 million lire in Italy alone (Brunetta 1982: 499–505).

Simple themes

The glorification of sport is obviously the best theme to examine first, as the film opens with it: the hero Philippides wins a series of Olympic Games contests, and it is in that capacity that he is granted 'the freedom of the city' and appointed chief of the Sacred Guard. Sport is the triumph of strength; but strength should be used only in the service of one's country (Philippides dedicates his laurels to Athena, the protectress of his city), whether in gratuitous competition or in defence of the nation (this is emphasized more than once by the dialogue). Sport also carries the notion of fair play, of distributive justice: Philippides recognizes the worth of his defeated rival, Eurus, who becomes his most reliable supporter in Sparta.

There is glorification of the people, too, and of their wisdom. Philippides comes from a peasant background, and in the very first sequence reminds

Plate 21 The glorification of sport: Steve Reeves (centre left) in *La Battaglia di Maratona*. By courtesy of the National Film Archive, London.

a city politician that intelligence is dangerous and difficult to handle (the smooth-talking politician naturally turns out to be a traitor). As a man of the people, he is capable of recognizing that the simple life involves both burdens ('I have my worries and my regrets here', he tells his friend Miltiades, who goes to see him at his rural retreat) and joys ('Bring me some good wine!'). But although a peasant he also knows how to think and talk: because he is honest and sincere, he wins the trust of the people and convinces the Spartans to come to the help of the Athenians, despite their past antagonism.

Finally, there is glorification of virility, which, combining wisdom and strength, nevertheless recognizes the primacy of love. This is the only point at which the feminine appears in the film. We find it in the docile yet provocative purity and grace displayed by the beautiful Andromeda, who disobeys her much-loved father, Creus, only because he is weak and allows himself to be led astray. We also find it in the seemingly perverse yet maternal seductiveness of the courtesan Charis, who has been told by the evil Theocritus to betray Philippides. She falls in love with him instead and ends up sacrificing herself, not only for him but for the Athenians as a whole, in other words all the Greeks, and even in the name of freedom!

Philippides has allies not only in women, who are close to nature despite

165

Plate 22 The glorification of virility and the primacy of love: Mylène Demongeot and Steve Reeves (right) in *La Battaglia di Maratona*

the danger into which they can be led by their desire to seduce, their make-up and their finery (we are treated to a scene where Charis is massaged and dressed), but in animals as well. His horse is like an extension of his own body when he is riding fast; it is prepared to risk its own life if necessary (while swimming across a turbulent river), and it even pokes fun at him (Philippides' white charger stamps its foot ironically as he dreamily takes his leave of the pretty Andromeda). The composition of the shots, too, often stresses the close relationship between the hero and trees, the sky and the earth.

In short, we are given an idyllic view of a man of the people, who tends to prefer the country but is not hostile to the city, as long as it is his polis, a place where civilian life is organized. He believes in a pure and chaste form of love that leads to a 'well-matched' marriage, while the sinning woman redeems herself by her self-sacrifice.

Politicians, on the other hand, are shown either in a poor light (the elegant traitor, Theocritus, with his delicate grey draped tunic) or as weaklings who are easily taken in by fine talk (Andromeda's father Creus) or unreliable oracles (the Spartan council); the best of them (Miltiades) is powerless without the support of the people.

An instructive film

The thematic simplicity of the film is combined with an instructive function. It states its message from the start: a superimposed rolling title at the end of the credits stresses the aim of the hero's struggle: to defend 'intelligence and freedom against despotism and brute force'. It is a lesson on the role of the citizen in the city and on the need to defend democracy against all attempts to introduce a dictatorship, and to protect the fatherland from foreign invaders whose power is based on strength alone.[2] It would be easy to examine the various possible ways in which that message may have been interpreted in 1959–60, but the main point at issue here is that the film derives its message from history.

We are in the domain of 'learned culture'. It is necessary, at the risk of sounding pedantic, to appraise the image of the battle of Marathon offered by the film, compared with that pieced together by historiography. Even when one is relying only on rather hazy memories from school, it does seem rather peculiar that in addition to the land battle there is a sea engagement so spectacular that it is the climax of the film. A *Cahiers du cinéma* critic rightly saw it as 'a conflation of the battles of Marathon and Salamis'. Moreover, the hero turns into a rather odd 'Marathon runner' to say the least: instead of announcing a victory and breathing his last, he simply carries out a liaison mission. Research by Claude Aziza and Michel Eloy has shown just how erroneous the representation of the battle is and how blatant its anachronisms are.[3] Leaving aside archaeological

167

details and various implausibilities in the technical and chronological organization of the fighting, it is easy to see what the film sets out to do: it condenses, displaces, and creates an epic dimension. By locating the model (and problems) of democracy in ancient Greece, it supports the idea that democracy is rooted in a European time and space. Aziza rightly points out that the screen writing techniques of the peplum are not all that different from the practices of traditional history writing, where successive additions and condensations are often made in the interests of pointing a 'moral'.[4]

Efficient narrative organization in a repetitive system

La Battaglia di Maratona divides into two parts: the first is devoted to the hero's disappointments as his honesty is thwarted by political scheming, and the second to a description of two battles (in theory the battles of Marathon and Phaleron) with Philippides' dash from Marathon to Athens slotted in between. The narration relies on a clear differentiation between sequences (indicated by fade-outs) and on the establishment of conventional situations. Its relatively simple organization combines a structure of contrasts and a linear chronological continuity. Let us see how it works at the very beginning of the film.

After the hero is introduced (during the credit titles), three sequences provide the elements necessary for the narrative to get under way: (1) the situation: the popularity of the winner of the Olympic Games causes jealousy (on the part of the traitor Theocritus) and puzzlement (on the part of one of the archons, Creus); (2) the prizes at stake: a pure young woman (Creus' daughter Andromeda, who is betrothed to Theocritus) and the rule of Athens (Theocritus is on the side of the exiled tyrant Hippias); (3) the meeting of Andromeda and Philippides, which radically changes the situation. Everything is there: the initial order (Athenian democracy welcoming the wise victor), the threat (Theocritus' ambitions), and the object of the quest (the young woman, whose threatened freedom symbolizes the fragility of Athenian democracy).

Antagonism between the good and bad guys is indicated not only by their discourse (the wise man offers his wreath – and his strength – to Athena; the traitor dreams of subjugating the city and the young woman) but also by their relationship to space: the good guys are shown in the open (in the stadium, in front of the temple, then in the sun-drenched countryside), while the plotters operate in the shadows (in Creus' house). The film subsequently specifies the nature of the conflict and the logic that governs the way the narrative unfolds. Just to make sure no one gets it wrong in the course of the various developments that mark the narrative, the good guy's horse is white, just as Andromeda is blonde, and the bad guy's is black, just as the courtesan Charis, through whom an attempt is made to corrupt Philippides, is dark-haired. Philippides wins the first contest (a sporting one) but loses the next (which is political and amorous) to Theocritus, who persuades Philippides that Andromeda is party to a plot against democracy and not in love with him as he thinks. He is so discouraged he abandons both Andromeda and Athens. Only a major development can now crank the narrative into action again, and it comes with the announcement that the Persians have landed. The straightforward opposition between the traitor and the hero is now paralleled by the opposition between the enemy and the defender of a country that stands for freedom. This triggers off another series of contests (two battles and Philippides' 'marathon' to Athens that comes between them), from which the good guy eventually emerges victorious.

The structural characteristics of the narrative described above are reminiscent of those of the fairy-tale. They have the same kind of effectiveness, while at the same time relying on contrasts with a didactic function. It is true, however, that not all the elements of that structure are easy to spot at a first viewing of the film, because of the imbalances caused by the spectacular developments which I shall discuss later. These developments are often lengthy, and sometimes cause the spectator to lose the thread of the story. Fortunately, certain indicators regularly remind us of the situation and suggest what may happen next. The credit titles themselves function as a system of foretokens: the first images show successively the arrival of a swimmer, a stone-throwing exercise, a hand-to-hand combat between two men, men running, and finally the triumph of the victor: this is obviously an elliptical description of the Olympic Games, but it also anticipates the main episodes of the film (the importance of the hand-to-hand fighting scenes, and above all the evocation of the 'Marathon runner' and the underwater fight).

The recurrence of musical themes associated with characters or typical situations is a simple method of recognition used so often that there is hardly any point in lingering on it, except to stress the mediocrity of the musical score. Finally, some identical shots are used more than once. They are very frequent in the two battle scenes (for example, the shot of the Persians striking the enormous drum which summons them to battle), but also play a role in the first part of the film. The most obvious repetition is a wide-angle general shot centred on the temple and 'representing' the city. It has to be admitted that the main purpose of such shots was probably to save money during shooting, but that does not preclude a wish on the part of the directors to let spectators find their bearings again, in case they have been thrown by the film's *longueurs*.

169

The *mise-en-spectacle*

While the film has didactic ambitions, as we have seen, it aims above all to appeal to the public. The simplicity of its themes and the efficiency of its narrative structure help audiences to enjoy it as they would a fairy-tale. Also instrumental in this is its *mise-en-scène* of performances, or *mise-en-spectacle*.

Performances can be organized within the film itself (in this case, there is the evening's entertainment of dancing and all-in wrestling which the courtesan offers the hero). But above all it is the events themselves which, because of the exaggerated way they are treated, become an excuse for major 'attractions': the whole of the second half of the film, which is justifiable from a narrative point of view (the Greeks defend themselves against the Persian attack, first on land at Marathon, then under the sea near the Piraeus), is in fact constructed like a series of spectacles. The submarine battle in particular is irresistibly reminiscent of the water ballet in *The Black Pirate* (US 1926): men of the Sacred Guard, dressed in elegant white loincloths, move about gracefully despite the spears which transfix them, causing red clouds of blood to swirl prettily in the blue water.

The most striking recurring feature is the way the male body is valorized: the credits begin with a shot of Steve Reeves's impressively muscular torso, which fills the whole screen diagonally as he hurls a spear into the sky (shot 2); it then lands, to applause from the spectators (shot 3). A whole series of shots of Philippides running from Marathon to the Piraeus have the same exhibitive function, as do the very many long-drawn-out scenes of hand-to-hand fighting. Here, the lingering on the grappling bodies is enhanced by the costumes (the men wear short fluttering skirts), the composition (close-ups), and the quick cutting which has the effect of making the brawling balletic.

The *mise-en-spectacle* is further accentuated by the technical resources available, Eastmancolor and Dyaliscope (an Italian wide-screen process). The composition and editing also serve a specific purpose: they are used not to make cuts from one shot to another imperceptible, as they are in the classical cinema of transparency, but on the contrary to make them stand out. Violently contrasting images succeed each other, with close-ups or close shots alternating with general shots. Through these visual effects, which are generally underscored by superfluous music, the film succeeds in increasing the emotional, almost instinctive simplicity of its narrative structure.

An 'exemplary' peplum?

Many of the features described in this brief analysis are to be found in peplums in general. Drawing on a few examples, I propose to identify those that are most frequent and to pinpoint their function.

Eros' biceps

One of the dominant themes of the genre is that of virile strength. As we have already seen, it is sometimes valorized as a sporting asset (sport is an important activity accessible to the working class). But it is often defensive: Hercules, the favourite hero of Italian peplums, fights, like Philippides, only when it is strictly necessary or unavoidable (for example, he postpones as long as possible the fight with Antaeus at the beginning of *Ercole e la regina di Lidia* (*Hercules Unchained*, Italy 1958).

In any case, Eros fares better in peplums with masculine attributes. True, they feature brutish, unwholesome louts (like Theocritus' henchmen, or Antaeus, who is played by ex-boxer Primo Carnera, at the beginning of *Ercole e la regina di Lidia*), and the good guy is not always sexy. Hercules can sometimes look a bit of a wimp, as in *Ercole e la regina di Lidia* or at the beginning of *Ercole alla conquista di Atlantide* (*Hercules Conquers Atlantis*,[5] Italy 1961). Maciste, one of his Italian cousins (who first appears in Italian silent films), is a nice enough guy but rarely pretty. Yet directors patently linger on their actors' physique, often highlighting it by drawing a parallel with statues (as, for example, in the fourth shot behind the credit titles of *La battaglia*, where Steve Reeves is flanked by two superb male nudes as he emerges from a pool). There is a connection between this emphasis on 'biceps appeal' and the vogue for body-building: Reeves, who had already starred in two films by Francisci – *Le Fatiche di Ercole* (*Hercules*, Italy 1957) and *Ercole e la regina di Lidia* – was a former Mr Muscle and Mr Universe. A man once described as 'the sexiest Apollo in the world', Reeves turned down the chance to star in the next Hercules film, as he did not want to become type-cast. But he was replaced by other musclemen like Mark Forest, who was endowed with 'a very beautiful physique, where each muscle is finely chiselled', in *La Vendetta di Ercole* (*The Revenge of Hercules*,[6] Italy 1960), Reg Park in *Ercole alla conquista di Atlantide*, and Mickey Hargitay in *Gli Amori di Ercole* (*The Loves of Hercules*, Italy 1960) (Aziza and Eloy 1986: 81–7). While not ruling out elegance and sometimes even a certain sartorial affectation, physical strength has a powerful erotic function, which is exploited in the scenes of (very) close combat, where the sexual component of two clinching men is clearly emphasized. Is this done to appeal to women spectators? Or, under the cloak of ancient customs, is it a way of alluding to the delights of censured homosexuality? Another feature of peplums is their love of violence, which very often results in fairly sadistic

171

scenes. Some such scenes serve to characterize the bad guy – for example Theocritus' brutality in *La Battaglia di Maratona*, as when he kills one of his henchmen or ties the poor Andromeda to the prow of a fighting ship. Other such scenes, however, are gratuitous: the overemphasis on the impaled bodies during the naval battle has been seen by critics as the hallmark of Mario Bava, who was to make his name chiefly as a director of horror films. In fact it turns out that there are similar scenes of brutality or torture in almost all peplums, but the results of maltreatment are not emphasized (there is usually a discreet cut away from the battered bodies). Although in the case of sadism, homosexuality and possibly even sex in general (which is treated with great modesty despite the quantity, and sometimes quality, of alluring women in such films), everything is left to suggestion (censorship was strict at the time), excessive violence probably has a cathartic function anyway. Indeed, Domenico Paolella, himself a filmmaker, has even described the peplum as 'the poor man's psychoanalysis'. In more down-to-earth language, it could be called a way of working off one's pent-up feelings.

From (grand) spectacle to cultural tradition

Spectacle, which is often based on eroticism and violence (to wit the Greek dancing woman and wrestlers laid on by Charis to stimulate Philippides), and is a compulsory thematic element of peplums, has a cathartic function too. One of the rules of the genre, like its pompous décors which do not always respect historical accuracy, is that it treats us to scenes of ancient Greek festivity and merry-making in all their barbarian splendour (which varies depending on the film's budget). It is one way of providing modern audiences with 'bread and circuses' at a relatively low cost. It is even quite frequent for there to be a seemingly unending series of dances, feasts, fights in the arena, chariot races and victory parades. An exhibition of sporting prowess, like the one summarized during the credits of *La Battaglia*, is a common feature. There is often a titillating sadistic element in the countless circus scenes to be found in such films, where gladiators are subjected to the brutal whims of the spectators.

My remarks about the way spectacle is organized in *La Battaglia di Maratona* are systematically valid for peplums as a whole. Major events, and notably battles, are included only because of the *mise-en-scène* they authorize. The *mise-en-scène* is concerned not just with organizing movements within general shots, but with the orientation of the spectator's gaze: repeated cross-cutting emphasizes the 'live circus' feel of battles, which is often further underlined by shots of one or other of the military leaders watching the fighting and predicting its outcome (as Miltiades does during the battle of Marathon). The same is true of violent and contrasting editing effects. Of the countless examples that occur, let me mention only the spectacular juxtaposition of a close-up of Mickey Hargitay's pectorals with a wide-angle shot of Deianira's city in *Gli Amori di Ercole*: contrast and contiguity make the muscles of the torso look as spectacular as the group of buildings with which they are equated.

The technical and aesthetic quality of filmed spectacles depended on the studios' choreographical potential, just as the scale of the parades was governed by the film's budget. In this respect, American blockbusters are more effective (for example, Rita Hayworth's dance in *Salome* (US 1953), the chariot race in *Ben Hur* (US 1960), or the Roman triumph in *Cleopatra* (US 1963)), whereas the standard of spectacles in Italian peplums sometimes leaves much to be desired, and the anatomy of both male and female extras is often more interesting than their rather feeble performance – as in the dance in *La regina delle Amazzoni* (*Queen of the Amazons*, Italy 1960).

On the other hand, Italian peplum directors often seem to be offering us 'a feast for the eyes', in the form of tableaux which rely on compositional devices, colour relationships (reds and greens, yellows and blues), back-lighting and *sfumato* effects which are all common features of pompier paintings. An example of this in *La Battaglia di Maratona* is the shot of Philippides ploughing, with his 'great white oxen'[7] on the left, which evokes the kind of landscape painting where a Graeco-Roman scene might be set against a 'naturalistic' background (reproductions of such landscapes are very common, especially in the form of colour prints which decorate the walls of working-class homes). This kind of device is very obvious in films by Francisci (who was trained as a painter); and certain movies, such as Giacomo Gentilomo's *Brenno, il nemico di Roma* (*Brennus, Enemy of Rome*, Italy 1963), are masterpieces of the genre, almost like a compendium of the Musée d'Orsay.

The references are not purely pictorial. True, all films reuse material from various sources, but peplums are full-blown cultural patchworks. The titles, themes and heroes of the 1950s and 1960s were taken from the silent spectaculars, which had already proved highly successful. Above all, the peculiarity of the genre is that it reuses knowledge which is traditionally the preserve of the educated, but which has just as traditionally been popularized by all the arts: ever since the Renaissance, opera and paintings have drawn on themes from the ancient world (Aziza and Eloy 1986: 37–69), which were also exploited in popular nineteenth-century novels with religious overtones like *The Last Days of Pompeii*, *Quo Vadis?* and *Fabiola*. Using the chromo or novel as an intermediary, peplums are another example of how learned culture is reused by popular culture, through what Pierre Bourdieu has called contemporary 'ordinary popularization', which derives its force from references to 'legitimate' culture disseminated in the form of universally accessible 'arrangements' or 'adaptations' (Bourdieu 1979: 371).

173

The lessons of history

The characteristic peculiar to peplums is not so much their choice of historical subjects as their specialization in the ancient world. In this respect, *La Battaglia di Maratona* is far from being typical: the ancient Greeks were not in fact a great favourite with producers, though it is true that the ingredients of *Helen of Troy* (US 1954) and *Alexander the Great* (US 1956) were spectacular enough to interest Hollywood. It was rather the great empires that fascinated them – the Roman empire of course, especially in Italian movies, and the Pharaohs at least as much in the US. The extent to which Hollywood movies were inspired by Egyptian and biblical subjects certainly had something to do with the high proportion of Jewish filmmakers in the United States, and above all with the tradition of reading the scriptures there, while the number of Italian films set in ancient Rome was clearly connected with the historical antecedents of Cinecittà.

As with the choice of theme, the morals drawn from the stories and the treatment of the historiographical referent are appreciably different on either side of the Atlantic. Problems are not perceived in exactly the same way by the Americans and the Italians. The Americans are shocked by the immoderation of virtually totalitarian power, which carries within itself the seeds of its own destruction (Anthony Mann's *The Fall of the Roman Empire* (US 1963)); *raison d'état* may clash with divine considerations (this is very clear in the conflict between Rameses and Moses in *The Ten Commandments* (US 1956) (Lagny 1988: 21–5)); a dictatorial regime, where the power of a single person is based on brute force, is an insult to democracy and to the equal rights that are every person's due. More particularly, the theme of rebelling slaves, whether Hebrew or not, is a very frequent source of inspiration, the most brilliant example being of course Kubrick's *Spartacus* (US 1960). The Italians, on the other hand, often focus on warring brothers and on the internal dissensions that weaken the political structure, as in Sergio Corbucci's *Romolo e Remo* (*Duel of the Titans*, Italy 1961) and Giuseppe Vari's *Roma contro Roma* (*War of the Zombies*, Italy 1963). Indeed, this is a theme found in *La Battaglia di Maratona*, with the conflict between Miltiades and Hippias/Theocritus in Athens itself, and between Sparta and Athens in the context of the whole of Greece. European films are also aware of the danger of invasion by barbarians, whether they come from the west, south or east: in addition to Darius in *La Battaglia di Maratona*, there is *Brenno, il nemico di Roma, Annibale* (*Hannibal*, Italy 1959), and *Attila, flagello di Dio* (*Attila the Hun*, Italy 1954). The lessons of history always carry a political moral, but obsessions are clearly somewhat different on either side of the Atlantic.

This historical lesson is above all a 'popular historical lesson'. I have already pointed out that the way the 'events' of Marathon are transformed results in epic condensation. While this epic tendency, like the heroization of characters, is a constant feature of peplums, it also goes back to a historiographical tradition that is still alive and well in primary school textbooks and illustrated popular history magazines. So we should be concerned not so much with checking the films' factual accuracy as with examining how they maltreat, to a varying degree, the referential material. It would seem that the Americans take a more serious approach and that the Italians are freer in their intepretation. Hollywood peplums sometimes disguise a veritable history 'lesson' behind their visual splendour.[8] This didactic approach is justified by the painstaking work carried out by the studios' teams of researchers, as can sometimes be deduced from the credits (in *The Ten Commandments*, for example, De Mille indicates his sources (Lagny 1988)), whereas those responsible for *La Battaglia di Maratona* admit that they 'interpreted the facts freely' and turned history into epic.

Myths and flights of fancy

Liberties taken with history encourage other flights of fancy, which take us into the domain of ancient, collective fantasies, that is to say the area of myth. *La Battaglia di Maratona* allows itself only a few fantasies in order to heroize its characters. However, we have glimpsed in the persons of Philippides and Charis two fundamental mythical figures who are all the more effective because they function as a couple: the wise and just strong-man, who can turn into a 'good giant', and the *femme fatale*, who can become a man-eater. Many other peplums opt more decisively for the fantastic, for which they give woolly mythological justification. Italian directors were particularly fascinated by Hercules and by the queen of the Amazons.

Although we do not find 'the authentic or primitive version' of the myth, which, as Lévi-Strauss (1958: 240) pointed out, does not in fact exist, these films do contain its academic sources, the attested legends that serve as a point of departure, and its cultural mediations. Michel Eloy has already studied the ancient figure of the 'strongman', Hercules (whose biblical counterpart is Samson, who was exploited by De Mille, or even Goliath) (Aziza and Eloy 1986: 37–69). But the cinema is an ideal terrain for phantasmagoria. Not only are traditional elements of the legend included in various films, but the indefatigable demi-god is sometimes credited with new adventures: we find him fighting Ulysses or the vampires, siding with Samson or Ulysses, consorting with Maciste, Samson, Ursus and so on. He has a human double, 'the strongest man in the world', Maciste, 'the new Hercules', who can take on the most extravagant kinds of enemy – mole men, stone-age men, giants, Mongols.

I shall merely indicate here his difficult relationship with the *femme fatale*, who is at once a powerful queen and a willing slave. She takes on various identities in peplums, some of which are 'historical', such as Semiramis,

Messalina and Theodora. A great favourite is Cleopatra, who ranges in style from the somewhat vulgar Linda Cristal in Vittorio Cottafavi's *Le Legione di Cleopatra* (*Legions of the Nile*, Italy 1960) to the Shakespearean Liz Taylor as directed by Mankiewicz. The reason for this is that this beautiful and formidable queen, who is so venomously undone, perfectly suggests the complex relationship between women and (male) power. As for Hercules, he encounters the female danger in various guises. One of its finest incarnations is the shapely Jayne Mansfield, in *Gli Amori di Ercole*. She plays not only Deianira, the weak queen of Oichalia who is threatened by the wily Lycos, and defended and loved by Hercules, but also Hippolyte, queen of the Amazons, who tries to bewitch Hercules when he is brought to her, unconscious, by her warrior women after his gruelling fight with the Hydra. There could hardly be a clearer enunciation of the theme of the two-faced woman: on the one hand there is the diurnal, reassuring Deianira (who is all the more reassuring because she is the spitting image of Megara, Hercules' wife, whom Lycos kills at the beginning of the film – and who is also played by Mansfield); and on the other there is the nocturnal, dangerous Hippolyte, who rules over a subterranean kingdom and turns her lovers into petrified trees. In this, she closely resembles Antinea in Cottafavi's *Ercole alla conquista di Atlantide*. There, her characterization by Cottafavi is directly inspired by the French novelist Pierre Benoit (author of *L'Atlantide*):[9] not only does she subject her lovers to radiation from the stone of Uranus and turn them into decerebrated albino mutants beneath their Black Guard uniforms, but she proves to be an unworthy mother as well as queen of the night and tries to•kill her daughter Ismene!

In all these cases, (female) Eros and Thanatos are brought together in a nocturnal atmosphere, in the cave, a subterranean or submarine labyrinth. These borrowings from the great fund of mythology (which are very numerous, and which I have made a point of only touching upon) could be manifestations of the 'anthropological structures of the imaginary', the 'archetypes' of Jungian origin which are so dear to Gilbert Durand – and which are often hotly contested (Durand 1984).[10]

Games of derision

But it would be a mistake to take all this too seriously. The often intentional, emphatic extravagance of some peplums, which critics so love to deride, throws new light on to the already formulated remark, with reference to traditional culture, about the 'revisions, excesses and subversions' (Chartier 1986: 175–8) which occur when popular culture takes over certain objects or certain codes; more particularly, there is often a vulgar dimension which weakens the 'archetype'.

The most respectable characters can be ridiculed with impunity. A little humour makes them more approachable, and the 'half serious, half jokey'

Hercules is, in Cottafavi's eyes for example, 'a heroic-cum-comic figure' who is 'obsessed with the idea of having a home, a family and children'. In other words, he is also a man like anyone else, who sometimes has to deal with the lavatory (one of his most unpleasant labours is the cleaning of the Augean stables) (Siarri 1986: 407). Similarly, in contrast with the *femmes fatales* mentioned earlier, the diurnal female figures are colourless or domesticated. In *La Battaglia di Maratona*, Andromeda occasionally takes on a solar dimension (notably when she drives her chariot); but she is very quickly cut down to size by psychological touches which rob her of any aura. The same could be said of all the other 'wives' or 'brides-to-be': there is no room in peplums for courtly love or Wagnerian passion.

The genre in fact has a ludic dimension which is indicated in several ways, and which appears from time to time in *La Battaglia di Maratona* (the rather grotesque character of Creus, the impatience of Philippides' horse). There is a veritable anthology of derisive effects in Vittorio Sala's *La Regina delle Amazzoni* (once again). It opens with a sporting contest (which has nothing to do with the story that follows) set to a jazz soundtrack. The hero, who is lumbered with a caricatural, cowardly double (the Egyptian), lets loose a Tarzan-like cry. We are treated to all the well-worn clichés about role reversal, both male (slaves who do the washing) and female (women warriors who choose their sexual prey). They are accompanied by appropriate comments on the kick the men get out of a task which is after all relatively pleasant in hot weather, and on the sexual frustration of the queen, who is doomed to a life of chastity. Each point is rammed home with occasional inserts of little caricatural animated drawings in strip-cartoon style.

This is clearly the realm of 'big noisy and colourful machines constructed in the vein of strip cartoons for children' referred to by Cottafavi himself (Siarri 1986); in other words, the realm of products which appeal both because one believes in them and because one does not believe in them. This is quite evident from the importance given to the sets and special effects themselves, which I have hardly discussed here, but whose sheer stylishness enhances the stories by lending them a marvellous, 'unbelievable' aura. While they are sometimes very impressive, as dazzling and baroque as great Italian decorative paintings, they are also on occasion slapdash and artificial-looking. Monsters in particular can be quite pathetically unconvincing. That does not stop them being effective, like the feeble Hydra in *Gli Amori di Ercole*: the model is so badly made that the monster looks ill; what is more, it has only three heads. It is hard to say whether this was so for budgetary reasons, or whether its grotesque appearance served to remind audiences that the whole thing was 'play-acting' – unless of course its tricephalism was a conscious or unconscious allusion to the three faces of woman played by Jayne Mansfield (as Megara, Deianira and Hippolyte successively). Let's give the film the benefit of the doubt.

The films I have been discussing, then, contain many contradictory features which, compared with those of other successful productions (and not just film productions), may give some idea of 'popular taste' as seen from the inside (of the texts) and of its possible functions: to allow spectators to reassure themselves while letting off steam, to have fun while educating themselves, and to consume without any risk of indigestion.

Similarly, Richard Hoggart's remark about popular reception being ironical and distant applies here: irony can be detected in the games of derision I have just drawn attention to, while the 'oblique attention' and 'ecliptic approval' which are typical of 'casual consumption' (Passeron 1970: 7–26: Hoggart 1957) are reflected in the various devices that are used to try to maintain the spectators' interest, such as the repetitive structure of the films themselves or the making of series (Hercules films, Maciste films, even Steve Reeves films) with frequent references from one movie to another.[11] The peplum genre, which is based on a 'nudge and wink' system via various cultural mediations, could serve as a basis for a study of the tactics which delineate the 'transformation of the social architecture of knowledge into a multilocation of culture', in Michel de Certeau's words (de Certeau 1974), and for an evaluation of 'the culturally differentiated uses of common materials' which Roger Chartier would like to define (Chartier 1986: 175–8) – irony or second-degree enjoyment among 'educated elites', and diffuse perception, even if the references cannot be formalized, by a working-class public which has been imbued, to a varying degree depending on its nationality, with references to the Bible and the ancient world.

Also evident is the differentiation, within mass culture, of tendencies which can be analysed only in relation to the cultural milieux of production. This is true of the contrast between the very serious big-budget American movies, shot by directors who did not specialize in peplums (including De Mille), and the ironic Italian productions made by specialized filmmakers (some of whom, like Cottafavi, would have liked to break out of the genre) who were thoroughly familiar with traditional culture.

There still remains a major question: why does this or that formula (in this case, the mythical/historical film) go down particularly well with audiences at a given time (1910–20 and 1950–60)? The only productive line of enquiry here would be an external analysis that might suggest how peplums should be seen in the context of 'a whole period's cultural artefacts' by analysing them 'as one of the components of a complex and shifting network of social artefacts constantly interacting with each other' (Revel 1986: 451). But, just as they involve local and maybe sociologically interpretable specificities and differences, peplums prompt another question – that of the permanence of ancestral reserves organized into 'constellations' which can take on varied and historically dated superficial forms. In that case, the products of popular culture should be approached from an anthropological angle, 'by locating them . . . in the obstinate recommencement of human endeavour' (Ariès 1988: 177), in what they reveal in the way of superimpositions, double exposures and 'non-simultaneities' (not to be confused with flashbacks) making up a cultural 'long duration' (*longue durée*) which Fernand Braudel (1958) defined as 'the prison of mentalities'.

Translated from the French by Peter Graham.

Notes

1 Editors' note: We have decided to retain the word 'peplum' (a Latinized version of the Greek *peplos*) used by Michèle Lagny to designate the genre. This is a term with wide critical currency in France, where the genre has received considerable attention. No similar common term has emerged in theory or criticism written in English.

2 The rolling text also indicates that the film is a tribute to Olympic athletes – a topical touch, as the film was released at the time of the Rome Olympics.

3 Aziza and Eloy demonstrate that the temple, symbol of the city, bears no relation with what the Hecatompedon might have been like in 490 BC (what is more, it is placed at the top of Roman-style monumental steps), that the Sacred Guard is an invention, that there were no Olympic Games that year, that Hippias had been expelled from Athens nineteen years earlier, not the previous year, that Athenian hoplites would never have formed themselves into rows protected by large Roman-style quadrangular shields nor would they have used pitfalls, and that the account of the battle has only a vague connection with what actually happened, in so far as that can be established for certain (Claude Aziza and Michel Eloy, *Bulletin de l'Association Régionale des Enseignants de Langues Anciennes de Paris* (ARELAP), Paris, Censier, n.d.

4 While the run from Athens to Sparta embarked on by Philippides (who was well known as a professional messenger in antiquity) is well attested by Herodotus in the fifth century BC and by Pliny the Elder in the first century AD, the Marathon runner was invented by Pliny's contemporary, Plutarch, and the condensation of the two was made a century later by Lucian of Samosata.

5 US: *Hercules and the Captive Women.*

6 US: *Goliath and the Dragon.*

7 The great white ox is a pompier stereotype and symbolizes the peacefulness of rural life.

8 For example, the endless presentation of the chariot race contestants in *Ben Hur* enables Wyler to present a pageant of the Roman empire at its height.

9 For a discussion of this film, of the political and technological interpretations to which it gave rise and of the cinema's treatment of the Atlantis myth, see Claude Aziza and Michel Eloy 'Les interprètes d'Hercule au cinéma' and 'Les avatars d'Hercule de l'antiquité au XIXème siècle', *Hercule: Mythologie – Littérature – Opéra – BD – SF – Cinéma*, September 1986, supplement to *Bulletin de l'ARELAP* 12, Paris, Censier.

10 For the opposing view, see Beckmesser's introduction to G. Durand, *Beaux-Arts et archétypes*, Paris, PUF, 1989, 8–26.

11 In *La Battaglia*, Steve Reeves-Philippides throws the wicker ball out of sight, just as Steve Reeves-Hercules hurls the discus in the palaestra in *Le Fatiche di Ercole*.

179

REFERENCES

Ariès, Philippe (1988) 'L'histoire des mentalités', in Le Goff, J. (ed.) *La Nouvelle Histoire*, Paris: Editions Complexe.

Aziza, Claude and Eloy, Michel (n.d.) *Bulletin de l'Association Régionale des Enseignants de Langues Anciennes de Paris (ARELAP)* (a roneotyped dossier), Paris: Censier.

Aziza, Claude and Eloy, Michel (1986) 'Les interprètes d'Hercule au cinéma' and 'Les avatars d'Hercule de l'antiquité au XIXème siècle', *Hercule: Mythologie – Littérature – Opéra – BD – SF – Cinéma*, September 1986, supplement to *Bulletin de l'ARELAP*, 12, Paris: Censier.

Bourdieu, Pierre (1979) *La Distinction, Critique sociale du jugement*, Paris: Editions de Minuit.

Braudel, Fernand (1958) 'History and the Social Sciences: the *longue durée*', *On History*, London.

Brunetta, Gian-Piero (1982) *Storia del cinema italiano*, vol. 2, *Hollywood sul Tevere: il ritorno di Maciste*, Rome: Editori Riuniti.

Chartier, Roger (1986) 'Culture populaire', in Burguière, A. (ed.) *Dictionnaire des sciences historiques*, Paris: PUF.

de Certeau, Michel (1974) *La Culture au pluriel*, Paris: Gallimard.

Durand, Gilbert (1984) *Les Structures anthropologiques de l'imaginaire*, Paris: Dunod.

Hoggart, Richard (1957) *The Uses of Literacy*, London: Chatto & Windus.

Lagny, Michèle (1988) 'Cecil B. De Mille historien', in Laurent Aknin, Claire Aziza and Claude Aziza (eds) *La Bible au cinéma*, Catalogue of Festival du Film Biblique, Paris: Centre Rachi.

Lévi-Strauss, Claude (1958) *Anthropologie structurale*, Paris: Plon.

Passeron, Jean-Claude (1970) Preface to Richard Hoggart, *La Culture du pauvre* (French translation of *The Uses of Literacy*), Paris: Editions de Minuit.

Revel, Jacques (1986) 'Mentalités', in A. Burguière (ed.) *Dictionnaire des sciences historiques*, Paris: PUF.

Siarri, Nadine (1986) 'Entretien avec Vittorio Cottafavi, Rome, mai 1983', 'L'antiquité latine au cinéma: histoire et histoires dans le péplum romain', unpublished thesis, Université de Provence, Aix-Marseille.

13

NATIONAL ROMANTICISM AND NORWEGIAN SILENT CINEMA

Anne Marit Myrstad

Norwegian films have seldom attracted international praise or attention. Film production in Norway has been unstable, and continued often in spite of, rather than because of, economic and practical conditions. Certain Norwegian films have, however, enjoyed great domestic popularity. The first such group were the rural films from 1920 on. The popularity of these films can be partly explained by many of them having a classic, melodramatic structure but the group also contains vaudeville-inspired comedies. The common denominator of the rural films is their national character. This chapter suggests that the popularity of the films is to a certain extent related to the impact of the nation and will indicate that the national in the texts relates to changing notions of nationalism in the cultural history of Norway.

NATIONAL ROMANTICISM IN NORWAY

The political and ideological complexity of nationalism is strongly represented in Norway in the cultural field. The nation as a concept was ideologically strengthened in the period of romanticism in nineteenth-century Europe. German romanticism developed the idea of the nation as an organism and part of a harmonic, universal structure. This ideology inspired national movements in several countries. The soul of the organism was to be found in the nation's ancient popular poetry, folk music and traditions. This branch of romanticism had a great impact in Norway as late as 1840–50. The discovery of traditions and culture that had survived centuries of Danish rule was a vital inspiration for the Norwegian bourgeoisie in their fight for independence from the Swedish king (Norway had been handed over from Denmark to Sweden in 1814). 'True' Norwegian culture was to be found in farming communities in remote valleys. The farmer and his traditions thus provided the link between the proud past of the Vikings and early Norwegian kings, and the free state to come. The Norwegian farmer had in a European context a position of freedom. With no tradition of serfdom, the Norwegian countryside was inhabited by peasant proprietors and cotters hiring their own piece of land from the bigger farm where they worked. A provision in the Norwegian constitution of 1814 had put an end to the aristocracy. In terms of class distinctions the Norwegian countryside was thus relatively homogenous. The bourgeoisie sought to strengthen their political alliance with the farmers, and developed the myth of the rural district as an idyllic reservoir of the original, Norwegian culture and folk character.

The nationalist impulse also had the effect of arousing the farming population, provoking the beginning of a political opposition towards the bourgeoisie. The linguistic works of a peasant's son, Ivar Aasen, provided the foundation for this radical movement. In 1814 Norway had been under Danish rule for 400 years. This had made Danish the written and official language. As a revolt against this linguistic repression, Ivar Aassen created a written language based on certain 'unspoiled' country dialects. He, and the movement he inspired, held that it was unworthy and disadvantageous for Norwegians to be forced to learn a foreign language at school. Danish was more common among the urban bourgeoisie, and thus the youths from the countryside were left behind in the fight for education and position. As a result of this linguistic controversy, we still have two written languages in Norway: Dano Norwegian or Norwegian, which is the standard language, and then New Norwegian built on Ivar Aasen's work. Two national 'cultures' were thus developing with differing notions in regard to the focal point of national romanticism: the farmer. For analytical purposes we may distinguish a Dano Norwegian, urban upper-class culture nurturing the myth of the countryside as an idyllic reservoir of the past, suitable for recreation, as opposed to a New Norwegian culture fighting for the farmers' share in the prosperity of progress. This radical, rural culture both shared and resisted the bourgeoisie's image of the farmer. To achieve respectability they shared the notion of the farmer as the true human being, but to be politically just it was important to convey the fact that life in the countryside was a hard fight for survival, not idyllic leisure.

From the start the New Norwegian movement revolted against the idyllic myth of the farmer in the literature of writers from the bourgeoisie, and welcomed a rural poetry of greater realism. New Norwegian romantic literature came to differ from the comparable Norwegian or Dano Norwegian literature in portraying the countryside in a less idyllic, more naturalistic and critical way.

The New Norwegian culture still prospered in the first decades of this century. In 1913 the Norwegian Theatre was established as the first professional New Norwegian stage. In the same period conservative notions of the nation seem to have been strengthened. Full sovereignty from Sweden was achieved in 1905 and the radical potential of bourgeois nationalism was thus fulfilled. The first decades of the century also meant the final breakthrough of the working class as an organized, militant, political force. Internal struggle as well as political attacks against this class were in the interwar years often related to the complexity of nationalism. International workers' solidarity on the one hand threatened the bourgeoisie and on the other hand intensified the solidarity between a rural and a recently urbanized working class. The interwar years were a period when the alliances cut across the two national 'cultures'.

The rural silents will be discussed against this background as an ideologically significant and popular group of films displaying the representation of differing, ambiguous notions of the farmer, the countryside and rural tradition.

FILM IN NORWAY

The first decades of the twentieth century were a period of growth, as regards the screening and distribution of film in Norway. The wonders of the screen found a devoted audience here as elsewhere. Throughout the country cinemas were established. Around 1913 the bigger cities would have had from ten to twenty cinemas. If the population of a district was too scattered to make up a regular audience, travelling entertainers would arrange screenings in community houses.[1] The production of Norwegian films, however, never experienced the same growth. Official concern was restricted to questions of morality and censorship, and to the possibilities of channelling the profits from film exhibition into the budgets of the desperately poor state and local authorities. The 1913 law on film censorship established that to run a cinema you had to get a licence from the municipality. This led to an increasing number of officially run cinemas, which today has become Norway's unique municipal cinema system.[2] Private capital was limited. Investors were not interested in film production at a time when cinemas were taken over by the municipalities. The municipalities used the profit from film exhibition to build hospitals, to subsidize the theatre proper and to build art institutions. To illustrate the problem of officially run cinemas, it has been stated that Norwegian film production lies buried under the largest statue in the Gustav Vigeland Sculpture Park in Oslo, a park financed by the profit from film exhibition in the 1920s. (The first state subsidies for film production in Norway were organized by the German occupiers during the Second World War.)

Between 1907 and 1919, eighteen features had reached a limited audience in Norway. These films seem to have taken their strongest inspiration from the popular Danish social melodrama, showing the temptations and dangers of lower-class city life. These Norwegian films did not always get the best of receptions, and were not widely distributed.

The national breakthrough in Norwegian film

Fante-Anne (*Anne, The Tramp*, Norway 1920) is a vital turning point. For the first time in the history of Norwegian feature films the countryside was explored. Of the twenty-nine features produced between 1920 and 1930, only five concerned the city. One of these, a detective story, was set in the streets of Oslo. The other four showed the bourgeoisie in mansions pleasantly distant from the town centre, or on holiday in the mountains. *Fante-Anne* was the first Norwegian film adapted from literature, being based on a novel by the New Norwegian writer, Kristofer Janson, written in 1879. The film was also the first to make use of professional actors and the first to get moral and – to a modest extent – financial support from an official institution, namely the newly established distribution company for the municipal cinemas, Kommunenes Filmsentral A/S. This company welcomed national films for distribution throughout the country and neighbouring Sweden and Denmark. Statistical material from this period is scarce, but available sources confirm that the rural films achieved great popularity. They ranked close to the top in competition with masterpieces by Charlie Chaplin and Cecil B. De Mille. Further investigation into the reception of the films is one vital source for the discussion of this popularity, but this chapter will be restricted to a presentation of different thematic and stylistic traits in the textual representation of national setting and national symbols.

Fante-Anne was apparently a response to what had been going on in Swedish film production in previous years. What we now call 'the golden age' of Swedish film began with *Terje Vigen* (*A Man There Was*, Sweden 1917). In 1919 the Swedish film *Synnøve Solbakken* (the story of a young woman of the same name) had an even greater success in Norway. This led to a vital conflict for the national, cultural milieu of Oslo. These Swedish successes were adaptations of works by two of the greatest Dano Norwegian writers, respectively Henrik Ibsen and Bjørnstjerne Bjørnson. The Swedes had chosen the best-known and most popular works of these writers, who were also national heroes. A common opinion in this period was that these films should have been made in Norway. An actor and musician at the Norwegian Theatre, Rasmus Breistein decided to do something about this. He took out a mortgage on his house, and then invited his fellow-actors to spend a holiday in the beautiful village of Vågå. With all kinds of assistance from the inhabitants, the scenes for their 'true' Norwegian film, *Fante-Anne*, were shot during their summer holiday. The production staff was limited to a director, who also wrote the script, and a photographer who was responsible for the décor and finally edited the film. With this, the director, Breistein, and the photographer, Gunnar Nilsen-Vig, started a collaboration that by 1940 had resulted in eight feature films. Breistein is one of the few Norwegian directors who made a

Plate 23 An unconventional heroine: Anne 'the tramp' in *Fante-Anne*. By courtesy of the Norsk Filminstitutt, Oslo.

profit on every film. He, himself, screened *Fante-Anne* in community houses all over Norway and in the Norwegian settlements in North America, and thus raised money for new film productions. Breistein thus circumvented the municipal screening system which, as already mentioned, turned the profit of film exhibition over to the local authorities.

As a representative of the New Norwegian movement, Breistein did not go to Ibsen or Bjørnson to find material for his film. Instead he chose, as already mentioned, the New Norwegian writer, Janson. This author never earned the praise of the literary critics, but he was a popular writer often telling stories from the farming community. In the written story as well as in the film, *Fante-Anne*, we meet a girl quite different from Bjørnson's Synnøve Solbakken.[3] Synnøve is the bourgeoisie's typical romantic female character; fair-haired, beautiful and mild, but with physical and moral strength, a farmer's daughter. Anne is a rough, unruly, inventive, dark-haired girl of unknown origin.

Fante-Anne opens on presenting the children, Anne and her brother, Haldor. Anne is constantly creating funny but, for the children, illegal situations, and Haldor has to follow Anne's commands. One day Haldor's mother loses her temper with Anne, and divulges that she is not her daughter but that of a tramp and beggar who died in the barn when Anne was a baby. From this moment, if she has not already, unruly Anne gains the pity and sympathy of the audience. Next we meet Anne and Haldor as grown-ups. Anne is still at the farm, working as milkmaid. The two are in love, and Haldor one day asks Anne to marry him. As expected, his mother has other plans and manages to persuade him to marry the daughter of the rich neighbouring farmer. When Anne realizes she has been cheated, she sets fire to the house Haldor is building for his wife-to-be. As a parallel to this tragic love-story we have been presented with another, equally tragic love. The good Christian cotter, Jon, who cared for Anne and Haldor as a father when they were growing up, has come to love Anne as a woman. In a dramatic scene Anne turns down his humble proposal. On the night of the fire Jon happens to meet Anne running from the place. She threatens to kill herself if he tells he has seen her. At the trial Jon tells the court that he is the guilty one, and thus has to go to prison. The film then very briefly shows Anne taking a job in town so that she can visit Jon during the years of his imprisonment. She meets him on the day of his release, but Jon knows that he cannot return to his home village after being in jail. His mother has also come to town for this occasion, and the closing picture shows the three of them on a big ship going west. The preceding title informs us that they are going to the USA, 'the land where every man can be himself independent of rank or prejudices'.

The ambiguity of *Fante-Anne*: radical rural representation and bourgeois national romanticism

With this ending, we are given the possibility of believing that Anne and Jon are now a couple. However, this is not made clear or given weight either in titles or images. The USA is here presented as the Utopian society and the final conclusion can thus be seen as a social romantic[4] statement about America, and a critique of the Norwegian village perhaps, more than as a romantic love-story ending. In *Fante-Anne* the characters are shown at work rather than enjoying themselves at folkloric dances, and the film thus shows its relationship to a radicalism in Norwegian photography where the hard work and misery of the peasants are focused on rather than the pictorial scenery demanded by tourism (although the beauty of the landscape is also a feature of the film). Most of the film is shot out of doors. The village of Vågå provides numerous possibilities for exciting compositions: the snowy mountains in the distance, and a silvery lake at the bottom of a valley, where fields and farmhouses lie in steep hills. Wherever possible, the motif is presented framed by birch leaves, to make the most of the beauty and perhaps also to give the film image the greatest possible depth. But whereas the opening shot of subsequent rural films will usually be a long-distance one of the actual farm framed in birch leaves, *Fante-Anne* opens with a low-angled frame of a birch obstructing the view. This is followed by a closer shot of Anne in the tree, and then a close-up of her angry face shouting to Haldor, certainly a less idyllic introduction than its successors.

The narrative of the film is built round melodramatic confrontations. The audience is 'sutured' into the narrative through a shot/reverse-shot technique in these confrontations. The technique, developed to perfection in US talkies, is here effectively used to present looks and reactions in close-ups underpinned by the fewest possible titles. Such structural homogeneity is, however, in contrast to the antagonism of the characters. Haldor, the farmer's son, is weak and cowardly. The complexity of Anne especially represents a radical tendency of this film. She is not portrayed as a nice child or a good woman. She often treats Haldor badly. She commits a crime and gets away with it. She even shows contempt for the law in the court scene. By contrast the (Dano Norwegian) bourgeois Synnøve Solbakken character is the incarnation of woman as undoubtedly good and morally supreme. In spite of Anne's antagonism, the film evokes pity on her behalf, this pity conflicting with pity for Jon when he is rejected by her and is later sent to prison for her sake. The moral lesson of this melodrama is not obvious or ideologically unambiguous.

In the written story, Anne's years in the city constitute a large part, nearly half the volume. Whatever the director's reasons for giving priority to the rural part of the story, the choice underlines the tendency of the films of this period to eliminate the city. A survey done on reprinted books of the 1920s reveals a predominance of works dealing with a precapitalist, farming community (Andreassen 1980). This could indicate certain national romantic needs in the book market on a parallel with those in the film audience. In this respect *Fante-Anne* is not radical. But the film adaptation differs further from the novel's strongly religious flavour. When Jon takes on Anne's punishment, this is described in the novel as a parallel to what Christ did for humanity, a point not made in the film. Devout Christianity is not a common value among audiences of the 1920s. The adaptation from literature to film is thus marked by a modernization and an adjustment to a nationalism freed from possible religious limitations.

In *Fante-Anne* we find traits from both radical and the bourgeois nationalism. The national landscape is portrayed, but not solely as idyllic. The national characters are the centre of interest, but they are not all supreme human beings. This first film contains all the visual signs of the subsequent rural films. It is, however, especially interesting in that it also includes some radical traits. After a short presentation of the 'typical' rural film, I will proceed to a chronological overview of examples of rural films that depart from this norm in more ideologically conservative ways compared to *Fante-Anne*. As we shall see, the radical potential of *Fante-Anne* was not taken up by subsequent examples of the genre.

THE RURAL FILM AFTER *FANTE-ANNE*

The typical rural film is a melodrama that relates strongly to the themes and structures of certain folk-tales and popular literature. The male hero is usually a cotter like Jon. He is poor, but has physical and moral strength. To win the girl he loves, he has to pass through a number of trials. In these films, this often includes going to prison for a crime he has not committed or being on the run from an unfair verdict. As part of these trials he may be forced by circumstances to stay for a while in the city where he of course is very unhappy. He is humiliated and misunderstood, but at last his virtues are revealed, and he wins the praise of those who humiliated him. He can return to the village where he belongs, and marry the 'princess', usually the rich farmer's daughter. These narratives with a poor hero turning rich can, to a limited degree, be seen as social romantic and radical in supporting the lower classes in their hope for a better future. The projects are, however, strictly individualistic, excluding the concept of social change. The beautiful scenery of the Norwegian valleys plays a vital part as the national background in these films. Other common national symbols are the medieval architecture, national costumes, folk dances often ending in a fight among the men, going to church and the farmer's wedding. The films were accompanied with music by the national romantic composers, Nordraak, Kjerulf and Grieg.

Plate 24 The romanticized peasant: *Til Sæters*. By courtesy of the Norsk Filminstitutt, Oslo.

Markens grøde (*The Growth of the Soil*, Norway, 1921) is atypical in lacking the national symbols mentioned above. This adaptation of the Nobel Prize-winning Norwegian author Knut Hamsun is one of the most ambitious projects in this selection of films. It was a Danish actor, Gunnar Sommerfeldt, who dared to take the risk. (Not without bitterness, one of the Norwegian directors from this period complains of how easily this Dane got financial support in Norway, just by being a foreigner (Sinding 1972: 25).) Even actors from the respectable National Theatre of Oslo could take part in this prestigious film. Two famous Danish actors were also hired. The film and the novel share European romanticism's idea of the peasant as the only true human being transcending time and place. The novel was well received in Germany, and it has been claimed that it was an inspiration for the Nazi 'Blood and Soil' ideology (Giersing *et al.* 1975). The first title of the film illustrates the eternal, universal framework of romanticism: 'Since the beginnings of human life on earth two forces have waged a ceaseless and titanic struggle against one another – the Soil versus Man.' From the mountain glacier the camera takes us downwards into the woods of the valley below, where in a long-distance shot we see the Man walking into the valley – from nowhere to the site where he decides to stay, and where he builds his farm and his future. He may represent a version of Adam, the first farmer on earth. With his own hands he builds his farm and he sticks to his fundamental values. When a small city grows up in his neighbourhood, he is not tempted by the modern, urban way of life. The film is lyrical in nature, and succeeds in communicating the strength of eternal values by portraying simple events. When his wife is sent to jail for seven years, his yearning is expressed by

189

superimposing her at his side while he is ploughing the fields alone. What this film lacks in presenting the national symbols and scenery it gains, as regards nationalism, by holding forth the ideal farmer. He is strong and wise enough to protect traditional values. He represents a deep layer in the mythic, Norwegian folk character.

Til sæters (*To the Mountain Pastures*, Norway 1924) represents the opposite of *Markens grøde* as far as national symbols and ideological depth are concerned. This vaudeville-inspired play was written in 1850 by the Norwegian academic Claus Pavel Riis, and was, in the 1920s, one of the most frequently staged plays in amateur theatre companies all over Norway. Harry Ivarson, previously a journalist in Oslo and director of a film in Germany, persuaded a new company of film distributors and private cinema owners to go into the production of films. National romanticism had by then proved its popularity in previous films, and with a well-known play they could expect success. Every single scene was shot out of doors, partly in the open-air Folk Museum in Oslo. In this film, the peasant is the faultless hero, while the schoolmaster representing the educated class is an old, ugly and evil-minded authority figure, trying to capture the rich farmer's daughter. The schoolmaster has the consent of the girl's mother, but the girl loves the poor peasant. When the schoolmaster is revealed as the thief of the girl's crucifix (a gift from her lover), the mother must give in to her daughter's wish. A double marriage can be celebrated: the girl's sister is also betrothed, to the richest young man in the valley. The lack of emotional conflict and melodramatic suspense overemphasizes the rural idyll and thus underlines the conservative traits of the bourgeois national romanticism.

The next example *Fjeldeventyret* (*The Mountain Story*, Norway 1927) is based on a vaudeville from 1824 written by a Norwegian student in Copenhagen, Henrik Anker Bjerregaard. The director Leif Sinding, also previously a journalist in Oslo, had assisted on the production of *Til sæters*. A student is the hero of *Fjeldeventyret*, while the peasant, an aspiring country policeman, is a stupid and comic figure. Traditional Norwegian scenery is once again the backdrop. The student is hiking in the mountains with his friends. They plan to visit the student's girlfriend, the daughter of the country policeman. She has stayed the winter in the city to acquire some refinement. Her father has promised her to his stupid assistant, if the latter succeeds in catching three dangerous criminals on the run in the district. The assistant mistakes the students for the criminals, and this cardinal offence leads to his downfall and the student's success. *Fjeldeventyret* expresses the upper-class and urban view of the rural areas and their inhabitants before the advent of national romanticism in Norway. In 1820 the potential radicalism of national romanticism, namely the virtues of the farmer, had not yet been discovered by the bourgeoisie. The farmer here is barbaric and stupid and all the virtues are attached to the aspiring city intellectual. The national romantic setting of the film may explain why this 'unromantic' message about the farmer has none the less been labelled rural romanticism.

Laila (Norway 1929), by the Danish director George Schneevoigt, is one of three films concerning ethnic groups in the last years of the decade. Throughout the decade the audience had seen films from all over Norway. The films of the Lapps in the north of the country represent a continuation of the constant display of new parts of Norway, and at the same time correspond to an international trend in the 1920s towards the exotic and primitive. *Laila* is once again an adaptation of a very popular book, this one from 1881. The writer, Jens Andreas Friis, was a professor of Lappish, who lived with the Lapps for many years. *Laila* tells the story of the daughter of a Norwegian salesman in Lapland. The family with their Lapp nurse, are caught in a blizzard and attacked by wolves on their way to church to have Laila christened. The nurse loses Laila from the sledge, and the parents have no reason to doubt that she has become the wolves' easy prey. Laila is, however, rescued by a Lapp servant whose master has dearly longed for a child, and he raises Laila as his own. The Lapp also raises a Lapp boy as his foster-son and when they grow up, a marriage between Laila and the son is planned. Laila has, however, secretly fallen in love with a Norwegian she has met in the village. This Norwegian learns of her true heritage, and on the day of the marriage he reaches the church with information that can halt the ceremony: Laila is a Norwegian! The marriage is then carried out with the new bridegroom of the 'correct' race.

The film is a photographic and dramaturgical achievement, although the eugenic ingredient is today quite offensive. Nationalism here is connected to the myth of Norway as a wild, dangerous and challenging part of the world, with a fascinating ethnic group. In spite of the fascination, a marriage between a Lapp and a Norwegian is inconceivable, and this concept can therefore function as an element of the plot.

SUMMARY

The contradictions of aspects of nationalism in this selection of films relate to conflicts in the cultural history of Norway. *Fante-Anne* is nationalist in its choice and use of a rural setting, while the complexity of the character and the modest use of idyllic love and national symbols connect the film to the radicalism of the Norwegian Theatre and the New Norwegian language movement. This radical influence seems, however, not to have been strong or unambiguous. The naturalist elements of *Fante-Anne* are modest, as is the use of national symbols, and the radicalism is not strengthened, but rather weakened, in the subsequent films.

Markens grøde relates to radical photography in not using the motifs of contemporary tourism, but still the portrayal of the farmer relates to, and reinforces, the myth of the farmer as the ideal human being.

With *Til sæters* all traces of the ideology or aesthetics of the New Norwegian tradition have disappeared. The dominant use of pictorial, national symbols – national costumes, mountain pastures, folk dancing, etc. – gives the film an obvious, Norwegian look related to the bourgeois rural romanticism, and the promotion of Norway as a pleasant land for tourists. The comedy *Fjeldeventyret* continues the praise of rural scenery, but at the same time displays the bourgeoisie's old disrespect for the farmer. This disrespect did not disappear with romanticism's discovery of the farmer, but continued alongside the somewhat superficial approval of the 'true' Norwegians of the countryside. The eugenic ingredient of *Laila* can thus be regarded as the continuation of a reactionary development in the films, and a hint of the growing acceptance of fascist ideology at the end of the 1920s in Norway, an acceptance which eventually led to the creation of a Norwegian Nazi party under the leadership of Vidkun Quisling in 1933. The Nazi party had a lot in common with the general bourgeois ideology of the period. The Nazis drew heavily on the national symbols and the notion of the protection of the true Norwegian soul, inherited ideologically from national romanticism. The nation as a concept transcending class was used in every bourgeois party to counteract the current and frightening working class. This nationalism was not easy to separate from the nationalism of liberal or radical policy, which encouraged the unity of the urban and rural working class. The bourgeois romantic concepts seem to have gained ground even in the radical language movement of the time.

Traces of a radical nationalism are easiest to find in the earliest films of the 1920s, and the fading of these traces corresponds to the growing dominance of conservative nationalism in contemporary Norwegian society. As a popular phenomenon, rural nationalism could meet a wide range of ambiguous needs and imaginations. The bourgeois audience were given a fictional rescue from the moral and political threats of the city. The working-class audience had their nostalgia nurtured. In a recently urbanized country many Norwegians shared a rural homesickness. It is the conflicting elements within nationalism in the period that account for the wide appeal of rural films to the audiences of the 1920s.

NOTES

1 The Norwegian countryside consists to a large extent of single farms in a huge area with no particular centre or village and thus no daily social gatherings. Gatherings are organized officially around the church and school; groups also run community houses for entertainment, dances, amateur theatricals, film screenings, etc.

2 For further information in English on this subject see A. Elton and P. Brinson, *The Film Industry in Six European Countries*, Paris, UNESCO, 1950. The authors

praise the system giving the Norwegian audience good access to international films. The only Norwegian film history till now (S. Evensmo *Det store tivoli*, Oslo, 1967) stresses, however, the damaging consequences of the municipal cinema system for the production of films in this country.

3 *Synnøve Solbakken* is a romantic short story from 1857, the first published of Bjørnson's works.

4 Social romanticism in literature is inspired by the ideas of the Utopian socialists of the French Revolution. The image of the ideal society is contrasted with the deprivation and misery of contemporary society.

REFERENCES

Andreassen, Trond (1980) *Nyutgivelser av romaner og noveller 1920–30. En litteratursosiologisk undersøkelse*, Bergen: Hovedoppgave ved Nordisk institutt, Universitet i Bergen.

Elton, Arthur and Brinson, Peter (1950) *The Film Industry in Six European Countries*, Paris: UNESCO, Publication no. 597.

Evensmo, Sigrud (1967) *Det store tivoli. Film og kino i Norge gjennom 70 år*, Oslo: Gyldendal.

Giersing, Morten, Thobo-Carlsen, John and Westergaard-Nielsen, Mikael (1975) *Det reaktionære oprør. Om fascismen i Hamsuns forfatterskap*, København: GMT.

Sinding, Lars (1972) *En filmsaga. Fra norsk filmkunsts begynnelse. Stumfilmårene som jeg så og opplevet dem*, Oslo: Universitetsforlaget.

14

THE ATLANTIC DIVIDE

V. F. Perkins

I want to examine some consequences of setting up popular European cinema as a category for scholarship. Popular cinema might be thought a contradiction in terms. 'Cinema' carries more of the elite status of art with it than 'films' or 'movies'; it also emphasizes the institutional and industrial aspects of film production and exhibition while significantly excluding television. Cinemas have owners and managements; they belong – usually – to corporations, never to filmgoers. One attends the cinema as a customer or at most a patron. The institutions of cinema determine what is available for one's patronage: the choice between *Batman* and the latest *Indiana Jones* could appear quite marginal. 'Let the buyer beware' governs the purchase of a cinema ticket more powerfully than it rules in most consumer transactions; satisfaction is not guaranteed and no compensation is offered if the items purchased prove unsuitable or cause distress.

Popular cinema brings with it the sense of 'popular culture', but only the 'mass culture' sense. It has to exclude that part of popular culture which depends on communal involvement in making and circulating songs, jokes, games and stories. There is no folk cinema to parallel folk music or folk-tale since access to the apparatus of production is so restricted by its cost and complexity. Even the creators can use the apparatus only as employees and under conditions governed by stringent contractual arrangements. The contract here is not with the people, however conceived, but again with the financiers. The absence of contract between the supplier and the consumer is in stark contrast with the abundance and complexity of contracts between the various agencies of manufacture. On the other hand the industry presents itself as giving the public what they want. Whatever one's scepticism towards this suggestion of creation by proxy, it also strains belief to suppose that the interests of cinema-goers have been without influence on the form and content of movies.

A Darwinian model would show this influence working as an adjudication at the box-office to determine the viability of mutations generated

194

by the film industries as they try to repeat and vary past successes, and to avoid replicating past failures. Ticket sales have been interpreted as guidance in terms of projects and personnel (not only, though importantly, stars and star-combinations) with sufficient perceived force to give rise to the notion that 'you're as good as your last picture'.

But the products of a selection-survival system offer an imperfect mirror of audience desires since box-office arbitration can come only in those forms and between those films that the structure of the movie business promotes or accepts. (That is one reason why popular cinema is almost always the current cinema.) Film industries have never been entirely governed by perceptions of what the public wants; systems of censorship presuppose an appetite for the products whose supply they restrict. The internal dynamics of movie-making communities put other values into play alongside and sometimes in preference to immediate financial consider-ations; prestige attaches to forms of work in ways that can be out of harmony with the drive to profitability.

Moreover, the movie business supplies only what it can supply, since it suffers worse problems of quality control than any other manufacturing industry. Think of the financial disasters incurred by attempts to respond to the successes of *The Sound of Music, Funny Girl* and *The Deer Hunter.* Box-office indications of a desire for funnier comedies and more suspenseful thrillers are without effect since it was never by design that the producers offered a yawn a minute. We can never know what parts of the British audience in the Rank–Korda era might have been open to or eager for British movies created in independence from the values and propensities of the London theatre. The British industry was so constituted (in partial reflection of British society) that it did not generate the mutations to put to the test. The British Gainsborough Studios melodrama of the 1940s, for instance, was available only in a form where an energetic politeness set the limit on the enactment of passion. The sad distinction of the Gainsborough movies was to rediscover the stiff and insipid within the luridly contrived. We cannot know whether that was part of their appeal, or a tolerable drawback.

Movies may be commercially successful without being widely or greatly enjoyed. A film that fails does so in the terms set by the structures of the industry and not necessarily because it is incapable of offering pleasure. Thus 'popular' may be thought to evade – where 'commercial' would confront – the difficulties of characterizing the products of a mass medium as a cinema of the people.

Yet 'of the people' is important for its emphasis on a constituency. A film may be popular/well-liked or popular/well-attended through its appeal to the prosperous, the powerful and the conventionally cultured. Popular cinema, though, is importantly a category of access identifying films whose comprehension and enjoyment require only such skills, knowledges and understandings as are developed in the ordinary processes of living in society – not those that come with economic or cultural privilege. The terms of access unite the formal with the cultural since what is learned in the ordinary processes of life varies with place and time. Thus a film fully accessible to its French audience will no longer belong to the popular cinema when it arrives in England equipped with subtitles. To correlate the meanings of words printed on the image in English with the inflections of foreign speech, so as to arrive at a vivid understanding of dramatic interaction, calls for abilities not acquired in the ordinary processes of English life. The significance of the passage from *vous* to *tu* is effortlessly registered by any French spectator, and quite recondite for an English audience. Conversely, English audiences will have a nuanced alertness to speech patterns that imply dramatically significant variations in economic and social status.

Factors of those kinds contribute to the processes whereby movies popular in their countries of production enter the structures of art cinema abroad. It is an advantage of the access approach that it can account for the presence within popular cinema of many films – *Raise the Titanic* and *Absolute Beginners* would be British instances – which have been neither popular/well-attended nor popular/well-liked. Of course there is some circularity in the notion of access that I have advanced since what is learned in the ordinary process of life includes what can be routinely derived from the mass media.

The popular can legitimately be polarized against the esoteric but not against the good or the bad and not against art, unless restricted address and exclusivity – availability only to specially developed skills and knowledge – are definitive for one's understanding of what art is. This would limit the art of film to the generic and commercial structures of the art cinema, and would thereby exclude many of the finest pictures.

Historically such a limitation has been in force. The sense of the popular has often been of work which does not so much meet the needs of the people (positively valued) as feed the appetites of the mob, understood as debased and mindless. The figure of the 'lowest common denominator' has been much used to characterize the appeal of the mass media to a coarse and uninstructed taste. The corollary to a suspicion of the accessible has been a valuation of the 'difficult' and the 'experimental', with these latter seen as the product of the more properly artistic motivations. The tendency to imagine that quite distinct impulses, aims and processes operate in the production of popular movies and of film art perhaps reflects a secularized hangover from the belief in art as the product of divine inspiration. As recently as 1981 the sociologist Janet Wolff could comment on 'our commonsense view of the artist as genius, working with divine inspiration' (Wolff 1981: 25). Divine inspiration is an all or nothing concept; we can hardly expect it to occur in small or moderate quantities or variously adulterated by mundane calculation. Thus the art/commerce divide may have some of the shadings of the opposition of the sacred and the profane as well as the class connotations of the noble and the base.

Within British culture the aesthetics of R. G. Collingwood reflected this kind of absolutism, insisting on a separation between art ('art proper') and amusement. Amusement was one of 'three kinds of art falsely so called' (Collingwood 1938: 11) and was identified as a form of corruption. But Collingwood was only more rigorous than most in enforcing a division that ran right through the alarmist discourses on mass entertainment. There was some instability within these discourses between the view that the art of the film was degraded by the demands of its low audience and the belief that the popular taste was being corrupted by continuous exposure to vile work.

> The producing companies made their great mistake when they decided to cater for the taste of the music-hall patron. . . . The cinema lost a public who loved it for itself and what it meant to them. . . . In place of the old filmgoer there arose a new type of audience, a vacant-minded empty-headed public who flocked to sensations, who thrilled to sexual vulgarity, and who would go anywhere and pay anything to see indecent situations riskily handled on the screen.
> (Rotha 1949: 129–30)

That was presumably not regarded as a hysterical view since it occurs in what served as the standard English-language history of cinema from its first publication in 1930 through the revised edition of 1949 until the mid-1950s. What I think it encapsulates – certainly in extreme form and perhaps too neatly – is an image of the bad audience, the public of the lowest common denominator, as members of an alien class. Evidently if the features of this audience were projected on to the films it favoured one would expect nothing of major – or even modest – artistic interest to be visible.

For some British commentators the image of the popular audience as threateningly other was matched by the foreignness of the popular films, overwhelmingly American. If the clients were an undiscriminating class, their supply came from a whole society which was held to lack class and culture.

An article that proposed a picture of the audience in apparent contrast with Paul Rotha's of 1930 was written for the 1947–8 edition of the *British Film Yearbook* by C. A. Lejeune, then the recognized leader of high-brow British film reviewers. Called 'A word in friendship', the article offered itself as a warning and defined its own sense of precarious context: 'Now, at the beginning of 1947, the British film industry is standing at the parting of the ways. Its present position is secure. Its past record is proud. Its future is a matter of urgent speculation' (Lejeune 1947a). Lejeune went on to warn of the dangers of competing with Hollywood on its own grounds and so becoming its parochial echo. Commercial wisdom was claimed to indicate a rejection of Hollywood's methods which were both curiously artificial and out of touch with reality.

> British audiences . . . are probably the most sensible and selective audiences in the world. . . . The thousands of British men and women and boys and girls, who will tell you today that they prefer British films, will tell you just why they prefer them. And the reason is nearly always the same – because they are more 'real'; because they deal with the sort of people we know; behaving in a way we under-stand; against a background of the things we cherish and recognise.
>
> (Lejeune 1947a: 31–2)

This portrait of the audience, apparently so different from Paul Rotha's, in fact carried most of the same implications. Like Rotha, Lejeune imagined the audience as stable and coherent, always in the same mood and having the same objectives – as one audience. But the most interesting aspect of Lejeune's picture is that it was knowingly false. It strategically ignored the mediocre commercial performance of some highly approved movies. Lejeune herself in acclaiming *Brief Encounter* (1946) had declared 'I doubt very much if it will be generally popular. . . . Nothing the producers can contrive is going to make *Brief Encounter* an understandable film for the practical millions' (Lejeune 1947b: 161–2). More boldly still, her picture wished away the box-office triumph of critically despised British films like *Madonna of the Seven Moons* (1944) and *The Wicked Lady* (1945). Instead 'Hollywood' was made to stand for the popular trash that a sensible and selective audience could be expected to reject. My point is not to examine the particular conjuncture that made this strategy useful, but to indicate the availability – for a wide range of polemical purposes – of the equation between Hollywood and the worthless popular, even when it was made in Britain. Hollywood cinema, on this view, was overpaid, oversexed and over here.

'Over here', at least, is surely right. If we take an audience rather than a production perspective, popular European cinema must include – and will in many or most places be dominated by – Hollywood products. American pictures provide the striking exception to the role pronounced earlier whereby movies popular in their countries of production enter the structures of art cinema abroad. Research, as relevant to American as to European interests, could well pursue the problem of the mysterious accessibility of the Hollywood film. I believe it would at some point confront questions as germane for *Liebelei* (Germany 1933) as for *Notorious* (USA 1946), as pointed in *It Happened One Night* (USA 1934) as in *La Grande Illusion* (France 1937), of the processes whereby the finest popular movies reconcile availability to a relaxed enjoyment – often but wrongly characterized as passivity – with a densely worked structure that can reward close, most sustained and informed scrutiny.

The popular, considered in terms of its ranges of accessibility, is aesthetically and critically neutral. Accessibility can be an artistic as much as a commercial aim, but that a work is broadly or narrowly accessible says nothing of the values that may be found in it once access is achieved. The kind of attention a work requires is not identical with the kind of attention it may reward. Value is neither ruled out nor guaranteed.

Not long ago this point had to be stressed in resistance to a blanket condemnation of commercial cinema. More recently it has come to need affirming in face of the tendency within academic film studies to reject aesthetics except as sociological data on formations of taste. Various groups of movies have been proposed for rescue from critical neglect on the grounds that their success suggests and their internal structure confirms the closeness of their issues and images to the concerns of their audience. A relevant instance is that of the Gainsborough melodrama which a growing number of revisionist essays on British cinema offer for sympathetic reassessment. The defence typically presents the claim that the contemporary reviewers' derision of Gainsborough reflected an inability to take popular culture seriously. I have chosen to discuss *Love Story* (1944) whose screening at the Warwick Popular European Cinema conference held it up for scrutiny in the light of the understanding that, 'Most European countries have produced a vigorous tradition of popular film . . . fully as capable of high aesthetic achievement as Hollywood.'[1]

The contemporary press – with Lejeune prominent among them – poured scorn on this film and on its plot, which contrives a wartime romance between a dying concert pianist and an invalid airman doomed to lose his sight. But such extremities of condition and coincidence, with the indifference to mundane probability that makes them usable, provide the conventional basis for the eloquence of the best weepies. The reassessment of melodrama that has progressed with the development of film studies has involved a validation of the expressive possibilities in narrative contrivance and in boldness of formal and emotional design.

Moreover the thematic material of *Love Story* is far from trivial. Lissa (Margaret Lockwood) faces the issue of what can count for her as the fulfilment of her life, and faces it urgently in the immediate prospect of death. Kit (Stewart Granger) presents the male action hero wedded to stereotypically masculine sources of self-esteem but threatened with incapacity and banishment from the valued sphere of prowess. Each of them confronts conflict between the private realm of romance and the social arena of the war effort as the ground on which fulfilment and consolation are to be sought.

These are significant issues, and the twists of the film's narrative and imagery draw in plenty of others. But then, snobbish prejudice aside, it is

Plate 25 Stewart Granger, Margaret Lockwood (centre) and Patricia Roc in *Love Story*. By courtesy of the National Film Archive, London.

hardly believable that any film could appeal in the way that, in 1944, *Love Story* did to a very large British audience unless it made contact with hopes, anxieties, beliefs and concerns whose pertinence was widely felt. It is not credible that a dramatic entertainment might elicit a strong or wide response while being thematically empty or insubstantial.

But to say this much is not to establish that the film treats its themes intelligently or honestly, nor that it realizes the potential of romantic melodrama by developing depth and subtlety within its broadly and boldly drawn effects. *Love Story* strains after emotional force by repeating established information with ever more insistent emphasis. The resulting imagery is flat and grossly contrived, as when the film reminds us of Lissa's consciousness of doom by answering a close-up of her distracted frown, during a romantic buggy-ride along a Cornish lane, with an inserted viewpoint of a graveyard.

What particularly distinguishes *Love Story* from the more trenchant and inventive romances is the absence of a critical or even enquiring perspective on the motives and perceptions of its lovers. Most damagingly, the film can do nothing with its pivotal contrivance, the lovers' silence. Kit will not tell Lissa that he is going blind; Lissa will not tell Kit of her terminal heart condition. Acts of concealment are a constant but unexplored centre of the dramatic action. Lissa takes Kit to be a coward because of his apparent disengagement from the war effort. A mine accident allows him to prove his courage and then Lissa discovers him practising his Braille. Kit claims to have dreaded her reaction of pity and he gives that as the motive for his deception. Pity is lavishly displayed in Lissa's movements and intonations, but the film observes no moment of concern over this realization of Kit's worst fear, nor – the lively alternative – does it follow up the possibility that Kit may have misrepresented or misrecognized his own motives. (Pity is an emotional currency, I suppose, that it is not prepared to bring under scrutiny.) If *Love Story* were alert, and were expecting its audience to be alert, it would also need to do something at this point about Lissa's continued deception of Kit. But 'Why didn't you tell me?' at the scene's start and 'Thank you for telling me' at its end are not allowed to provoke Lissa into an inspection of her own silence, or to prompt the film to an independent valuation. Indeed the immediately following scene has her enter into a dumb bargain that involves further deception of, and separation from, Kit. Inability to find an animating dramatic focus for actions crucial to the plot deprives *Love Story* of the subtext that can deepen and enrich the romantic tear-jerker.

The subtexts that the film does have carry it from ineptitude to ugliness. It is oppressive and dishonest in pursuit of propagandist goals. So Kit's detachment from the war effort has to have the alibi of sickness if it is not to be contemptible. No other position is acknowledged and the appetite for disapproval that disfigures so much of English life and culture is meanly indulged. Lissa's resolve to become Kit's lover is shaken when he refuses to manage the dangerous but patriotically significant mining works. She is troubled as, once more, the pony-trap carries them along a lane. They come upon a squad of war-wounded soldiers out for a hike on their sticks and crutches. The lantern-slide function of two insert shots of these cheerful, bandaged simpletons is confirmed by Lissa's declaring that she can't go on, and objecting to Kit's attitude 'after what we've just seen', as if someone, somewhere might have needed a visual aid to remembrance that the war has victims.

This exploitative and hectoring rhetoric is called in to validate Lissa's decision that she will not, after all, be sharing Kit's bed. The device gives an early indication of the film's unrecognized project which is to divert sexuality onto sacrifice and military heroics. At the picture's end when surgery has lifted the threat of blindness, and other impediments to (however brief) union have finally been dissolved, the film celebrates Kit's re-enlistment in the airforce much more emphatically than it welcomes the satisfaction of desire. All talk of living for the moment resolves into a decision to marry which then yields no image of fulfilment in love. Instead the film affirms its preference for transferred gratification by moving straight from the accepted proposal to the image of Lissa standing alone on the Cornish cliff tops and fondling her wedding ring before waving to the flight of bombers that passes over her head.

The final choice of distance over intimacy, and aggression over tenderness, is made on behalf of an England depicted with great complacency in rigidly hierarchical terms. Every public incident is handled with a steady concentration on the needs and concerns of the officer class. When an emotional crisis delays a theatrical performance a slow hand-clap is started by an aged squire (A. E. Matthews) and taken up by the crowd until it is converted to applause by the intervention of the mine-owner (Tom Walls). When the mine falls in, the escape attempt below ground is managed by Kit in partnership with the owner and with virtually no reference to the skills or judgements of the miners themselves; above ground all interest in the progress of the rescue is filtered through Lissa and another of Kit's friends, the actor-manager Judy (Patricia Roc), as if their status as upper-class outsiders gave them sure title to first news of events. The crowd of Cornish wives and colleagues at the pit head are present precisely as extras who dutifully yield all initiative along with the foreground of action. This blinkered concentration on the privileged treats their interests alone as serious and real. The film clearly looks forward to business as usual at the end of the war. Rapture itself turns out to be an elite preserve in Kit's proposal of marriage: 'Happiness such as we can have is worth grasping. . . . If you can stand on the highest peak for one moment you've had what most people strive in vain for all their lives.'

Evidently my contempt for this film could be misplaced. No critical case is ever conclusive, but the critical discussion would have to be advanced through descriptions and understandings like – even if opposed to – those I have offered. It cannot be resolved through an appeal to the adjudication of the box-office or by demonstrating the neatness of the picture's fit with some particular reading of cultural history.

On the other hand while *Love Story* is, on my account, a bad film it was surely not bad to enjoy it. The 'bad audience' view seems to assume that the work is relished for precisely those aspects that the commentator deplores: it is the badness of bad work that is taken to constitute its appeal. Thus one could proceed from the observation that at the end of *Love Story* Lissa's entranced affirmation that she will 'never be afraid any more' has no connection with the preceding two hours' drama in which fear has not been the declared or implied source of any of her actions. Lissa's declaration will be understood – correctly, in my view – as a climactic instance of the film's emotional opportunism whereby effect is pursued without a disciplined regard for relevance or shape. But a spectator who invests emotion in this moment is surely not responding to its incoherence. It seems more likely that the crudity passes unnoticed by an audience immersed in the grand (and not contemptible) aspirations embodied in Lissa's vow. Willingness to take the film's devices for granted would allow an unchecked response to the fantasy of release from timidity and anxious expectation. The crudity, the exploitation of feeling that is unearned dramatically, is not – on this account – the source of the fan's enjoyment (though it may be the precondition for the abundance and variety of big emotional moments throughout the film). It would be, rather, passed over in the focus on against-the-odds romantic fulfilment. Stewart Granger:

> My next epic was a film called *Love Story*, shot on location in my beloved Cornwall. On the train I shared a compartment with the director who asked me what I thought of the script. Not knowing he'd written it, I told him it was the biggest load of crap I'd ever read. . . . I was wrong of course. It was a smash hit and there wasn't a dry eye in the house.
>
> (Granger 1981: 75–6)

If it is not to trap itself in a position as contradictory as that of *Love Story*'s star, film studies will need to find ways of reconciling its critical and its socio-cultural aspects. That will involve discussing the appeal of shoddy work without recourse to assumptions of depravity or feeble-mindedness in the spectator, but also without attempting to redeem the work by giving it undue credit for being what it must always be, a product of its time. An incautiously erected category of popular European cinema threatens to aggravate the difficulty rather than contribute to its solution. If it is not constructed as a category of access (which would for good reason acknowledge a polarization against avant-gardism) but is established in opposition

Plate 26 'Art', 'popular' or 'popular art'? Jean Gabin and Simone Simon in Jean Renoir's *La Bête humaine*. By courtesy of the National Film Archive, London.

to the art/auteur film, then it risks reconstructing within the discussion of European movies the old opposition between European art and Hollywood show business. Many films by directors such as Lang, Lubitsch, Ophuls, Renoir and Visconti can be excluded from the category of the popular only, I would have thought, by declaring them too good! It is important to dismantle the opposition between popular film and film art. But is any useful purpose served by reversing its polarities?

NOTES

1 Quoted from conference brochure: Popular European Cinema Conference, University of Warwick, September 1989.

REFERENCES

Collingwood, R. G. (1938) *The Principles of Art*, London: OUP.
Granger, Stewart (1981) *Sparks Fly Upward*, London: Granada.
Lejeune, C. A. (1947a) 'A word in friendship' in Peter Noble (ed.) *British Film Yearbook 1947–48*, London: British Yearbooks.
—— (1947b) *Chestnuts in her Lap 1936–1946*, London: Phoenix House.
Rotha, Paul (1949) *The Film Till Now*, London: Vision Press.
Wolff, Janet (1981) *The Social Production of Art*, London: Macmillan.

15

EARLY GERMAN CINEMA
Melodrama: Social drama
Heide Schlüpmann

In the years before the First World War there developed in Germany a form of narrative film production very different from the Weimar cinema with which we are familiar. If we want to bring to light again (as Patrice Petro (1989) has done) the female public's connection with films made under the rubric of *Autorenkino* (auteur cinema), we may do so on the basis of the surviving examples from before the war. In particular between 1910 and 1912 German film production seems to have focused on stories portraying love and marriage; not until 1913 were they pushed aside by crime and adventure films. It is evident from the film publicity of the time how controversial women's participation in cinema-going was. Indispensable from an economic standpoint, their very presence among men in the dark space of the cinema seemed a danger to culture and society. In this chapter it will be argued that this conflict over women's participation in cinema is evident in the films themselves: on the one hand in the recognition in the films of their everyday lives, their interests and needs, and on the other in the regulation and suppression of this presence of female desire. Two modes in which early German cinema dealt with love stories may be distinguished: social drama and melodrama. The former has its origin in Danish film, the latter in traditions of light fiction and art. The coexistence of both forms indicates that aesthetic development is not a single process in which expression and censorship are inextricably linked. Cinema of this period displays rather the power of the expression of social reality against an official culture that denied reality, a power over and against which the new medium's mechanisms of reality denial were soon used to advantage.

In the course of the early 1910s, melodrama asserted itself against the documentary use of the medium. A series of films was made in 1911 which constituted the beginnings of melodrama in German cinema. *Der Müller und sein Kind* (*The Miller and His Child*), *Im Glück vergessen* (*Forgotten in Happiness*) and *Tragödie eines Streiks* (*Tragedy of a Strike*) were all Messter productions starring Henny Porten and directed by Adolf Gärtner. In these films, the narrative cinema that was just establishing itself intersected with the inheritance of the so-called *Tonbilder* (sound images), which were first introduced in 1903. Messter was known for its *Tonbilder* and Henny Porten made her first appearance in these one-reelers. The *Tonbild* – a combination of film and recorded sound – was a genre of the pre-narrative cinema for which Tom Gunning (1986) has coined the concept, 'the cinema of attractions'. The cinema of attractions developed between 1895 and 1906 within the context of variety shows and yearly fairs. Its forms are those of exhibition, not voyeurism. It worked through visual effects in front of the camera, but also through effects created by the camera and through montage, and not least through the attraction of being able to exhibit reality. It did not yet subsume the new potential of the technical medium within the older interests of narrative. The attraction of Oskar Messter's *Tonbilder* lay above all in their connection of the image with sound. At the same time, however, these films banked on appealing to bourgeois taste through their choice of subject matter. From its prehistory in the cinema of attractions, the melodrama appropriated precisely this moment that connected the 'lower art' to the 'higher' bourgeois culture. Many *Tonbilder* draped the offerings of an 'art of the body' (*Körperkunst*) in the forms of classical opera and ballet, orienting themselves around images from bourgeois art history. For example, the attraction of *Meissner Porzellan* (*Meissner Porcelain*, 1906) lay in the movement of living bodies which appeared as the marionette-like dance steps of delicate rococo porcelain figures.

Just as with the representation of bodily movement in *Meissner Porzellan*, so melodrama froze the movement of female (self-)representation at the beginning of narrative cinema. As in the *Tonbild* the cinema of attraction had acquiesced to bourgeois culture through references to traditional art, so in narrative cinema melodrama acquiesced to patriarchal forms of culture. In German cinema, it had from the very beginning a disciplinary function. It was not a genre that came from below, from the realm of the popular, but instead placed women's history in the service of nationalism and, later, National Socialism.

Melodramas in Germany have always had a second-hand effect.[1] They did not build their tragedy out of life; rather, the tragic structure into which they compressed all reality ultimately consisted in nothing other than the collapse of a female narrative perspective within the restrictions of the dramatic form. The tragic element was an a priori attribute of the protagonist, before any particular content; it developed neither from the reality in which the film placed her nor from her story. Melodramatic heroines were static. They were not 'narrators' but rather the representatives of an always already determined femininity. Even their aura of suffering did not refer to historical-social experience outside the cinema – precisely during this period, women were realizing that the feminine character was not a destiny – but on the contrary mystified the suppression of the female narrative perspective within the films.

The reactionary element in a melodrama like *Tragödie eines Streiks*, a Messter production starring Henny Porten and directed by Adolf Gärtner, is obvious: the woman, who from the very beginning has been in favour of order and against the uprising, is able in the end to convince even the male protagonist that social struggle will bring nothing but disaster. But she does so only at the cost of losing her child. Not only is the suffering of the woman in a male society transfigured by the melodrama, but the transfigured image of female sacrifice also serves to domesticate male oppositional perspectives. The actress, representative of femininity, i.e. of a male projection rather than an articulation of female experience, no longer represents her own narrative perspective, but enforces the dominant order. The 'reason of the heart' (the title of a 1910 film) is thus transmuted from a historically specific voice into a projective defence, all in the name of a speechless female sensibility.

Henny Porten, the embodiment of this sensibility, already scores a victory in her initial appearance in *Tragödie eines Streiks* as the star who bows and smiles during the credits. The clumsy antics of the male protagonist are no match for her. He acts the communist official in a Russian peasant smock, proletarian cap and wild moustache. Only at the outset are we treated to some snippets of 'realism': the first shot, when life still seems to be in order, shows the everyday site of a proletarian one-room apartment which is at once living room, bedroom, and the woman's work space, as well as the nursery. The mother works at the sewing machine, her son playing at her feet. But when he falls ill, the film resorts to emotional, suggestive devices. It anticipates the dismal ending in that the camera devotes less attention to the details of the trip to the hospital than it does to the logo of a coffin manufacturer that has obviously been created in the studio.

The presentation of the strike must have seemed too 'realistic' to the censors, since they excised the better part of it.[2] Only one shot remains that shows the gesticulating labour force from above: a view from the position of dominance onto insurgent reality. The enticing image of woman in this film functions, analogously to the camera angle, to reinforce the idea of industrialization from above. One of the intertitles tells us that 'light and power' are indispensable, thus putting in writing the admonition that was voiced by the female protagonist before the strike. The text has the effect of a caption that might come from the mouth of an allegorical statue representing 'Electricity' that decorates the entrance of a power plant. The sequence in the hospital's operating room makes reference to the blessings of electricity; the operating table looks impressive in the bright light of the lamp.[3] To the same extent that little of the text touting the indispensability of the new technology comes from the mouth of a real woman, so too the protagonist fails to communicate the view as the film proceeds that this technology could belong to women – or, for that matter, to the workers. The mother who fears for the life of her child sits waiting passively outside the operating room, a portrait of the madonna hanging above her head, and as the light goes out, the 'god in white' appears in the doorway, ominously blood-spattered: the workers' strike is more than anything else a blasphemy against higher powers. It makes no difference if, in this context, the female spectator senses within herself a higher right *vis-à-vis* the 'politicizing' man, seeing herself reconfirmed in her domestic concern for private well-being.

And yet, melodrama was not the only form in which cinema was oriented towards a female public. The social drama approached this public differently. Although the concept of the social drama stemmed from Scandinavian cinema, Emilie Altenloh used it more generally in her 1913 sociological study of the cinema. For Altenloh, the term 'social drama' referred to a form that related particularly to the life contexts of women (1977: 58).[4] Unlike melodrama, social drama maintained a proximity to newsreels; its documentation of reality broke with conventional dramatic form. Altenloh described this similarity to the newsreel as follows:

> Viewed from one perspective, the interest in the cinematic image in German newspapers and newsreels is not so very different from the interest in German dramas. Certainly one important cause is the reference to the present. Film drama speaks to people in the context of their everyday lives.
>
> (ibid.: 57)

In contrast to melodrama, the social drama responded solely to an external censorship, one that restricted a genuine female narrative perspective, but yet did not force it to recede in favour of a stereotypical representation of femininity within a dramatized story. Social drama appealed to the curiosity of female spectators and gave the subjectivity of the actress a spatial framework.

The strength of the female narrative perspective in the social drama derived from its foundation in the forms of the cinema of attractions with which it entered into a pact against the bourgeois superimposition of the dramatic form. The first kind of cinema did not give way that quickly to the bourgeois interest in cinema: from film to film, even within a single film, documentary qualities could disappear in favour of a theatrical effect.

In keeping with the social division of gender roles, social dramas concern themselves with the theme of the mistress, on the one hand, and the married woman, on the other. But they also resist this division. *Heimgefunden: Von Stufe zu Stufe: Lebensberichte einer Probiermamsell (The Way Back Home: Step by Step: The True Confessions of a Model*, 1910) is one example of such resistance. Perhaps more than any other film, *Heimgefunden* shows how the independence of the story, in the face of attempts to dramatize it, is based on the continuation of elements of the cinema of attractions and goes hand in hand with the suspension of moral prejudices. The subtitle, *Lebensberichte einer Probiermamsell*, could have been taken from the enlightened women's literature of the period. The story of the film as well – a decent female employee allows herself to be seduced and becomes a mistress – corresponds to many cases that were reported by the women's movement in their publications so as to set in motion emancipatory processes of reflection and self-reflection. The rehabilitation of 'fallen' women, rather than their social condemnation, was the goal of radical sexual politics at the time. In 1914, for example, the journal *Die neue Generation (The New Generation)*[5] published a series entitled 'From the life of a prostitute, as told by herself' (Hermann 1914).

The formulation 'as told by herself' has the same effect as the subtitle *Lebensberichte einer Probiermamsell*. Filmed, on the one hand, with a documentary camera that utilizes the visual values of outdoor shots and directed, on the other, at sexual curiosity, the film maintains a complete distance from melodramatic elements. The female protagonist is seduced, but she is not presented as a victim who will meet a certain death; on the contrary, she will return to her family and marry her fiancé, as if nothing unusual had happened. Instead of representing patriarchal morality, her story conveys sexual and documentary attractions to a female public.

Heimgefunden tells the story of Elise, a girl from a simple home, who works in a dressmaker's studio. Her promotion to model (*Probiermamsell*) brings her into contact with upper-class customers. A count who comes into the shop with his matronly wife is less interested in the latest fashions than he is in the girl who models them. Elise agrees to a rendezvous, and soon thereafter becomes the count's mistress. He rents her a flat of her own and provides her with clothes and jewellery. This helps her overcome her guilty conscience about having abandoned her parents and fiancé. While out for an evening of fun at Maxim's, she meets the engineer Natas, who makes advances towards her. The count surprises the couple when Natas is paying her a visit at home, and not only throws out his rival, but also decides to break with Elise. She switches over to the engineer, who turns out to be a less than serious candidate, eventually gambling away her jewellery. Thus disappointed, Elise longs for home. Her father shows her to the door, but her fiancé runs after her and prevents her, in her state of anguish, from throwing herself in front of a train. Eventually she and her father are reconciled as well.

The narrative in *Heimgefunden* draws its strength from an undercurrent linking it to the cinema of attractions; in so doing, the film constructs the rudiments of formulating a first-person narration on the part of the female protagonist. Generally, the film is shot in tableau style, presenting its story in a simple sequence of scenes that are arranged and shot autonomously,

Plate 27 Probiermamsell: the camera observes – Elise waits for the count. He lights a cigar as he enters the frame. By courtesy of the Deutsches Bundesarchiv, Koblenz.

emphasizing their visual values over their function within the film's narrative totality. 'At home' as the intertitle comments, Elise is 'her parents' sunshine' and also that of her fiancé. She is fascinating to the public as well. In the dressmaker's studio we are offered an insight into the working conditions and mode of production of a trade shop. Rows of sewing machines are set up, fabric and finished articles of clothing are strewn about, fashion drawings hang on the walls; we even catch a glimpse of a tailor's dummy wearing the design being produced at the moment. A number of women are busy working when a man, the boss, enters the room. A brief dramatic scene has been embedded within the presentation of the milieu, which is retroactively attributed to the supervisory male gaze. The boss scrutinizes his employees – he is looking for a new model, and suddenly chooses Elise.

At Elise's first rendezvous with the count, the camera is alongside the gentlemen waiting on the other side of the street, attention fixed on the somewhat self-conscious, indecisive Elise as she stands in front of the café. The camera assumes the voyeuristically possessive male gaze, but, at the same time, pushes the woman into the open bustle of a big city; its interest in documenting the atmosphere outweighs the interest in formulating the male gaze. The count lights a cigar as soon as he enters camera range (his pleasure while waiting); he crosses the street, cigar in hand, while the camera remains fixed, recording the couple as they disappear into the café. Once inside, the man and woman sit at the window at equal distance from the camera, which reveals behind them the undulating traffic of the street and the flow of passers-by. The light from outside illuminates the faces of the lovers.

Another scene that seems primarily to provide the viewer with narrative information is the following, in which Elise's parents and fiancé receive a letter from her, telling them about her new life. Even though Elise is not visually present, the scene centres on the written communication from her that the fiancé has received: 'Forgive me, I have found my happiness; I won't be coming home any more.' The scene thus reinforces her fictional authorship.

The most elaborate scene in the entire film is devoted to the situation of the suffering mistress, a scene which characterizes the milieu just as it provides insight into the subjective perspective of such a woman – an attraction in its own right. Elise sits in her dressing gown in front of her dressing table mirror, which proudly reflects her new status. She takes up a small hand mirror. But instead of it affording a multiple view of her external features, she sees in it figures from her own inner life. Magically, there appear within the mirror's oval frame, in miniature and one after the other, her weeping mother who is wringing her hands, and then her angry father. The camera engages us through this minor bit of artistry; it shows us the conscience through a visual attraction rather than by means of the gesturally mimetic expression of an inner self. After this brief excursion into special effects, the film returns to her milieu. The door opens, and the count enters the room laden down with hat boxes and new clothes. The apparition has vanished, and Elise takes delight in unwrapping the packages.

This special effect is one example of how the film continues to develop its narrative on the basis of the principle of Variety rather than subordinating it to the dramatic form. The conflict evoked by the old ties, despite the protagonist's clear decision to opt for a new life, is articulated by means of the montage of subjective images which preserves the unity of the woman's point of view. The autonomy of the scene supports that of the woman in the film; parallel editing would have withheld the realization of the reactions of the parents from the gaze of the heroine, and thus from her control. This would have also given an opportunity to the public to turn against the protagonist, to identify with the parents instead of with the gaze that their 'lost daughter' directs upon them.

The film, far from reasserting the power of the moral superego over the narrator/heroine, goes on to show her and the audience the enticements of leisure. We are allowed a glimpse into Maxim's. There the women enjoy themselves at least as much as the men: they become exceptionally animated while drinking wine and champagne and dancing with one another. Elise too enjoys this unrestrained erotic atmosphere. Ultimately she is

Plate 28 Probiermamsell: special effect – Elise sees her weeping mother in her fancy mirror. By courtesy of the Deutsches Bundesarchiv, Koblenz.

Plate 29 Probiermamsell: Maxim's, women enjoying themselves as much as the men. By courtesy of the Deutsches Bundesarchiv, Koblenz.

accompanied to the cab not only by her count, but by her new suitor as well.

Although discovered in the act of being unfaithful, the woman is not represented as the helpless victim plagued by a guilty conscience. In view of all the indications that the enraged count will abandon her, she leaves the flat in a rage. She seems helpless for the first time two scenes later, when the engineer imperiously demands her jewellery, her only joy, so as to meet his gambling debts. Intimidated, she brings him the jewellery box. Yet as soon as he is gone, she vents her indignation and decides that under such circumstances she no longer wants to continue leading the life of a mistress. The memory of her old way of life intensifies, and, as the intertitle reminds us, 'Elise longs for home'. Whereas the two older lovers – both corpulent and sporting moustaches – were already reverse mirror images of the father as moral authority, the film's ending enforces the father's disempowerment. 'Get away, you miserable woman!' is his predictable response to his daughter's return home; the fiancé pleads in vain on her behalf. We see her leave the house through the front garden on an entirely ordinary late afternoon. In the next scene she is in an open field criss-crossed by railroad tracks. A train approaches in the distance, but even before the viewer has realized what the purpose of this walk through the field might be, we catch sight of the fiancé who runs behind her and takes her in his arms. The train passes by. This sequence in its entirety does not achieve its effect through drama, through the creation of emotional tension, but instead, once again, through the appeal of the outdoor shot of the railroad yard and the train roaring past. The dispassionate poetry of the camera's gaze, within which technology and nature appear momentarily reconciled, accompanies the heroine up to the very end. It could not be further removed from the suggestion of a higher power of fate that will ultimately catch up with the woman who has strayed from the proper path. At the end of this film, the desire of the men for the woman – now transferred from the lovers to the fiancé – is allied with the self-affirmation of her life against paternal authority. In the early narrative cinema that concentrates on social drama, the exhibition of the female body for voyeuristic male desire is not necessarily incompatible with the establishment of a female narrative perspective prompted by the appeal to a female public.

Marriage, which *Heimgefunden* no longer shows but instead allows us to imagine at the close of the film, would not re-establish the patriarchal order, but consummate physical love between social subjects. Other social dramas deal with ordinary married life in patriarchal society: narratives representing the lives of married women often display a similar blend of sobriety and fascination as do the stories of mistresses. *Perlen bedeuten Tränen (Pearls Mean Tears*, 1911) shows the development of the marriage of a lieutenant – from the delirium of the newly-weds, through the boredom of everyday married life, to the errant husband and the patiently faithful behaviour of the wife, concluding with their reconciliation. *Um Haaresbreite (By a Hair's Breadth*, 1912) presents an upper middle-class marriage in which the husband's club is as important to him as his wife and his home, his child and domestic help. This creates problems. His male friendship is destroyed by the advances his friend makes toward his wife. The life of the family is threatened by this male relationship which has turned into hate. The security of the household rests solely on the self-assuredness of the wife.

Although both of the films discussed above are Messter productions with Henny Porten, the first directed by Adolf Gärtner and the second by Curt Starck, neither film represents the suffering of the married woman in a melodramatic way. Rather, the films narrate scenes from a marriage and offer descriptions of the milieu. The documentary camera counteracts a sentimentalizing perception of the staged drama of 'real life'. There is a wonderful street scene in *Perlen bedeuten Tränen* when the crisis in the marriage has reached its peak. The scene shows a jewellery store: the wares on display in the window can be gaped at in every detail. The heroine arrives and disappears into the store. The shot, which is photographically precise and poetic at once (an effect of chiaroscuro and multiple reflections of light), focuses the gaze on the woman's walk; it pre-empts the melodramatic sense of a 'victim's gait' (she is selling her pearl necklace to pay her debt). *Um Haaresbreite* devotes considerable time to delineating the dramatic events between the rivals – the death of one man from the bullet of a poacher, the flight of the other who believes himself to be under suspicion of murder – instead of tightening them dramatically. The film loses itself in the appeal of the landscape shots, the images of a seemingly endless flight and pursuit through the woods, fields and river.

And yet, these marriage films differ in form from the films about mistresses. In *Heimgefunden*, the dramatic form, as a framework for male judgement which restricts the female narrative perspective, becomes one element within the narration. *Perlen bedeuten Tränen* and *Um Haaresbreite* develop a new concept of drama out of an element of the story. Both films revolve around objects whose meaning transcends their narrative function and generates tension around the solution of their 'mystery'. The newly-wed young woman receives a pearl necklace as a gift from her mother-in-law along with a hand-delivered letter, telling her: 'They always say that "pearls mean tears", but to me they have brought only happiness.' From that point on, the female viewer will wait to see whether the superstition will be confirmed or whether the enlightened attitude of the mother-in-law will prove correct. In the end, the experience of the gift-giver rather than 'popular wisdom' proves true, so that the significant object generates a dramatic tension in the minds of the audience which both responds to and criticizes a deep-seated belief in fate.

In *Um Haaresbreite*, the rival who is dying alone in the woods writes a letter that exonerates the husband. The wind blows the sheet of paper away. From then on the audience wonders – will the letter be found, will it be able to fulfil its redemptive function? The couple's child, who is playing, picks it up and wraps it around a bouquet of flowers he has picked for his mother. In keeping with melodramatic convention, the pearls in the first film and the letter here generate the expectation that deflects the narrative from everyday life. Thus, the enjoyment of the individual scenes that have been meticulously observed and attractively staged and photographed is overlaid with an eagerness to find a solution to the 'mystery'. Inserted into a suspense-generating plot, the scenes finally take on tendentially a new quality that curtails the effect of the documentary camera.

This new quality lies in the stimulation of the voyeuristic libido without anything explicitly erotic being offered on the screen. The objects that are charged with meaning in the marriage stories tend to usurp the function of the suggestive scenes in the mistress films. Since bourgeois marriage is not an institution of sexual pleasure (on the contrary, it renders the married woman taboo as a public object of desire), the female protagonist cannot be staged openly as an attraction for the male gaze. The marriage films, therefore, relinquish a residual moment of the cinema of attractions, with which the female story had joined forces in opposition to the establishment of a bourgeois patriarchal cinema. The eagerness for the solution of the mystery revolving around the object thus replaces the erotic attraction that could be provoked by the heroine's negligée or by the hero's kiss upon her lips. But it is precisely this erotic stimulation that continues to have an effect, repressed and displaced within this eagerness.

It was more explosive for women than for men to be able to see the stories from everyday married life invested with this secret pleasure. Pleasure was defined as taboo for women within bourgeois marriage during the Wilhelminian period.[6] The situation was presumably different for men, who had access to mistresses and prostitutes. For women, however, the repression of sexuality in marriage amounted to a repression of their sexuality altogether. How much more a rupture, therefore, it must have meant in their everyday lives to be able to observe in the cinema with pleasurable expectation the complications of married life.

This form of marriage drama transformed and contained the elements of the cinema of attractions that still survived in the early narrative cinema because it responded to the gaze of the female consumer. The cinema opened up the perspective of mistresses and prostitutes to women, who constituted a financially potent (*finanzträchtig*) public. At the same time, the cinema organized a perspective on marriage not only as an institution of reproduction, but also as the dramatic form of their sexual life. It thus rechannelled the sexual curiosity that was released for the sake of consumption.

Such attempts at rechannelling were not simply repressive, but also productive. The inclusion of erotic attractions in stories about women allowed the social problematic of the sexes to be rendered visible; by the same token, the dramatization of the female narrative by means of an objective correlative reflected the social relationship – the marriage – back onto repressed sexual relations. Fundamentally, *Perlen bedeuten Tränen* and *Um Haaresbreite* are about nothing other than the deteriorating sexual interest of the husband and his homoerotically based leisure-time enjoyment. What the officer's casino is to one man, the club is to another; one relaxes with a ballerina, the other by going hunting.

The social marriage dramas mediated between a female narrative perspective and the cinema of attractions, and also between both of these and the dramatic form. In this mediation lay the real significance of objects which take on the status of actors. On the one hand, they are everyday objects that play a role as props in the course of the narrative. On the other, they possess a fetish character in so far as they appear in place of the openly erotic attraction in the mistress films. They substitute for the sexual element repressed in the representation of the marriage: the happiness that the mother-in-law promises with the pearl necklace on the wedding day is a reference to what the bride anxiously anticipates before the wedding night. The rival's letter stands for the sexual desires that intrude into the marriage from outside, as well as for the mending of the damaged marriage bond. Thus the meaning-laden object occupies the sexual fantasy of the public.

This tension, this provocation of sexuality through a special staging of an object within the cinema of attractions, is not the only tension, however. It is not only their fetish character that lends the objects significance beyond their function in the plot. Their significance also originates in the fact that, in the privileged status of the object *vis-à-vis* the story, a moment returns that might be a refuge for the dramatic frame as the representative of patriarchal power. Displaced by the female narrative perspective on the level of dramatic form, it remains present in the film as an ominous substance: will the mother-in-law's experience be productive for the young woman, or will the pearls only confirm the repressive role of the mother in patriarchy, i.e., preventing her son from forming a happy relationship with the opposite sex? The meaning-laden object mediates between erotic attraction and prohibition, the id of the female viewer and her superego; it dramatizes the gaze that is cast upon the story.

Heimgefunden demonstrates how the narrative revocation of the authority of patriarchal censorship made possible a representation of marriage as a voluntary association for what Kant terms the 'reciprocal use of the sexual organs'. Thus the new medium of film was reacting to social changes that were pressing for a liberalization of rights within marriage, as was being demanded by progressive social movements at the time, especially the women's movement. Patriarchal violence is ascribed to the past; the films retain it as the prehistory of their story in the form of a pearl necklace or a letter. The patriarchal order appears not only as something that has been conquered, but is simultaneously present as something that has been internalized. However, while melodramas were, during the same period, already attempting to psychologize in a way that made external fate into an internal one, these social dramas of marriage attach the continuing presence of outdated powers onto what is objectively visible. In their foregrounding of such objects, these films place the hope for a release from the 'return of the same' within the relationship between the sexes. The function of the significant objects oscillates between a release of the longing for earthly happiness and the blinding of sexual desire in the fetish object.

To the female public for whom the marriage dramas were chiefly produced, these objects ultimately stand for the male sex as patriarchal power and as sexual object. What seems to be at stake for the female spectator, who is uncertain about marriage and who seeks enlightenment or pleasure in the cinema, is that which the married woman is deprived of, that which seeks its satisfaction elsewhere, that which threatens and beckons outside marriage – that 'beyond' which has been rendered socially taboo. The bourgeois appropriation of German cinema through the melodrama developed a repressive distraction in the sublimation of the female gaze and its erotic power. By contrast, the dramatization of the female gaze through the social drama tended towards a representation of male sexuality, of the man as sexual object. This tendency obviously collided with the influence of the guardians of bourgeois culture; social drama, unlike melodrama, disappeared from narrative cinema after the First World War. Now the meaning-laden image world of film completely assumed the role of the taboo.

Translated by Jamie Owen Daniel (with Richard Dyer). Translation originally published in *Camera Obscura*; reprinted (with modifications) by permission.

NOTES

1 This is not due simply to their iconography which, similarly to that of reproduced oil paintings, is a mass-cultural popularization of classical bourgeois art.

2 On censorship, see the entry by Corinna Müller in Helga Belach (ed.) *Henny Porten*, Berlin, 1986:

> In the publication of the censorship decision of the Berlin authorities of 8/5/1911, the film entitled *Ein Streik und seine Folgen* is listed under the rubric, 'completely forbidden'. The censor's comment: 'Strike, the cutting of a cable, operation on a child'. In the publication dated 8/6/1911, the lifting

of the ban is announced: 'The picture is now only banned for children. The strike, cutting of the cable, and operation on the child have been cut'. In the last version, under the title *Tragödie eines Streiks*, the scene 'the cutting of a cable' is again included. The film was released with the restriction that it not be shown to minors.

(p. 178)

3 The operation on the child itself had to be cut in accordance with the censor's stipulation. See Note 2.
4 As Emilie Altenloh explains, 'Social questions are of essential interest. These dramas for the most part reflect a woman's struggle between her natural, feminine instincts and conflicting social conditions' (*Zur Soziologie des Kino*, Hamburg, 1977, p. 58).
5 A publication of the Deutsche Bund für Mutterschutz and the Internationale Vereinigung für Mutterschutz und Sexualreform (German Society for the Protection of Mothers and International Society for the Protection of Mothers and Sexual Reform).
6 On marriage, sexuality and the situation of women in Wilhelminian Germany, see, for example: Ute Frevert, *Frauen geschichte zwischen bürgerlicher Verbesserung*, Frankfurt, 1986; Isabel V. Hull, ' "Sexualität" und Bürgerliche Gesellschaft', in Ute Frevert (ed.) *Bürgerinnen und Bürger*, Göttingen, 1988.

REFERENCES

Altenloh, Emilie (1977) *Zur Soziologie des Kino. Die Kino-unternehmungen und die sozialen Schichten ihrer Besucher*, Hamburg: Medienladen.
Belach, Helga (ed.) (1986) *Henny Porten. Der erste deutsche Filmstar 1890–1960*, Berlin: Haude & Speners.
Frevert, Ute (1986) *Frauen geschichte zwischen bürgerlicher Verbesserung und Neuer Weiblichkeit*, Frankfurt: Suhrkamp.
Gunning, Tom (1986) 'The cinema of attractions: early film, its spectator and the avant-garde', *Wide Angle* 8(3–4): 63–70.
Hermann, Babette (1914) 'Aus den Aufzeichnungen einer Prostitutieren', in Helene Stöcker (ed.) *Die neue Generation*, Berlin: Nikolassee.
Hull, Isabel V. (1988) ' "Sexualität" und bürgerliche Gesellschaft', in Ute Frevert (ed.) *Bürgerinnen und Bürger. Geschlechtsverhältnisse im 19. Jahrhundert*, Göttingen: Vandenhock und Ruprecht.
Petro, Patrice (1989) *Joyless Streets: Women and Melodramatic Representation in Weimar Germany*, Princeton: Princeton University Press.

16

'FILM STARS DO NOT SHINE IN THE SKY OVER POLAND'

The absence of popular cinema in Poland

Anita Skwara

In the past four decades nothing like popular cinema in its typical western form existed in Poland. No genre in this country with its own tradition, classical examples and model texts can be singled out and labelled as popular in the way Charles Altman, for example, distinguishes this phenomenon in the context of US culture.

Till now what Polish commercial entertainment movies there were, were chance productions, generated by occasional social demand or a director's whim. The films of this kind that appeared sporadically did find an audience, but their culture-forming significance was minuscule, almost negligible. Put aphoristically: film stars do not shine in the sky over Poland. Popular cinema in Poland lived its precarious life outside a paradigm of filmic art which was a product of two circumstances, namely the economic conditions shaped at the turn of the 1940s and 1950s, and the cultural substratum embodied in the romantic tradition.

To establish the correct perspective, let us go back to the 1940s when contemporary Polish cinema assumed its institutional form in Sielce, a town on the Oka River in the Soviet Union. On 15 June 1943 the Czołówka Filmowa (Film Spearhead), an embryo of the future film studio, was created as part of the Tadeusz Kościuszko First Infantry Division. The first film produced by Czołówka Filmowa was the documentary *Przysięgamy ziemi polskiej (We Vow to the Land of Poland*, 1943). When this film was being made, hostilities were still in progress and the future shape of Poland was still unknown, although to all those billeted on the banks of the Oka its fate appeared sealed. The future of the Polish post-war film industry was also determined by the very fact that it was born on the frontline and was being developed by people who allied themselves with the Red Army and Soviet communism.

The time and place of Czołówka Filmowa's creation made the event paradoxical. A single institution combined two basic and in a sense opposing sets of values of Polish culture. The first and by far the more significant of these was the ethos of the struggle for national independence, ever present in Polish tradition and art, and pre-eminent since the end of the eighteenth century when Poland was partitioned and culture became the mainstay of national identity.

The other set of values in play in that June of 1943 was the ethos of proletarian class struggle beneath the workers' red banner, conducted in the spirit of Rosa Luxemburg's precepts. In Polish tradition the latter have a somewhat alien ring about them, placing class interests above national issues. Polish soldiers who fought alongside the Red Army, from their baptism of fire at Lenino to the storming of Berlin, wrote a dramatic chapter in this conflict of ideas, bringing freedom to their motherland (the former ethos) at the price of an alliance that was as merciless as enslavement (the latter ethos).

These events of what we now see as the distant past, together with their later consequences, shaped the paradigm of Polish post-war cinematography. The technologically provincial Polish film industry, annually turning out no more than thirty films, is fascinating in its many political, cultural and economic paradoxes, not least the conflict between preferences inherent in the model of socialist culture and in the Polish national style codified during the romantic period. Also evident was (and still is, despite the collapse of the previous political system) the peculiar phenomenon of central European culture, created by small 'provincial' countries whose spiritual and material existence has been under threat for centuries. As Yevgeny Yevtushenko recently wrote, 'a poet in Russia is more than just a poet'. In such ominous circumstances art was supposed to trigger immunity mechanisms, create moral authorities and hierarchies of values. Paraphrasing Yevtushenko, one might say that 'cinema in Poland is more than just cinema'. Or at least was – till yesterday.

To elaborate this metaphor, let us go back once again to the 1940s, to the days when fascism was in its death throes and when foundations were being laid for a new socialist state in Poland. In July 1944 the July Manifesto outlined principles of the state system, and the Wytwórnia Filmowa Wojska Polskiego (Polish Army Film Company) was set up in Lublin, with the participation of Jerzy Bossak and Aleksander Ford. A year later this film company was moved to Łódź, a city which eventually became the production capital of Polish cinema.

The productions in the years from 1944 to 1949 divide into three principal categories:

(1) filmic epitaphs depicting smouldering ruins and focusing on Polish martyrdom; an example here is Wanda Jakubowska's *Ostatni etap* (*The Last Stage*, 1948);
(2) filmic 'hymns of victory' depicting the deeds of Polish soldiers fighting

Plate 30 Polish martyrdom: *Ostatni etap.* By courtesy of the British Film Institute, London.

alongside the Red Army, for example Jerzy Bossak's *Zaqlada Berlina (The Destruction of Berlin*, 1945);

(3) the Polska Kronika Filmowa (Polish Newsreel), which was a kind of information service whose impact was extremely significant given the dramatic pace of transformations at that time.

Following the congress of filmmakers in Wisła in November 1949, Polish cinematography was almost entirely subjected to the aesthetics and thematic and formal preferences of socialist realism. This complete cultural leftward turn towards the most radical and univocal adaptation of art to the purposes of Marxism-Leninism made Polish cinematography a typically totalitarian phenomenon. Despite this, its guiding principles appear to be in paradoxical accord with the ideas behind the contemporaneous European cinematography. Setting aside, rashly perhaps, all the differences which arose in Europe in the 1930s and 1940s in the aftermath of fascism, Nazism and the earlier revolution in Russia, we see the universal conviction in European culture of those times that cinema is an extremely significant social, political and ideological factor.

A key to understanding these tendencies in Polish socialist realism is the concept of 'cinefication'. Today this is a linguistic curio, a relic word not to be found even in specialized dictionaries. In the 1950s, however, it was a watchword of cultural policy determined by strictly ideological mechanisms. Its sense is closely linked to its etymology. The word's origins go back to the famous and reverentially quoted aphorism by Lenin: 'Communism is Soviet power plus electrification of the entire country'. We may come up with a long series of related terms – electrification, gasification, cinefication – identical as to their word formation scheme, pedigree and relation towards designates. They were to refer to mass-scale processes organized by the authorities (the socialist state) and meant to serve the newly forged society presided over by the working class. The processes were launched along the lines of the economic and ideological principles of Marxism-Leninism. Moreover, they implied the belief in their positive outcome, in the coming of a better future when gas, electricity and the cinema would be at last universally available commodities.

The placing of cinema in such company predefined its function in society and the character of its products. The filmmaker was classified as 'cineficant', again by analogy to 'gasificant' and 'electrificant', functionaries of the respective processes. And here we come to a specifically Polish paradox. This filmic craftsman, so ranked by the appellation applied to him, turned out to be destined not for mass and serial production but rather for the creation of films truly great in their obligatory typicalness, works displaying individual traits despite the 'loyalty' imposed upon them, spontaneous within the framework of totalitarian codes. In manifestos of socialist realism one encounters the categories of 'creative inspiration', 'pathos', 'heroism'

223

Plate 31 The 'second Polish cinema's social realism': Krystyna Janda, Jerzy Radziwitowicz and Lech Wałesa in *Czloziek z żelaza*. By courtesy of the British Film Institute, London.

(usually in the context of labour) and even 'the subconscious', a concept which sounded suspiciously reactionary to the Stalinist ear. An illustration of this is a speech by the then president Bolesław Bierut:

> What would be the worth of artistic creativity, or art, knowledge or literature, which would overlook, which would fail to comprehend, fail to draw inspiration from the profoundly revolutionary transform- ations and phenomena which live in the minds of millions of simple people, which subconsciously jolt their psyches?
>
> (Kierczyńska 1951: 161)

This peculiar marriage of lay materialist ideology and mystic terminology proved viable. It was motivated by the need to conform to national style, to a language which was natural to Polish culture. This phenomenon in fact reflected yet another paradox: film in a people's, a proletarian country was to emerge as a powerful and ambitious artistic discipline, and the artist was destined to become a socialist visionary driven by materialist inspiration. On the other hand, the receiver of this art was pictured as a proletarian sensitive to tradition, familiar with the works of Diderot and

Mickiewicz, and also well versed in Marx and Stalin. As in Italian neo-realism, the foundations for this all-embracing revolt were to be laid down by a complete reconstruction of awareness: 'The Marxist-Leninist world outlook ought to recast the psychology of society' (Kierczyńska 1951: 162).

Effective barricades were in those days being erected to keep out all qualities and phenomena smacking of capitalism. Today we smile at stories of musicians being persecuted for playing jazz, a music pulsating with the rhythms of 'dastardly imperialism'. Similar ostracism was applied to Coca Cola, a beverage which, as Roland Barthes would say, is mythology from everyday American life. The consumer of western mass art was seen as a manipulated individual fed lies and illusions of an invented world (e.g. westerns, adventure movies) or deluded with the false glitter of a bourgeois and reactionary culture. In cinematography, complete institutional trans-formation (nationalization, monopolization, centralization of management) was accompanied by a thorough reappraisal of objectives and ideals held up to Polish cinema. A theoretical model of cinema was created, defining its rights and duties as well as its manner of existence, from the moment of the pre-filmic encounter of the artist with reality all the way to the social functioning of the finished screen work. As one provision of the relevant law put it, film was to be 'a means of information and social upbringing, and a means of dissemination of education and culture' (Zajicek 1968: 35). Cinema as an element of commercialized entertainment was unthinkable within this paradigm.

If we were to seek something like the Hegelian 'absolute idea' in Marx-ism, we would arrive at the category of work. Heidegger's assertion that for Marxism 'the entire being is a matter of work' (quoted in Tischner 1981: 49) explains why work is at the top of the Marxist hierarchy of values. Art determined by this ideology focuses on the work ethos. The emerging communist empire grimly resisted anything that was not work or was an alternative to work. The heroes of 'production art', another description of socialist realism, practically rid their lives of the problem of free time, time outside work. Myth-creating everyday reality embellished their existence: work champions doing 300 per cent of their quotas, plans being exceeded, Stakhanovites. Culture stood side by side with them, aimed floodlights at them, finding nourishment in 'class passion, love for the people, hatred of the bourgeoisie, fidelity towards the working class – the leader of progress' (Żółkiewski 1950: 248).

To underscore the Marxist interpretation of work, we will contrast it with a text from an entirely different culture; we may even say from an entirely different civilization: 'To invoke the notion of "entertainment" is to call forth our Puritan heritage, according to which anything which is not *work* has no value: only productive activity deserves society's full sanction' (Altman 1977: 31). This quote from Altman, applicable to an exegesis of American genre film, would be a perfectly acceptable slogan of socialist realism. The question now arises: what mechanisms made two different cultures, the US and the (Stalinist) Central European, both erected on a work ethos, differ so widely in their attitudes towards that which is not work, towards entertainment, show business, mass culture? The United States, exhibiting the nonchalance of a culture aware of its attractiveness, power and stability, developed a gigantic mechanism of commercial culture. As Altman puts it: 'Treated as play by the Protestant ethic, forms of entertainment are considered marginal, and thus somehow unreal' (ibid.: 33). Also, as a consequence, entertainment is perceived as something harmless. No such luxury could be afforded by Marxist ideology, deprived of a sense of security and a sense of humour in the areas it conquered.

One other aspect of socialist realism in Poland is that new contents were partly injected into forms already assimilated by mass imagination and by the nation's cultural awareness. During the past two centuries Poles have been historically conditioned to absolutize preferred attitudes and concepts. The nineteenth and twentieth centuries were in Poland a time of an 'autocracy of warriors', a time when the ethos of struggle dominated all others. Once independence was officially restored in the mid–1940s, only the weapons and military strategy changed. The struggle continued, only this time on the 'front of labour'. Campaigns proliferated, waged on the battlefields of culture, economy, reconstruction of consciousness. A concrete enemy materialized – the 'class enemy' – exceedingly dangerous because of his omnipresence. Hence the pioneer call of 'Be vigilant', applicable to social, political and cultural life. The arms in these battles, and also insidious weapons in the hands of the 'enemy', may equally well have been a rifle or a poem, a film or a musical score, or even the way a person looked.

Thus there is a great difference between the western 'productive activity' of which Altman speaks and the absolutist interpretation of work in Marxist dialectic, a philosophy which in Poland was additionally filtered through the religion of struggle universally embraced in this country. To put it simply, if work is treated pragmatically, then work time is followed by time for rest which one has 'earned', for something that is not work. However, if work is also 'struggle', then it is a total activity, an activity taking over its subject entirely. It is thus inconceivable that socialist realist art could be reconciled with entertainment, with mass culture containing elements of spontaneity and ritual, of revolt, a culture often fascinated by designs of worlds turned upside-down.

On the other hand, an obvious aspect of these forms of cultural activity is subordination to an official system of values and preferences as well as a strategy aimed at consolidating an existing state of affairs. For that reason in the Poland of the 1950s entertainment, including popular cinema as the most potent form of entertainment, could not be attractive to any of the parties involved. Marxist-Leninist culture rejected those cultural forms as too reactionary, incapable of severing ties with the bourgeois mentality. For any opposition that might arise, for the cultural dissidents (whose potential activity was effectively paralysed by the state monopolization of cinematography), to dabble in such forms would be pitifully infantile revisionism.

I should perhaps explain why I devote so much space to the socialist realist episode in the history of Polish culture and cinematography, especially since the turn of the 1950s and 1960s witnessed the most celebrated chapter in our cinema, namely the 'Polish School' with films by Wajda, Munk, Kawalerowicz and Kutz, all of which betray their romantic origin in both content and form. In Stalinist Poland, socialist realism was the most spectacular example of totalitarian strategy in such diverse domains as economy and culture, politics and art, industrial production and philosophy. It was, moreover, intended to be the great Polish aesthetic and ethical revolution. Individual awareness and the social archetype were slated for remodelling. Looking back on socialist realism, it is amazing to see how the opposite of the intended goals was achieved. The trend brought defeat upon itself by its caricatural prophetism, and Polish cinema emerged from it with a shameful achievement, the *produkcyjniak* (trivial film extolling production), which was supposed to create a new kind of national epos but ended up as a grotesque vehicle of crude propaganda, a self-ridiculing fiasco.

The Polish School was a counterposition to socialist realism, devastating in its effects, evidence of the durability of national traditions and myths. This triumphant return to Polish roots, to romanticism, occurred in a system shaped in the 1940s and consolidated in the 1950s – another paradox. It was the same institutions and the same production model as before that made decisions about Polish cinema, and this situation continued into later decades. Like the whole Polish economy, Polish cinematography was in the grip of insurmountable problems caused by the absurdities of the political economy of socialism.

Let us proceed, however, from the economic order of things to aesthetics. The Polish school reinfused Polish cinematography, laid barren by socialist realism, with that national cultural paradigm which the 1950s stood on its head. The 'engineer of souls' again became a prophetic bard, in both calling and name, and the cineficant assumed the role of 'organizer of the national imagination'. Andrzej Wajda, with his *Popiól i diament* (*Ashes and Diamonds*, 1958), *Lotna (1959)* and *Kanal* (*The Canal*, 1957), is naturally placed alongside the three great romantic poets, Mickiewicz, Słowacki and Norwid. Everything in these films by Wajda is a protest against socialist realist aesthetics: the organization of filmic language is different, as are the story and the protagonist. The attitude shared by the two opposing orientations is one of disdain for commercial art which is seen as a playground of vulgarity, cheapness and poor taste. Also shared is a negative reaction against cinematography as an industry, the artist seen as a man of show business, and gauging the value of a work of art by market categories.

The phenomenon of the Polish school and its amazing viability in the mainstream of Polish culture hinges also on something else: the works of Wajda, Munk and Kawalerowicz sit at the intersection of two orientations: artistic and 'cult' cinema. The latter tendency has been characterized by Umberto Eco:

> It must provide a completely furnished world so that its fans can quote characters and episodes as if they were aspects of the fan's private sectarian world, a world about which one can make up quizzes and play trivia games so that the adepts of the sect recognize through each other a shared expertise.
>
> (Eco 1986: 198)

The Polish School did indeed furnish and order national imagination. Its content and form were the peak and crowning of two centuries of insurrection. The artists creating this film trend tackled grand issues, addressed questions on the philosophy of history, and made statements about the conflict between the individual and history. In his *Popiół i diament* Wajda made admirable use of ancient tragedy, filling categories like guiltless guilt, fate, the moral norm and catharsis with modern Polish reality. It is surprising that despite the inner consistency of works produced by the Polish School, despite their unequivocally high art character, their structure contains elements typical of a cult film such as *Casablanca* (USA, 1941), which, according to Eco 'must be already ramshackle, rickety, unhinged in itself' (ibid.). In film history textbooks, *Popiół i diament, Lotna* or *Kanal* evoke a concrete, noble and artistically fruitful direction. In the audience's memory, in mass imagination, these films exist primarily as 'visual icebergs', as 'disconnected series of images, of peaks' (ibid.), such as the mounted uhlans charging tanks in *Lotna*, Maciek Chełmicki lighting alcohol in glasses and then dying on a rubbish heap, and the dance at the end of the party (*Popiół i diament*), the bars blocking the only remaining way of escape in *Kanal*, and Jaś Krone committing suicide by jumping down the spiral staircase in *Pokolenie* (*A Generation*, 1955). Let us not, however, succumb to the illusion that the Polish School conforms fully to Eco's theoretical model. Eco writes that the addressee of cult cinema

> must suspect it is not true that works are created by their authors. Works are created by works, texts are created by texts, all together they speak to each other independently of the intention of their authors. A cult movie is the proof that, as literature comes from literature, cinema comes from cinema
>
> (ibid.: 199)

Here we come up against a clear divergence of objectives and origin. The formal and thematic reciprocity characteristic of the western version of cult cinema is definitely of secondary importance in films by Wajda, Munk and Kawalerowicz. Paraphrasing Eco, one might say that 'the Polish School of cinema is the proof that film comes from the nation's cultural awareness'.

The Polish School phenomenon, combining artistic and a kind of cult cinema, was a direct consequence of the historical and political circumstances affecting all of Polish culture, a culture that was obliged, or perhaps condemned, to speak out on behalf of the nation or a community. Polish film was sworn in as national art, expected to deliver syntheses of the past and forecasts for the future. Surrounded by the giants of History, Fate and God, Polish cinema could not live by the phrase, 'Was that artillery fire, or is it my heart pounding?' The melancholy of the New York gangster would leave the Polish audience cold. This specifically Polish syndrome was admirably expressed by Adam Zagajewski, a chronicler of Poland's spiritual reality: 'Crime stories are impossible here. You always know who the culprit is: the state' (Zagajewski 1986: 91). Thus the two diametrically opposite formations – socialist realism controlled from above and the spontaneous 'neo-romanticism' of Polish cinema in the 1960s – went hand in hand in excluding the third standard of show business as it evolved in the west. This hypothesis appears to be confirmed by the more recent history of Polish cinematography, by films of the 1970s and the very beginning of the 1980s. Neither the so-called second Polish cinema, nor the cinema of moral concern, nor films settling old accounts, aspire to be commercial productions. Nothing can be more remote from fun than the atmosphere pervading films like Zaorski's *Matka Królów* (*The Króls' Mother*, 1987), Bugajski's *Przesłuchanie* (*The Interrogation*, 1982) or Wajda's *Człowiek z żelaza* (*Man of Iron*, 1981).

When martial law was imposed in Poland, these films became what German expressionism was for fascism (*toutes proportions gardées*). The date 13 December 1981 is a symbolic turning point in Polish history and culture, hence also in cinematography. The national style, the paradigm that could accommodate both socialist realism and the critical assessment thereof, dating to the turn of the 1970s and 1980s, was badly, possibly even critically shaken. For the first time since the war, cinema stood overwhelmed and powerless before this fact, so unprecedented in character. Also for the first time in the post-war period the authorities (or rather the powers running the country), part of the public and a certain group of artists announced the need for mass art in Poland. Censorship became extremely tolerant of steamy eroticism and brutality which suddenly permeated the abruptly revived Polish entertainment cinema. The great directors fell silent while cinemas reverberated with trivial, sometimes hysterical laughter triggered by imported and domestic commercial productions. The neologism 'Polish-made American film' was coined to describe clumsy imitations disgusting the more refined audience and generating in the more average cinema-goer complexes and desires impossible to satisfy.

The poetics of American genre cinema transplanted to Poland turned out to be disfunctional, alien, astonishingly naïve or vulgar and simplistic. Polish cinema stands a chance of survival and development only when it is national in character, when it arises directly from the traditions, culture and myths forming Polish awareness. Rather than stories haltingly delivered in some Polish-English tongue, it must deliver messages in a distinctly Polish idiom.

Today, in the early 1990s, Polish film is in a 'state of exhaustion', an expression once used by John Barth to describe modern prose (Barth 1967). Let us hope that Polish cinema, like prose in Barth's predictions, will again be filled with content, form and ideas after a period of decline. A change of tack is obviously necessary. If Polish cinema intends to retain its presence in Europe, it must devise for itself an entirely new formula of post-totalitarian art. This will require a new filmic idiom, a kind of formal revolt which will not make life easy for artists or the public, since it would run counter to the engrained habits and canons of national tradition.

If Polish art, cinema included, is to retain its spiritual and artistic autonomy, it must permanently rid itself of the Polish complex of the giants: of History, of institutionally understood Providence, and the Insurrection ethos. Already in 1983 Adam Zagajewski described the coming decade as 'the time of shattering of mirrors' (Zagajewski 1986: 90), or rather the huge surfaces reflecting the nation but failing to show individual faces.

This long awaited post-totalitarianism of culture, politics and social life has led to atomization, to the disintegration of communities. The collective nature of our existence, so amplified by the blow that came on 13 December 1981 and later in times of martial law, requires radical change. Yet the Poles of the 1990s spare neither effort nor sacrifice to lay the foundations for a society of consumption and democracy, or rather of democratic consumption, chanting the slogan, 'Catching up with Europe', with the same reverence as Polish knights once invoked 'God, honour and the motherland'.

We are thus saddled with the duty to preserve our provincialism, a provincialism not in the usual sense of the word but in the sense arising from the Latin word *provincia* meaning possessions. Our culture possesses a place in central Europe, experience gained in the yoke of two totalitarianisms, the fascist and the communist, and on the currently negotiated twisted road towards democracy. Polish art, Polish cinema must be a product of all these factors. That this is in fact desirable is confirmed by the praise lavished on the most successful recent Polish film *Ucieczka z kina*

Wolność (*Escape from Cinema 'Freedom'*, 1990). Wojciech Marczewski tells his story of a censor in the form of a moral play abandoning didactism and propaganda for even the most noble truths. Viewers with their ability to use filmic material to construct answers to their own questions are respected to an extent few other Polish films can boast of.

Forms of mass popular culture alternative to western ones will probably emerge in Poland in the near future. The increasingly economic regulation of life, the activation of market mechanisms in the promotion of culture (in the widest sense of the word) and the very principles of pluralism and democracy will perhaps lead to the creation of Polish music halls, crime novels (in which, contrary to Zagajewski's observation, the perpetrator is not easy to guess) and gangster films. Most likely, however, what will emerge are new forms of cultural entertainment, hard to predict at this stage.

We will have to wait quite a while for a Polish *Casablanca* though. Before a film like that is produced a new cultural formation must appear, one no longer based on dates of national upheavals, meditations of freedom fighters, and a sense of the inviolability of national archetypes. This new formation will be rooted in the year 1989 which witnessed a civilizational turning point in Poland, bloodless for a change, which was marked by a kind of embarrassment at the official proclamation of freedom and a hidden fear of the discipline of western pragmatism. For the time being, however, the vision of Europe, a Europe that is happy, rich and protective, a Europe that is blessed by the heritage of Vermeers and Fellinis, and which at the same time is as carefree and colourful as a frame from an American movie, this vision is an axiological category in Polish everyday thought, a category that is in fact at the top of the hierarchy of values. Let us just hope that the paralysis of autonomous artistic expression that we are now witnessing is only due to a momentary dizzy spell.

REFERENCES

Altman, Charles F. (1977) 'Towards a theory of genre film', in *Film: Historical-Theoretical Speculations. The 1977 Film Studies Annual. Part Two*, Pleasantville, NY: Redgrave.

Barth, John (1967) 'Literature of exhaustion', *Atlantic* 220.

Eco, Umberto (1986) *Travels in Hyperreality*, London: Picador.

Kierczyńska, M. (1951) *Spór o realizm*, Warsaw: Książka i Wiedza.

Tischner, J. (1981) *Polski kształt dialogu*, Paris: Editions Spotkania.

Zagajewski, A. (1986) *Solidarność i samotność*, Paris: Zeszyty Literackie, Cahiers Littéraires.

Zajicek, E. (1969) 'Produkcja filmów', in J. Wittek, W. Swieżynski, W. Wertenstein and J. Trafisz (eds) *Kinematografia polska w 25-leciu PRL*, Warsaw: Redakcja Wydawnictw Filmowych Centrali Wynajmu filmów.

Żółkiewski, S. (1949) 'Aktualne zagadnienia powojennej prozy polskiej', *Kuźnica* 4.

17

VALBORGSMÄSSOAFTON

Melodrama and gender politics in Swedish cinema

Tytti Soila

Much work on popular cinema stresses the element of ideological struggle within filmic texts. Such an assumption implies the existence of innate, contradictory discourses and illogical statements in films, that a film can contain several ideological 'voices' enunciated in and by different narrative devices.

This study will concentrate on two such contradictory discourses within a single film: one is an offensive *patriarchal discourse* which I wish to call *dominating* (instead of the usual 'dominant') to stress the sense of an ongoing process, a struggle. The other is a female discourse, which I call the *harassed discourse*, quite fragmented and yet clearly present, dimly seen through the fissures or tears in the smooth web of the patriarchal discourse. The dominating discourse exhibits values that can be seen as corresponding to the dominant ideology in the society, and the harassed discourse can be understood as one that draws on ideas and thoughts based on the real, painful experience of oppressed groups, especially women.

The dominating discourse expresses itself at every level of the narration, including *mise-en-scène*, dialogue and plot. The harassed discourse on the other hand finds expression through jarring 'slips of the tongue', gaps and irrational moments. It has to be put together from split pieces of dialogue and seems to be there only in order to be countered. This arises because the dominating ideology in a society always needs to argue against other ideologies; it has to legitimize itself when confronted with the actual experience of the oppressed groups in society. Since the popular media form a kind of forum for ideologies to expose themselves, it is likely that values and ideas in a popular film will relate to values of the people in the society (Hall *et al.* 1980). John Fiske (1984: 165–6) states: 'The notion of popularity [is] an easy fit between the discourses of the text and the discourses through which its model readers articulate and understand their social experience.'

Such a model may be applied to the flourishing tradition of melodrama in Sweden, particularly the films of the 1930s. This was the decade in Sweden when the bourgeois conception of the world was mediated to working people thanks to accelerating social mobility, a rapidly expanding middle class and the greater accessibility of the mass media. Also, contrary to what might be a common understanding, social democratic ideals carried on bourgeois norms and values, slowly suffocating what might be called a genuine working-class life style and culture (Frykman and Löfgren, 1985: 101–16). This was reflected in the thematic contents of the Swedish film melodrama where the emphasis during the 1930s shifted from social protest melodramas of the silent era (such as *Ingeborg Holm*, 1913) to the private problems of middle-class people. Characteristically, the social/political issues remained in the background of many films while being expressed and resolved within the private family sphere.

One of the best examples of this is *Valborgsmässoafton (Walpurgis Eve)*, a highly successful release of 1935 which earns a further incidental place in international film history for being Ingrid Bergman's fifth film and according to the leading film critic Robin Hood her definitive breakthrough on the screen, giving her credit for the first time as an independent artist: 'The most beautiful, most fervent lines are formulated by Ingrid Bergman who (in this film) has her great breakthrough. She seems to have freed herself from superfluous instruction' (*Stockholmstidningen*, 24 October 1935).

Valborgsmässoafton was a success and remained in the top twenty of the most popular domestic films made during the 1930s. Gustaf Edgren, the director of the film, was a well-established master of comedies during the 1920s who had an infallible feeling for the popular. At the beginning of the 1930s he had turned to directing more 'serious' films dealing with contemporary issues. A year before *Valborgsmässoafton* he had directed *Karl Fredrik regerar (Karl Fredrik Governs*, 1934), a comedy about a farm hand who becomes a Member of Parliament and later a cabinet minister. The film is a classic for its tendentious propaganda for the social democratic spirit and socio-political consensus on the Swedish model. Himself a conservative, Edgren was the brother-in-law of a distinguished social democratic politician called Spångberg and his next, more serious undertaking was the melodrama, *Valborgsmässoafton*, using a story that addressed the decreasing birth rate in the country.[1]

In the early 1930s the birth rate in Sweden was decreasing year by year as a consequence of the depression, unemployment and lack of decent housing. The Social Democrats had gained a majority in the 1932 Parliamentary elections and an extended reform programme was presented. Edgren's film was released only a year after Gunnar and Alva Myrdal's famous *Kris i befolknignsfrågan (Crisis in the Population Question*, 1934) had initiated a major debate over the living conditions of young families. (Both authors were well-known social democratic ideologists, who suggested several reforms to check the decline in the birth rate.) The film was not

233

perceived to have lived up to the Myrdal programme, and the social democratic newpaper *Socialdemokraten* (25 October 1935) stated in its review that the film's approach to the problem was quite naïve. Nevertheless, the film can be seen as an emotional contribution to the debate. This study is limited to one aspect of that, namely family reproduction and the way mechanisms embedded in the narrative of the film debate the problem.

The patriarchal set of values in *Valborgsmässoafton* is constructed by the male characters in the narrative. This verbal expression in the dialogue is supported by the formal topography of the movie. Against the background of these particular values concerning home, family and childbirth there is a binary opposition constituted of/by two women, around which the plot revolves. The opposition is emphasized by juxtaposing (through editing) the different situations the two women are involved in. One of them, Clary, is married but unwilling to have a child, claiming her right to her own body, which resolves itself in an abortion. Lena is unmarried wishing for nothing else than to become a wife and a mother.

My aim is not to discuss the quite obvious fact that there is a patriarchal male discourse dominating the narrative, but to show how the cinematic devices forward this patriarchal configuration and how the spectator is implicated in it, and to point to where and how the harassed discourse is occasionally enunciated and treated within the film.

THE OPENING SCENARIO

The opening image of the film implicates the spectator in the dominating discourse by means of an ingenious trick. Five women are walking on a street in Stockholm, each one with a pram. 'What a lot of mothers and babies!' the spectator observes. The promenade is accompanied by a popular children's song, 'Baa Baa Black Sheep' by Alice Tegnér,[2] which seems to confirm the spectators' assumption of the women being mothers with their babies. This immediate perception is, however, shown to be wrong. When the procession has passed the camera, there is a cut, and the camera tilts down to reveal that instead of babies the prams contain newspapers. The surprising arrangement of the melody – faster than is common, with a kind of mocking quality – can now be understood. 'Really, I thought these women were mothers (but they weren't)!' thinks the spectator: the prams are not being used for the purpose they were made for, but the women are using them in their jobs (they are newspaper distributors). The women are working instead of having babies, which is what they were made for. The trick of the two shots, the false initial implication and the revision of it, creates the fundamental thesis that is being confirmed throughout the film: '(These) women should (have) be(en) mothers!'

VALUES/PREFERENCES

The second scene is set in the office of the newspaper *Morgonposten*. The editor-in-chief, Palm, and the chief story editor, Bergström, discuss, half irritated, half friendly with each other, the problem of the decreasing birth rate.

At this point, at the very beginning of the film, extra-cinematic factors are of great importance. The spectator has to orient him/herself in the world of the film and establish the hierarchy of different characters. When the film was shot, Ingrid Bergman was still just another young actress playing ingénue roles. Bergström and Palm, on the other hand, were played by very popular actors of their time, the latter by Bullen (the Bun) Berglund, an actor who, even if he mostly did comic roles, was a more or less compulsory character in all the main productions of Svensk Filmindustri. Victor Sjöström in turn, as Bergström, gives the character his great authority as the Grand Old Man of the Swedish cinema. He was, along with Mauritz Stiller, the person who had brought Swedish film artistic world fame. As Victor Seastrom he had directed films such as *He Who Gets Slapped* (1924), *The Scarlet Letter* (1926) and *The Wind* (1928) in the USA, and had now returned to Sweden as an actor.

The relationship between Bergström and Palm in the newspaper office is built on the difference between the categories that the two actors embody: Berglund (Palm) a comic character and Sjöström (Bergström) a dramatic one. The fact that Palm is standing up might imply his higher position in value terms but his statements are comic and he speaks unceasingly, walking around and gesticulating (except when he has his hands tucked in his pockets). Bergström on the other hand is sitting by his desk, busy with his work, only making an occasional retort – the spectator sees that he is quite industrious and does not waste words. These are characteristics of a reliable (male) person in popular fiction of the 1930s. The sympathies of the spectators are gradually transferred to him and his opinions thus grow in importance.

In Palm's opinion the low birth rate is the result of bad housing: people do not have decent homes in which to bring up a baby. A young editor comes in with a discussion article on the problem, and Palm is enthusiastic. Bergström, however, speaks contemptuously about the statistics, investigations and practical solutions that the young man suggests. His argumentation is emotional and anti-intellectual: 'When my wife and I solved the problem of the birth rate according to the "principle of seven kids", we only had a room and a kitchen – and there was no trouble with it at all!' He takes the young editor to task, pointing out to him that while he was still in nappies, he, Bergström, was fighting for better conditions for the poor. And, talking about bringing up children, the young man should get married instead of hanging around at the university, he adds.

As he talks, he is gradually excited by his words, and stands up. The camera tilts sightly upwards from behind the stunned young man, expressing the fact that the elderly patriarch has thus become the mouthpiece of the dominating discourse in *Valborgsmässoafton*. In his opinion the reason for the low birth rate is neither bad housing nor the depression but something quite else: 'lovelessness'.

THE IDEAL WOMAN

When Bergström pronounces the word 'lovelessness', there is a cut and a change of scene. The next act opens with a confirmation of Bergström's words: 'Quite right: lovelessness', says Superintendant Borg to his wife. The scene takes place in their bedroom, he is wearing a smoking jacket: he stands up looking down (in both senses) at his wife Clary.

Borg is played by Lars Hansson, one of the most celebrated actors at the Royal Dramatic Theatre. Just to recognize him is to realize that he is the hero of the story. He repeats and confirms Bergström's words. This transfers the authority and values of the older man to him.

The typical role for Karin Kavli[3] (Clary) had mostly been in the category of the spoiled, arrogant and often promiscuous upper-class woman. She is sitting on a stool in a white gown with flounces. Her dark hair is well done, she smokes and she has a name that sounds foreign. All these details have negative associations.

'I thought I got a wife when I married you, Clary', Borg continues.

The ideal image of a woman in the changing society of the expanding middle class, built upon an increasing segregation of labour and a separation between the public and private spheres, was that of a wife and a mother. A woman was hailed as complementary to a man, an owner of unique and specific characteristics that related to nurturing, pleasantness and leisure. This Manichaean construction of male and female roles was frequently expressed in the nineteenth-century bourgeois novel, and later in popular media, including film (Ambjörnsson, 1978: 32–61).

Nobody seems to have escaped identification with this female image. It is, for instance, interesting that when Queen Victoria of Sweden (not to be confused with Victoria of Britain) died in the spring of 1930, every commemorative article described her as in the first place a dutiful housewife: 'To the very last the Queen showed such a touching interest even in the smallest details in her far-away home. She gave orders concerning matters that an ordinary housewife would not have worried about at all if she had been as ill as the Queen was.'[4]

This is, then, the frame of reference that even a married fictional character like Clary was to be compared with. When she hears her husband's accusations, she stands up hastily, takes the few steps to her dressing table, still polishing her nails, and bursts out: 'I'm still young. I have the right to enjoy my life even if I happen to be married . . . I don't want to sit at home tied to a bunch of kids!' These are the first lines pronounced by a woman in *Valborgsmässoafton*, and the first manifestation of the harassed discourse.

Up to this point there has reigned a complete unanimity concerning the birth rate, so far the only subject of interest to the characters. Suggestions about the reason for and solution to the problem have been divergent: for Palm it is a matter of finding headlines that sell (and keeping stockholders, like a certain building contractor, happy), for his young editor it is a question of social science, for Bergström and Borg, finally, a matter of values: love, home, family and tradition. These different attitudes form a background of argument, which underscores the claim that every man in the film agrees on: more babies should be born in the country. It is only now that the spectator gets the opportunity to hear a woman's opinion on the question and it is impetuous, defiant and clear. She does not want any children because she thinks she is too young to have them and the responsibility of a child would restrict her too much.

In his essay on melodrama Thomas Elsaesser argues that, regardless of the fact that this genre enshrines bourgeois ideology, it is nevertheless possible to find subversive elements within it: 'Even if the form might act to reinforce the attitudes of submission, the actual working out of the scenes could nonetheless present fundamental social evils' (1985: 169). Within melodrama the rigorously conventional form with stereotyped characters and enclosed settings quite often presents a rigid frame that allows the appearance of rebellious expressions like Clary Borg's. The claim of a woman's right to her own body and own life is undeniably there even if it is forcefully contradicted by the patriarchal discourse.

Clary stands as one pole of the basic dichotomy that is constructed by the narrative. It is, of course, of great significance to note what kind of a woman she appears to be. Three negative components in her character have already been mentioned: the foreign association of her name, the colour of her hair and the character category of the actress, conventions common to the era. Her behaviour is quite significant, too: she does not look into her husband's eyes but keeps her eyes down with half-closed eyelids, she smokes and polishes her nails as if she does not have anything else to do. She even says she wants to enjoy her life, i.e. wants pleasure. A spectator in the 1930s with a Lutheran Protestant background would have found this very unsympathetic.

The following scene opens by presenting the opposite of Clary: Lena, the other pole of the basic dichotomy. It is around the tension between these two poles that the implicit values of the film revolve. Lena is the character who is going to confirm and reinforce the patriarchal discourse through her behaviour, while Clary will perish. (It is interesting to note that she just disappears from the screen and her death is casually announced in dialogue.)

The camera is directed at a diary in which one can read the following words: 'Why is it so difficult for men to notice those women who only long to be wives and mothers?'

A marital project was an indispensable component of Swedish fiction in the 1930s. The causal workings-out of the narrative are directed towards fulfilment of a goal, preferably a happy ending or reconciliation. Happiness was regarded as the foremost goal in people's lives, and this meant a home of one's own and labour for the benefit of 'one's own folks' (Frykman and Löfgren 1985: 275–8). Within this constellation, then, the foremost goal and mission for a woman was to be a mother and wife. For this reason, the unmarried woman is most often the focus of a story. It depends on her character and behaviour whether she achieves happiness, i.e. a promise of marriage guaranteed by a kiss, a proposal or both. I have identified in Swedish cinema of the 1930s thirteen female character types and the most frequent among them are the two variants of nice unmarried girls (it is only nice girls who get married). Lena Bergström is one of them: quiet, nurturing, respectful of her father and other authorities, but also proud, honest and chaste.

The young Lena Bergström (Ingrid Bergman, that is) is introduced sitting by her dressing table turning over the pages of her diary. Her shining, beautiful face is grave and the three-part mirror reflects it, under-lining her split feelings. She has secretly fallen in love with her employer, Superintendent Borg, and has now made up her mind: 'I cannot go on any more. If I do, something that shouldn't happen, will.' So she has decided to quit her job.

The image of the ideal woman as formulated above is unequivocal. Editor Bergström expresses it well when, later in the film, he compares his daughter with his late wife: 'Lena is the very image of her mother – the same sweet, sacrificing little woman – but she's also got the same hot blood . . .' Note that the patriarchal discourse does not deny the sexuality of the ideal woman. A central part of the plot is that Bergström suspects his daughter of being her employer's mistress and that she has become pregnant and had an abortion, a suspicion of sexual freedom that soon turns out to be false. The crucial aspect here, however, is to show that Lena is both willing and ready for reproduction, for building a family. Yet it was very unbecoming for a young woman to express her longing for a man aloud and so the film presents it in other ways. This is why the spectator reads her thoughts over her shoulder, surreptitiously, with a possible feeling of embarrassment coming over him/her, not Lena.

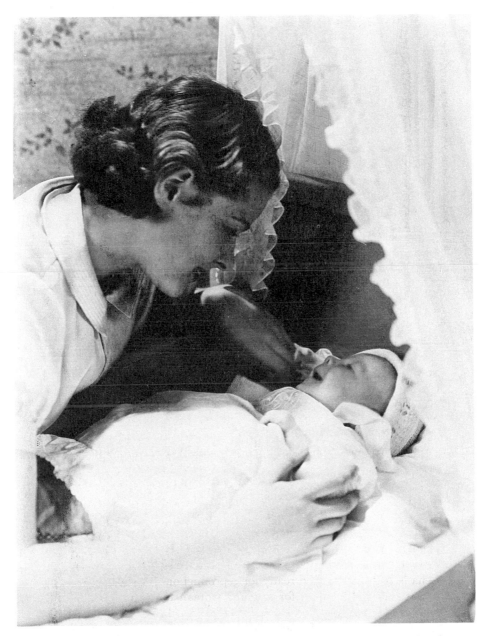

Plate 32 Walborgsmässoafton: the ideal woman – Ingrid Bergman, motherhood, white *mise-en-scène*. By courtesy of the Svenska Filminstitutt, Stockholm.

VICTIMS OF LOVE

Lena is the very image of her mother according to Bergström who on occasion sits in the twilight holding the portrait of his wife in his hands talking softly to her: 'Mama dear'. The portrait is deceptively like one of the young Queen Victoria. Through the resemblance, something of the official image of the late queen as self-sacrificing housewife is transferred to this fictional figure, Mrs Bergström.

It is at one of these moments that Bergström gives his definition of love: 'Love is not just a kiss on a spring night, it is tenderness, sacrifice, a thousand cares . . .' Here it is possible to find a vestige of the harassed discourse behind the idealized image that the dominating discourse carries with it. Nobody ever mentions the reason for the death of Bergström's wife, simply because it is irrelevant to the development of the narrative. But what the spectator does know of her relates to an ideal loving wife, whose life was filled with sacrifices and a thousand cares for her family. As the spectator finds out that these sacrifices and cares were practised during and between at least seven childbirths in one room and kitchen, there is no need to ask the reason for her early death.

When *Valborgsmässoafton* was made, it was still illegal to give information

Plate 33 Valborgsmässoafton: the bad woman – Karin Kavli, pleasure, dark *mise-en-scène*. By courtesy of the Svenska Filminstitutt, Stockholm.

on birth control. When the birth rate decreased, an attempt was made to improve the status of illegitimate children, but the fact is that shame and dishonour followed unmarried mothers almost half a century on. In the 1930s quackery was a booming business and 'angel makers'[5] still made their profits. Many young women gave their lives, became sterile or were severely punished as a consequence of illegal abortions.

Clary has become pregnant against her will and she visits a doctor. The doctor, a natural authority on behalf of his profession, sits behind his desk in his white coat. The camera points up to him and he keeps his spectacles in his hands when he speaks. He reproaches Clary because she 'seems to have such an erroneous conception of a "serious-minded" doctor's attitude towards problems like this'. Clary claims it is not her fault that she became pregnant, that she was against having a baby at all, but the doctor continues in a persuading voice:

> It hurts me, Mrs Borg, to find out that you don't want to realize that the child would mean an infinitely greater happiness to you than all these things you believe it is so difficult to be without – it surprises me that you don't understand that a child gives a woman the sign of nobility that cannot be compared with anything else on this earth!

Clary does not let herself be convinced. She consults a quack instead. She gets an appointment on Walpurgis Eve, which in old Bergström's world is the feast of love, reveries and romance. Moreover, it is Bergström who condemns her deed while he still suspects his daughter to be the one who had the abortion: a woman like Clary is 'no better than a common tramp, a common criminal'. The normative rules governing the narrative, dictated by this patriarchal discourse, punish Clary; as already mentioned, she commits suicide later in the film.

At every level in the plot Clary is being compared with Lena. By juxtaposing these two young women, it becomes clear that while Clary is always presented with negative connotations, Lena is completely brought together with positive ones. The spectator is gradually guided to accept and approve of Borg's disowning wife and marrying his young secretary.

The scene where the breach between the two spouses becomes definitive is interesting from the point of view of both discourses. Borg wants to mend his splitting marriage by arranging a romantic Walpurgis Eve in a fancy restaurant, just as he knows his wife would like. Clary has, however, made the appointment with the quack and has to tell a lie to conceal the real situation. As an excuse, she says she has a woman friend who absolutely wants to spend the evening with her and that she has already said yes. Borg is disappointed and claims, 'Don't you remember we'd agreed to spend the evening together? Please let's keep to it!' Clary gets tougher and a shadow falls over her eyes to underline her dishonest aims: 'You are so selfish never to allow me to feel myself free – I'm tired of your rule, tired, do you hear?' As their argument continues, Borg finally asks: 'Have you definitely decided to kill all the love that might possibly be left in my heart?' 'Love,' replies Clary scornfully, 'I know what your idea of love is!' 'You've never known it!' replies Borg, his arms crossed over his chest and his eyes fastened on his wife, who is staring straight ahead and not at him. Then she makes her last retort. 'Yes, I have the honour of knowing what it is and that's why I'm leaving!' Clary has indeed the honour of knowing what her husband's idea of love is: it implies a claim on her to give him a child against her will. Once again the harassed discourse makes itself manifest: Clary's bitter words express many women's experience of submission in marriage.

Instead of humbly accepting her destiny, Clary is going to do something about it – but her determination and willpower are drowned in a sea of negative associations. Instead, the conclusion the spectator draws is that she certainly does not deserve this man of honour, Borg. The breach between the two is sealed with a single cut. During the entire scene the camera has been cross-cutting between the two spouses with the walls of Borg's office as their background, as if there were no way out. But the very moment Borg has said his words about his feeling of love dying, there is a cut to him with a large window in the background, which gives an air of light and space encompassing him, implying that the withering of his feelings in fact sets him free.

The most common solution for marital problems in popular fiction of this time is that the spouses decide to go on with their marriage in spite of severe disagreements, especially if there are children or an agreement to raise a family. *Valborgsmässoafton*, however, is an exception to this rule, which implies that in this case the dominating discourse would value the presumptive couple's fitness for reproduction above the inviolability of matrimony. Similarly, it is quite common in Scandinavian fiction to give a kind of sacred aura to children who are born outside marriage, so long as they have been born of 'true love'.

Swedish melodrama of the 1930s may be nationally specific in its details and in the contemporary issues of its plots. It does not, however, deviate from a common pattern of a film melodrama with Manichaean oppositions, a causal structure and an Aristotelean dramaturgy of accelerating conflict that ends up in reconciliation or a happy end. Nor does the Swedish variant deviate from melodrama's historical tendency to express the ideals of the dominating bourgeois and capitalist ideology. Recent studies and theories of melodrama have also revealed that it is even capable of giving expression to categories of experience that cannot be manifested in intellectual or verbal terms. In most mainstream popular films, however, the patriarchal discourse is indisputable and the ideological claim manages to close itself around the narrative and expressive material of the story. The overdetermining power of the dominating ideology should not, then, be

underestimated in studies of melodrama as a possible expression of otherness. Nevertheless, in certain films such as *Valborgsmässoafton* the struggle
of the dominating ideology to conquer and conceal its innate contradictions
is sometimes less successful because of the struggle itself: the patriarchal
ideology in this film, through its tendency to make arguments for its
own legitimacy, has created an opposing discourse coherent enough to be
distinguished and understood, thus giving an enunciation to what exists
beyond and beside the dominating ideology.

NOTES

1 *Valborgsmässoafton* is a classic melodrama with a characteristically intricate plot.
  Superintendent Lars Borg wishes, after years of marriage, to have a child but
  his wife, Clary, wants to postpone such plans. At the same time Borg's young
  secretary, Lena, falls in love with him and decides to quit her job so that he
  will not find out about her feelings.
  Clary has, however, become pregnant and since her doctor refuses her an
  abortion she turns to a quack who offers her an operation on 30 April. Clary
  intrigues in order to free herself from the Walpurgis Eve celebration with her
  husband. The spouses end up in a bitter fight and Clary decides to leave. This
  is also Lena's last day at her job and when she wants to say goodbye to her
  chief, he invites her to the dinner his wife has just refused. In the course of the
  evening Borg realizes he has been in love with Lena all the time.
  Meanwhile the police have decided to raid the clinic belonging to the quack
  Schmidt, who gets wind of it and manages to send the newly operated-on Clary
  home. A crook called Roger finds Clary's patient card and picks it up to
  blackmail her. Clary is desperate and confesses everything to Borg who promises
  to help her out but refuses to continue their marriage. While at Roger's flat
  Clary becomes nervous and fires a gun she holds in her hand, killing Roger.
  The Borgs run away but leave a piece of the torn patient card in Roger's hand.
  In the newspaper office editor Bergström, Lena's father, encounters not only
  the front page news about the quack and the murder of Roger but also gossip
  that connects Borg and Roger (and therefore the quack) and, worst of all, his
  precious daughter Lena. He suspects his daughter of being the woman who had
  the abortion, a suspicion that Lena proudly denies though she admits her love
  for Borg.
  Borg himself joins the Foreign Legion but later deserts. He returns home to
  find that Clary has committed suicide, confessing in a letter to her part in the
  murder of Roger and the quack affair. Lena and Borg marry and within a year
  the happy couple have a son.
2 The song seems to be known all around the world with slight variations but
  was included in a collection of children's songs put together by Alice Tegnér
  that was extremely popular in Sweden at the beginning of the century (and even
  today).
3 Known at the time of the film as Karin Carlson but to posterity by her married
  name Kavli.
4 *Husmodern* 16 (1930): 23. 'Far-away home' refers to the Isle of Capri where she
  died of tuberculosis.
5 Many unmarried women left their newborn children to be taken care of by

women who let them starve to death or die 'accidentally'; these women were called 'angel makers'.

REFERENCES

Ambjörnsson, Ronny (1978) *Familjeporträtt*, Stockholm: Gidlunds.

Elsaesser, Thomas (1985) 'Tales of sound and fury: observations on the family melodrama', in Bill Nichols (ed.) *Movies and Methods II*, Berkeley and Los Angeles: University of California.

Fiske, John (1984) 'Popularity and ideology; a structuralist reading of Dr Who', in W. D. I. Rowland and B. Watkins (eds) *Interpreting Television*, London: Sage.

Frykman, Jonas and Löfgren, Orvar (eds) (1985) *Modärna tider*, Malmö: Liber.

Hall, Stuart *et al.* (1980) *Culture, Media, Language*, London: Hutchinson.

Myrdal, Alva and Gunnar (1934) *Kris i befolkningsfrågan*, Stockholm: Norsteds.

18

A FORKFUL OF WESTERNS

Industry, audiences and the Italian western

Christopher Wagstaff

Everyone who has thought at all about the Hollywood aesthetic wants to formulate one of its peculiar qualities: that of direct emotional involvement, whether one calls it 'giving resonance to dramatic situations' or 'fleshing out the cliché' or whether, more abstractly, one talks in terms of identification patterns, empathy and catharsis.

(Elsaesser 1972)

Elsaesser was writing about melodrama, but what he says applies to Hollywood films from other genres, including the western. It does not apply to the spaghetti western, however. Anthony Mann[1] said of *Per qualche dollaro in più (For a Few Dollars More*, 1965):

In that film the true spirit of the Western is lacking. We tell the story of simple men, not of professional assassins; simple men pushed to violence by circumstances. In a good Western the characters have a starting and a finish line; they follow a trajectory in the course of which they clash with life. The characters of *Per qualche dollaro in più* meet along their road only the 'black' of life. The bad ones. And the ugliness. My God, what faces! One or two is all right, but twenty-four no, it's too much! . . . The shoot-outs every five minutes reveal the director's fear that the audiences get bored because they do not have a character to follow. In a tale you may not put more than five or six minutes of 'suspense': the diagram of the emotions must be ascending and not a kind of electrocardiogram for a clinic case.

(Fenin and Everson 1973: 347)

Implicit in Elsaesser's observation and explicit in Mann's are some of the main terms in which critics and historians compare the spaghetti western with the American one. Much of what has been said about spaghetti westerns, however apparently superficial, has these terms of comparison at its heart, analysing the Italian films in terms of narrative unity, style, realism, conformity or reaction to a genre model, the viewer's empathy with the protagonist, and the ethical principles that support the narrative.

This view from above, in which the spaghetti western is characterized by what it is not, leads it to be deemed, for example, a 'critical' western[2] or else a debased and unsuccessful imitation.[3] Many aspects of the culture of study itself are responsible for these assessments and, where the study of popular cinema is concerned, these are shortcomings. The culture of study (its institutions, its methodologies and its economy) should fit us for seeing clearly and understanding the object of our study. About 450 spaghetti westerns were released in Italy between 1964 and 1978.[4] To see them all (even if copies were available) would take some 750 hours of viewing or five and a half months of thirty-five-hour weeks. Hunting down a copy of as many films as were still in existence might take many years. While the culture of study promotes research, it does not support investments on this scale in objects of study that possess the cultural status borne by the majority of those spaghetti westerns. Inevitably, the method applied is one of sampling. And just as inevitably, the sample is determined by the 'quality' of the individual film, box-office receipts and the amount of discussion that a given film has already generated. Hence, studies of the spaghetti western tend to be text-based (individual films, often identified by title, director and year of production), and to discuss films always taken from the same sample of about fifty films. Of these fifty, some forty comprise those which took the largest receipts at the box-office (in making this calculation, I have made allowances for annual rises in average ticket prices).[5]

The box-office receipts of spaghetti westerns can be looked at in two different perspectives, one of which I shall call 'commercial' success or failure, and the other I shall call 'box-office' success or failure:

A. A film that is a 'commercial' success makes a profit:
    (1) it cost a lot and makes a lot (decent profit);
    (2) it cost little and makes little but enough (small profit);
    (3) it cost little and makes a lot (windfall profit).
B. A film that is a 'box-office' success:
    (1) makes a lot in comparison with other films, regardless of its cost and how profitable it has been – in other words, it is purely a measure of where the film was shown and how many people bought tickets.

Italian cinemas in the period under discussion were divided into first run (*prima visione*), second run (*seconda visione*) and third run (*terza visione*). The majority of *prima visione* houses were in the sixteen principal cities, and that is where the big, immediate receipts were achieved, because ticket prices were high. In 1965 a number of spaghetti westerns were pulling in a billion (1,000 million) lire in *prima visione* alone. Hitherto no Hollywood western had ever made more than 0.5 billion lire in *prima visione* alone (rises in ticket prices over the preceding ten years – i.e. back into one of the heydays of the Hollywood western – are not big enough to strip that statistic of its significance). So certain spaghetti westerns definitely belong in category B1. *Per un pugno di dollari (A Fistful of Dollars,* 1964) cost 200 million lire to make, and received 3.18 billion lire at the box-office, which puts it into both category B1 and category A3. This film, and the others that I have just referred to as doing so well in *prima visione,* all belong in the 'sample' of fifty films commonly discussed. The 'box-office' success of *Per un pugno di dollari* took everyone in the industry completely by surprise, which guarantees that here we are dealing with a consumer-led phenomenon; people paid good money to see the film because they wanted to – the film was not imposed on them. But because *Per un pugno di dollari* was such a 'commercial' success (windfall profits), it led the industry into trying to repeat the phenomenon. In a period of falling attendances, producers and distributors saw the spaghetti western as a salvation, and proceeded to impose it on the Italian cinema-going public.

The notion of distributors 'imposing' a product on the consumer may seem too strong, but a knowledge of the history of Italian cinema gives support to the notion.[6] And I am not suggesting that the consumer was resistant. Instead, I shall suggest that the organization of production, distribution, exhibition and state support in Italy was such that it was in the interests of the industry to make a large number of these films for ten years. I shall also suggest that these films matched in certain important ways the habits and expectations of Italian cinema-goers.

First, however, spaghetti westerns have to be divided into two different types: on the one hand films directed primarily at the urban, middle-class *prima visione* public (which would then soak up further receipts in *seconda* and *terza visione*), and on the other hand films made cheaply, and distributed mainly through *terza visione* (sometimes with a brief launch in *seconda* or even a few days in *prima*). The *prima visione* 'box-office' successes cannot really be thought of as being imposed on the public, but they are relatively few. The small-scale *terza visione* 'commercial' successes may be a response more to the needs of the industry than to the spontaneous preferences of the public, and they are many. A characteristic of spaghetti westerns, and of other genre films of the adventure type, is that they got exceptionally large receipts from *terza visione* and the provinces over longish periods (four or five years). In this, they contrast with 'box-office' successes, which must make their money rapidly in *prima visione* in the major cities in order to repay their large production costs before interest payments eat away into revenue. One *prima visione* spaghetti western costing 600 million lire and taking 1.2 billion lire at the box-office is equivalent to three *terza visione* films costing 150–200 million lire each and taking 400 million lire each at the box-office. The difference is that the 1.2 billion lire taken by the three *terza visione* films represents far more tickets sold (ticket prices being far less in *terza* than in *prima visione*) than the same receipts of the single *prima visione* film. I cannot get complete data, but I would estimate that only about 100–150 films failed to break even for their producers. (I shall explain later how a cheap film that failed to make enough at the box-office to cover its production costs might still not always end up costing its producers anything.) Very few spaghetti westerns made as little money at the box-office as some of the films of Rossellini, Ferreri or Olmi at the time. The 'box-office' successes were distributed in *prima visione* in the principal cities. They were made to appeal to a certain kind of audience, they often cost more than twice as much to make as the run-of-the-mill films, and were often produced by a handful of solidly established production companies able to invest in marketing a quality product.

In 1970, *Vamos a matar, compañeros! (Compañeros,*[7] 1970), which took 1.5 billion lire at the box-office, would have been shown on the same *prima visione* circuit as Bernardo Bertolucci's *Il conformista (The Conformist,* 1970) which made 0.5 billion lire. *Vamos a matar, compañeros!* (a spaghetti western to which pretensions to political 'commitment' are attributed) is in certain respects rather more similar to *Il conformista* (almost universally acknowledged as one of the finest films of its period) than it is to *terza visione* spaghetti westerns, and it is not surprising that scholars who like talking about Bertolucci, when they get to talking about popular cinema, talk about films like *Vamos a matar, compañeros!*[8] This is not to deny that *prima visione* spaghetti westerns are 'popular', nor is it to deny the validity of applying the same kind of textual analysis to Leone's or Corbucci's spaghetti westerns that is devoted to Bertolucci's *Il conformista.* Indeed, nothing would be more delightful than to investigate the true 'authorship' of *C'era una volta il west (Once Upon a Time in the West,* 1968), directed by Sergio Leone, but whose subject was first written by Bertolucci, and consists of exactly the same same tight web of paternal and Oedipal relations and of symbolic castrations that we find in films that Bertolucci directed himself.[9] But the point that does need to be made is that there is a small group of what we could call 'quality' spaghetti westerns that has hitherto attracted all the critical attention, while the bulk of the films belonging to the *filone* (or 'formula') have been dismissed as *sottoprodotto* (a debased, ersatz product). These 350 or more films were very much 'popular cinema' in the sense that they were distinct from 'quality' cinema. Their existence tells us a lot about popular cinema-going and its industry in Italy. What is not clear is how far these films were an expression of popular culture,[10] and how far they were a mass consumer product imposed by the interests that controlled the market. It is probably a bit of both.

The notion of 'popular' cinema poses two main problems of definition. The first is whether the epithet 'popular' is a description of characteristics of the addressee of a given film or genre, or whether it is a description of characteristics of the film or genre itself. These alternatives require different critical approaches to the relationship between film and addressee, and historians are inevitably tempted to look very hard for a match between film and audience, and to be satisfied with after-the-fact conclusions (these must have been the addressees, because they are the people who went to see the films). The second main problem is the ideological one of distinguishing the 'popular' audience from the 'mass' audience. In this essay we are concentrating on the rather more limited question of commercial targeting of audiences, but the case of the spaghetti western might confirm Vittorio Spinazzola's observations:

> To the popular cinema belong works destined to be consumed by the lower classes exclusively; the mass cinema is instead designed to unify the public, bourgeois and proletarian, and therefore appears to have an interclass value. One derives from a small-scale system of production; the other is a product of a more advanced industrialisation. [In time] popular cinema gets squeezed into a smaller area, where it can still preserve some elements of autonomy, but where it loses its separate identity, and becomes predominantly a hasty imitation, at a very low level, of models furnished by current consumption.
>
> (Spinazzola 1974: 348)

Let us start with the market. The year 1964 saw annual ticket sales continuing to fall, standing at 683 million compared with the peak of 819 million in 1955. Television had existed for ten years, but only now were Italians beginning to own television sets in significant numbers. All three sectors of the industry were attempting to find the formula (the *filone*, or type of film) that would draw the public into the cinemas. The US cinema industry was going through a crisis and drastic reorganization. Therefore, to cope with a contracting US presence in the Italian market, Italian production expanded. Since the Second World War, the Italian exhibition sector had grown accustomed to having too many cinemas and too many films in circulation at any one time. There are a number of reasons for this, some of them political, but the result was that a feature of the Italian industry had always been a relatively low level of exploitation of a relatively large number of films. This stance on the part of the exhibition sector had been a millstone round the neck of Italian production, and was one of the reasons why Italian producers had never been able to persuade the government to give them adequate protection against imports. And it had led to the production of cheap films in large quantities rather than well-financed ones in moderate quantities. The medium-level, good-quality film was poorly represented in the Italian system of production. The expansion of production had to be accomplished without an increase in creative talent; there was no pool of undiscovered cinematic creativity waiting to be tapped. The way to increase output without any available increase in

249

creative resources was to have recourse to imitation and repetition. This is how the spaghetti western and its sibling formulas thrived.

US distributors had withdrawn from Italy, and were operating through agents. They were to return to Italy in the early 1970s, and force a concentration of the market. Italian distributors had traditionally been weak in the face of the restrictive practices of the US majors, and the large national distributors were distributing annually about twelve films each, which left little room for error. They had, therefore, tended to cling tenaciously to safe bets, and to go for films that had already proved their success with the public. Because of the system of financing films with guarantees from distributors, these distributors held complete control over production. Hence the success of a few spaghetti westerns led to a stampede to make and market more.

The production sector was extremely fragmented – this had always been a feature of the Italian industry since the beginning of the century. In 1967 forty-three production companies made only one film, a western, each. This meant that companies could not cover loss-making productions with the proceeds of profitable ones. This was another incentive to go only for safe bets. Small-budget production spends most of its money on the material and technical requirements of filmmaking, rather than on stars, for example. Because of their scale, and the way the system of guarantees worked, these productions had to pay cash on receipt for these technical items. It was a further pressure to keep the costs as low as possible. So an increase in the polarization of production was taking place: producers were moving even further towards more expensive films and very cheap films, and even further away from medium-sized productions. This was partly in response to the rapid growth of coproductions. Expensive films got international promotion, and very cheap films, because of the system of government aid, did not run much risk of ending up in the red (they also commanded a respectable export market, strong in Africa, South America and the Middle East). About half the spaghetti westerns made were coproductions, and of those, the majority were made with Spain. In addition, many were directed, or partly scripted and acted by Spaniards.

The Legge Corona, stipulating the relations between the state and the cinema, came into effect in 1965. This is not the place to explain it in detail, but for our purposes the important provisions were the various subsidies that films could receive, the credit facilities made available, and further extension of the subsidies to coproductions. These were not new provisions, but the Legge Corona improved conditions for producers in these areas. An Italian partner in a film could recover a lot of any losses that might result from poor box-office takings through state subsidies and tax rebates. The year 1965 saw the start of support for 'national' productions in Spain, and 1968 for those in Germany. Moreover, the film credit fund of the Banca Nazionale del Lavoro was enormously increased by the Legge Corona, and advances were sometimes not repaid in full. The situation I am describing is one in which there was an incentive to make very cheap westerns which offered a good chance of a reasonable return on investment and an outside chance of large profits, and a lessened risk of losses, for these might partly be covered by the tax-payer.

Some of the reasons why spaghetti westerns were so cheap to make are by now proverbial, and they centre on the lack of demands the genre made as far as sets, costumes, effects, scripts, story lines, personnel and acting talent are concerned. It is well known that even *Per un pugno di dollari* used sets from a more expensive production. Producers had a vested interest in keeping the genre alive for as long as possible.

Prima visione was much more responsive to fashion than *terza visione*, and so by 1970, for example, spaghetti westerns were less prominent in *prima visione*, but only slightly less represented in *terza visione* than in 1965. In other words, whether or not the public was truly enthusiastic about spaghetti westerns, the far slower cycle of *terza visione*, and the various financial cushions supporting the producers, meant that these producers were under little pressure to abandon the genre.

So far, we have looked at factors that supported the continuation of the spaghetti western. But in the 1970s, the industry suffered upheavals. Hollywood had reorganized, and the majors re-entered the Italian market, recapturing their hold over distribution, and forcing a concentration in the exhibition sector. The number of cinemas in Italy stayed fairly constant throughout the 1960s and 1970s but their make-up changed. *Prima visione* was greatly expanded at the expense of *terza visione*. Despite the fact that the total number of cinemas stayed constant, the number of communities without any cinema at all more than doubled. Those cinemas that disappeared or were transformed were great projectors of spaghetti westerns. With the 1973 oil crisis, inflation leaped from around 6 per cent to over 18 per cent. Average ticket prices in 1978 were four times what they had been in 1964. In 1976, the Constitutional Court made a judgement that had an effect equivalent to the deregulation of television, which led to hundreds of television stations, and wholesale broadcasting of films. In other words, the conditions that had favoured the spaghetti western came to an end, and so did the spaghetti western. The reason normally given for the demise of the spaghetti western is that audiences tired of them. They probably did, but they are still watching them on television – in Naples, at times about two or three are broadcast every day.

The spaghetti western is not a formula that existed on its own. Since the 1950s the Italian production sector has been characterized by its faith in formulas. With the rise of the peplum in 1958 there began an avalanche of adventure formulas, of which the spaghetti western is a subcategory. The peplum itself was a broad and diversified formula, containing mythological films and films about classical history, biblical times, the early and

251

late Middle Ages, Vikings, the Renaissance, Cavaliers, pirates and such like. These films were superseded by films about the American west, cold war spies, the Mafia, urban bandits, thrillers, detective stories and so on. At the end of the 1960s all of these formulas and subcategories were simultaneously being produced, distributed and exhibited. The films were made by the same personnel, and the stories are more or less the same. A promotional synopsis for *Robin Hood e i pirati (Robin Hood and the Pirates*, 1960) – already a hybrid, just in the title – reads like this:

> Lex Barker, already famous as Tarzan, is Robin Hood in an Italian version that is slightly different from the traditional legend. Here Robin is a nobleman who is kidnapped by pirates. He forms an alliance with them, however, in order to avenge himself on a rival who has usurped his title.

We are shocked or moved to mirth at reading this, because the hero is such a contamination, and as far from the stable stereotype that we expect from the Robin Hood formula as is the parched, rocky Mediterranean shore on which the film is shot. It would be absurd to interpret this in terms, for example, of an Italy that had abolished its monarchy and was experiencing nostalgia for an aristrocracy, or as an expression of sympathy for the Sardinian peasant tradition of extortion by kidnapping. The narrative units of these formulas and subcategories are interchangeable: villains threatening, heroes rescuing, changing of alliances, pursuits of quests, etc. It can sometimes be hard to tell from the credits of a film and its synopsis whether a particular film is a spaghetti western or an example of another formula such as bandit, gangster, Mafia, thriller or political suspense. A still, particularly if someone in the shot is wearing a hat, usually clears up the mystery.

There were other formulas too, such as horror. But alongside adventure formulas, the other two major components of popular cinema were sex and comedy. Even here, contamination was the rule, with the one important exception that in the second half of the 1960s all films had sex (female nudity) in them except westerns. Comedy, to a greater or lesser extent, pervaded all the genres. The adventure formulas were not entirely serious. Only in the genre of drama was this element of light-heartedness or burlesque absent, and that was a genre mainly directed at the *prima visione* elite (interestingly, the ingredient of sex was as prominent a feature of the elite drama as of the popular formulas). In 1970 and 1971, Enzo Barboni made two very successful comedy westerns, the second of them, *Continuavano a chiamarlo Trinità (Trinity Is Still My Name*,[11] 1971), Italy's biggest ever box-office earner. Commentators talked of a change of direction in the spaghetti western, but in fact Barboni's was not the first comedy spaghetti western, nor even the first successful one, and comedy had always been one of the optional ingredients of the formula.

Adventure formulas did well in provincial and *terza visione* cinemas, especially in the south of Italy. These audiences had not yet achieved the consumerist approach to sex and the display of female bodies that was being acquired by audiences in the industrial north and centre. This may explain the lack of sex in spaghetti westerns; and it is compatible with the ample but rather coy display of female anatomy characteristic of the peplum formulas. Meanwhile, in the 1962–3 season, a comic duo, Franco Franchi and Ciccio Ingrassia, had rocketed to box-office success, particularly in the south, with good-humoured, unproblematic burlesque of just about everything in Italian life and show business, and their many films amply motivate Barboni's effective experiments with Terence Hill and Bud Spencer.[12]

To look at the formulas in terms of gratifications offered to the viewer may clarify the picture. The viewer was being offered either one or a combination of three pay-offs: laughter, thrill, titillation. They are, as it were, three physiological responses, provoked not by whole films, but by items or moments in films. Italian formula cinema simply juggled with plot items to produce the required recipe that would stimulate the appropriate number and kind of these 'physiological' responses.

The audience for the cinema can be conceived in a variety of ways: first, the individual spectator, and his/her gratification; second, the audience in an auditorium; third, the audience over time and space for a particular film; fourth, the audience over time and space for a particular genre; fifth, the audience (clientele) over a period of time for a particular cinema.

If one thinks of the Italian industry as perceiving the spectator in terms of the first and fifth of these alternatives,[13] then the functioning of the system of interchangeable formulas that consistently offered the same gratifications becomes clear. The audience of the *terza visione* cinema was more like the television audience than like a *prima visione* cinema audience. The viewer (generally he)[14] went to the cinema nearest to his house (or in rural areas, the only cinema there was) after dinner, at around ten o'clock in the evening. The programme changed daily or every other day. He would not bother to find out what was showing, nor would he make any particular effort to arrive at the beginning of the film. He would talk to his friends during the showing whenever he felt like it, except during the bits of the film that grabbed his (or his friends') attention (the film would stop anyway at an arbitrary point for an intermission). People would be coming and going and changing seats throughout the performance.

This kind of cinema-going has a social context and function which needs to be taken into account in the study of popular films. Film studies have traditionally seen the individual film as the unit to be studied, and have assumed that the object of the spectator's attention is that unit in its integrity. Television studies have recently begun rejecting those assumptions. The Hollywood western is conceived of as a whole film, and the

253

gratification offered the viewer comes from that 'trajectory' of which Mann spoke in his observations on *Per qualche dollaro in più*. He put it well when he said 'the diagram of the emotions must be ascending, and not a kind of electrocardiogram for a clinic case'. The picture we have seen emerging of the situation in which spaghetti westerns were produced and marketed (and viewed) explains completely that deliberate seeking after the 'electrocardiogram'. The peaks in the electrocardiogram of the *terza visione* viewer's attention and gratification were supplied by the three 'physiological' responses (sex, laughter, thrill/suspense) that were as interchangeable as plot lines, and that a cinema would dose according to the cultural expectations of its audience: in the south, comedies were more common than erotic films. The music of the spaghetti western was important in signalling to inattentive viewers the moments when they should pay attention. The shoot-outs and sadism that offered the thrill could be replaced by Hill and Spencer's antics provoking laughter. Viewers could go to their local cinema and watch a comedy, an adventure story or a so-called 'erotic' film (for example, one of the 'documentary' formula (Spinazzola 1974: 318ff.)) and have more or less the same experience every time. The industry was furnishing a functionally homogenized product.

However, the whole structure depended on repetition. The audience had to return to the same cinema the next day. It had to be offered something different, but providing the same gratifications. In other words, a repetition with variation, a serial. Hence, the spaghetti western, and other examples of Italian formula cinema, must be seen in terms of both larger and smaller units than that of the individual film. The audience of a particular cinema was being offered a nightly appointment where it would receive a series of discrete gratifications that were part of a longer-term sequence. (It is easy to see how catastrophic the deregulation of television was for *terza visione*.) Hollywood marketed genres which were constituted by the meanings of whole films; Italy marketed *filoni* made up of items. The *filone* can be subdivided into a number of parts, often consisting of subspecies, but characterized in all sorts of ways, and generally living for a season or two. Here is not the place to illustrate this in any depth; but the changing titles of the films are a kind of symptom of the sorts of transformations and cycles that evolved. In 1966–7 titles were frequently the names of heroes. By 1970 they had become sentences consisting of statements about what the hero did, or else mocking or menacing addresses to a potential victim announcing the hero's imminent arrival. But these titles in their turn evolved into sentences that are descriptions of the hero, and then later into statements made by the hero. The title of the film *Giù la testa* (literally: 'Get your head down', 1971) shows Sergio Leone's team subtly exploiting an existing fad, preserved in the American title (*Duck You Sucker*), but lost in the flogging of a dead horse in the British title (*A Fistful of Dynamite*).

Just as an American television series like *Kojak* did not advertise each hour-long film with the title of the episode being transmitted, but rather with the title of the name of the hero, asserting a continuity with other films in the series, so spaghetti westerns used titles as a means of asserting continuity with other films of the *filone*, and with other films in specific subcategories (I have put the number of films in parentheses): names like Django (16), Ringo (14), Sartana (14); hardware like *dollaro* (53), colt (19) and *pistola* (21); injunctions like 'kill', 'die' (60); warnings like 'he's coming' (14); Spanish key-words like *hombre, adios, vamos* (22) – often several characteristic elements were combined. Each title had the duel function of identifying the 'series', and characterizing the individual 'episode'. The same parallel can be drawn with actors. Just as Telly Savalas had regularly identifiable side-kicks in the *Kojak* series, and villains were all played by actors recruited from a certain stable, so Fernando Sancho (30 films) and Klaus Kinski (17) functioned in similar ways with respect to Giuliano Gemma's hero (18).

Examining the industry shows that seriality was the most important mechanism available to the Italian production sector, given the way it was organized, for meeting the particular requirements of the exhibition sector. Whether the Italian man in the street really wanted to be fed what it suited the industry to provide is a much-debated question in Italy. It would appear to stand to reason that viewers could vote with their feet, and the production, distribution and exhibition sectors were obliged to scurry to satisfy their preferences. But this was only true up to a point. Whenever the Italian production sector failed to satisfy its customers, it did not automatically change its product, but rather would carry on regardless, go into debt and demand that the state bail it out. Cinema-goers had to accept what was on offer, and the only alternative was to watch American films – which is what they would tend to do, whereupon Italian production would hurtle into one of its periodic troughs, or 'crises', as they are called.

The bulk of spaghetti westerns, those never mentioned in the books and articles spawned by the formula, were made by a revolving squad of writers, actors, directors, technicians and musicians. To list five names (three of them Spanish, incidentally), Sancho, Carpi, Simonelli, Marchent, Balcazar – an actor, two writers and two directors – is to list names to be found separately or together in the credits of at least sixty-eight spaghetti westerns. These revolving teams did not set out to do the same things that the Hollywood westerns of the 1940s and 1950s did. The build-up of tension towards a final dramatic confrontation was something that Sergio Leone concerned himself with, but very few others. The long process of building the character of the hero, and drawing the spectator's empathy around it, was essential to the didactic and dramatic strategy of the 'classic' western, and the absence in spaghetti westerns of what Elsaesser calls 'one of [the] peculiar qualities' of the Hollywood aesthetic is striking. The

Plate 34 American icons in an 'Italian' genre: Rod Steiger (right) and James Coburn in *Giù la testa*. By courtesy of the British Film Institute, London.

Plate 35 Europe in Monument Valley: Claudia Cardinale in *C'era una volta il west*. By courtesy of the British Film Institute, London.

256

viewer is tempted to attribute this absence to hasty, slapdash conception and production. Another interpretation (though usually only applied to *prima visione* spaghetti westerns) is to see the films as 'critical' westerns, parodying and mocking the moralism of the American model. While there is truth in both conclusions, neither of them answers all the questions that are raised by the Italian films. If the films fail to develop patterns of empathy and identification in the viewer simply because they are hurriedly and poorly put together, one would expect to see in them failed attempts to achieve empathy and identification. Usually, there appear to have been no such attempts made. As for the absence of the moralizing, perhaps it is sufficient merely to interpret it as an absence, not as the presence of some alternative moralizing strategy, which is implied in the notion of the 'critical' western.

The aims of the makers of spaghetti westerns were comparable more with the aims of those who made Hollywood 'B' westerns in the 1930s than with the makers of big-budget Hollywood westerns in the 1940s and 1950s. The product was to be suited to a market. In the 1960s Italian society was undergoing a rapid transformation, which involved changes in almost all the values and assumptions that had hitherto underpinned social and economic life. In the 1940s and early 1950s, the debate over the reconstruction of post-war Italy had taken place as much in the cinema as in any other cultural medium. It is therefore possible that the characteristics of popular cinema of the late 1960s and early 1970s, a popular cinema in many ways imposed by the exigencies and habits of the cinema industry itself, were accepted and tolerated because what they eschewed matched the social situation in which the viewing public found itself. The avoidance of moralizing, the refusal to construct role models, the openness about the superficiality and construction of the stories are aspects of spaghetti westerns that made them enjoyable. Popular cinema held a moratorium on didacticism, and stopped propounding paternalistic values. The western could have a new lease of life as a source of adventure stories no longer weighed down with mythical and moral overtones. The viewer no longer went to see a particular story, with its meaning and dramatic closure. The seriality of the spaghetti western functioned like television series, and narratives had to obey new rules. No longer was the goodness of the hero built up; instead the hero merely encountered a large number of villains or rivals. The famous 'servant of two masters' plot[15] had the virtue of postponing closure: the defeat of a villain did not resolve the tensions of the plot, and confrontations could go on until the filmmakers had used up their ninety minutes. Much of the amorality attributed to spaghetti westerns comes from the fact that in order to have a large number of shoot-outs in a plot, characters had to keep changing sides and betraying each other. To attribute too much meaning to the violence would be to fail to see how much these films resembled, in that respect, American cartoons like *Road Runner*, for example.

258

Umberto Eco astutely pointed out how Superman comics needed to devise a way of holding off closure, and of producing conflicts whose resolutions did not lead to progress. Superman must not change, and the world cannot be made free of villains (Eco 1964). One of the essential requirements of serial narratives is that the story more or less begin again next week. The post-modernist implications of spaghetti westerns – the denial of progress, of narrative closure, and the parodic nature of the genre – are almost unintentional products of commercial necessity. While a few 'auterist' spaghetti westerns tried to pick up some of the levels of meaning, and some of the functions of the classic American western, the bulk of the *terza visione* spaghetti westerns picked up the comic-book functions of the western inherited from the 1930s. These films have been universally attacked by Italian critics and historians for their low cultural level and their poor production values. They have been seen as symptoms of what was wrong with the Italian cinema industry. But their passing has coincided with a concentration of the Italian exhibition sector, which now caters for a middle-class urban audience, and the severe contraction of the production sector. The production resources have not, like those of Hollywood, gone into large-scale production of films for television, and instead, Italian television has been invaded by the products of the United States. It is hard to avoid the conclusion that the cultural values of the critics and historians have prevented them from fully explaining *terza visione* formulas. For its part, film theory has tended to concern itself only with the fully attentive viewer, not with the social function of cinema-going, nor with the economics of down-market film exhibition. By applying some of the methods and concerns that have been developed for studying television, we may be able to achieve a better understanding of formulaic cinema and of its audiences.

Plate 36 (opposite) A fairly costly Italo-Franco-Spanish *prima visione* western, destined to earn a great deal at the box-office, is well-promoted in Milan's *Corriere della sera* for Friday 28 January 1966 for a first run Milan cinema, starring Giuliano Gemma, Italy's muscle-man answer to Steve Reeves. The director 'George Finley' is really Giorgio Stegani, and 'Evelyn Stewart' is Ida Galli.

Below it, this is all the publicity the *terza visione* films get. The list shows the range of formulae at this fairly early stage in the spaghetti western cycle: James Bond spin-offs, peplums and westerns jostling each other. Particularly interesting is the simultaneous presence (at the 'Zara') of the expensive but scarcely known 1964 Italian western, *Le pistole non discutono* (*Pistols Don't Argue*), with (at the 'Bruzzano') the cheaper film knocked off after that was finished, with the same sets and crew, *Per un pugno di dollari* (*A Fistful of Dollars*).

NOTES

1 Mann directed some of the classic Hollywood westerns of the 1950s.
2 Christopher Frayling (1981) takes this position, particularly with regard to the films of Sergio Leone, but his analysis of features of the *Django* cycle is not characterized by this perspective.
3 While basically taking this position, Micciché (1976) calls for a detailed study of the mass phenomenon of the spaghetti western.
4 It is difficult always to be sure from the title and credits whether a film is a western or not. Moscati (1978) lists 407 films for the period 1964–78. Della Fornace (1983) gives a total of 435 for the period 1965–78. Putting together Moscati and various *cataloghi* published by Bolaffi, I would estimate the number as around 450 for the period 1964–78. A good survey in English of Italian formula filmmaking is in Newman (1986).
5 For box-office receipts (of big money-earners only) see Della Fornace (1983). For receipts of all films, see the various editions of *Catalogo Bolaffi del cinema italiano*, and less accessible, but more reliable, ANICAGIS (1974). For ticket prices see Quaglietti (1980).
6 For the importance of distributors in the period 1945–54, see Wagstaff (1989).
7 Literally, 'Let's Go and Kill, Comrades'.
8 I am not trying to refute Baudry (1971) here; but it is interesting that his discussion of 'popular cinema' should be based on *Vamos a matar, compañeros!*
9 Leone asked Bertolucci to write the subject for *C'era una volta il west* because he met him at a *prima visione* showing of *Il buono, il brutto, il cattivo (The Good, the Bad and the Ugly*, 1966) in Rome. Thus does *prima visione* beget *prima visione* progeny.
10 Frayling (1981) discusses elements of 'popular' culture that he discerns in these films.
11 Literally, 'They still called him Trinity'.
12 Terence Hill is the pseudonym of Mario Girotti, Bud Spencer that of Carlo Pedersoli.
13 An Istituto Doxa (Institute for Statistical Research and the Analysis of Public Opinion) survey of cinema audiences carried out in 1953 showed that the public tended to know in advance, rather than what film they would go to see, what cinema they would attend. A third of the audience tended to go to the cinema on regular, fixed days of the week.
14 We know from audience surveys that among the lower classes (a significant part of the audience that we are hypothesizing for the *terza visione* spaghetti westerns), 70 per cent of people never went at all to the cinema. If we also assume that the south accounts for a significant part of our audience, we can guess that this huge absenteeism is made up in large part of women. From surveys of audiences and of exhibitors, we also know that adventure formulas were preferred much more by men than by women. This does not mean that in more modernized areas of Italy, women (especially young women) did not go often to the cinema. Unfortunately, I do not have enough good data to be more precise on this point.
15 Sergio Leone copied Kurosawa's *Yojimbo* (1961) for *Per un pugno di dollari*. He claimed that both films owed something to the comedy of the Venetian eighteenth-century playwright, Carlo Goldoni, *Arlecchino servo di due padroni (Harlequin Servant of Two Masters)*.

REFERENCES

ANICAGIS (1974) *Catalogo generale dei film italiani dal 1956 al 1973*, Rome: ANICA AGIS.

Baudry, Pierre (1971) 'Idéologie du western italien', *Cahiers du cinéma* 233: 55–6.

Bolaffi (1966, 1976) *Catalogo Bolaffi del cinema italiano*, vols 1945–65; 1966–75, Milan: Bolaffi.

Della Fornace, Luciana (1983) *Il labirinto cinematografico*, Rome: Bulzoni.

Eco, Umberto (1964) *Apocalittici e integrati*, Milan: Bompiani.

Elsaesser, Thomas (1972) 'Tales of sound and fury: observations on the family melodrama', *Monogram* 4: 2–15.

Fenin, G. N. and Everson, W. K. (1973) *The Western*, New York: Grossman.

Frayling, Christopher (1981) *Spaghetti Westerns*, London: Routledge & Kegan Paul.

Micciché, Lino (1976) *Il cinema italiano degli anni 60*, Venice: Marsilio.

Moscati, Massimo (1978) *Western all'italiana*, Milan: Pan Editrice.

Newman, Kim (1986) 'Thirty years in another town: the history of Italian exploitation', *Monthly Film Bulletin* 624: 20–4; 625: 51–5. 626: 88–91.

Quaglietti, Lorenzo (1980) *Storia economico-politica del cinema italiano 1945–1980*, Rome: Editori Riuniti.

Spinazzola, Vittorio (1974) *Cinema e pubblico*, Milan: Bompiani.

Wagstaff, Christopher (1989) 'The place of neorealism in Italian cinema from 1945 to 1954', in Nicholas Hewitt (ed.) *The Culture of Reconstruction*, London: Macmillan.

INDEX